THE
NETWORK
RESHAPES
THE LIBRARY

THE NETWORK RESHAPES THE LIBRARY

Lorcan Dempsey on Libraries, Services, and Networks

BY *LORCAN DEMPSEY* | *EDITED BY* *KENNETH J. VARNUM*

An imprint of the American Library Association
Chicago | 2014

LORCAN DEMPSEY has worked for library and education organizations in Ireland, the UK, and the United States. He manages OCLC Research and is also OCLC Chief Strategist. Before this, he managed the information division of JISC, the UK national agency that provides networking, information, and innovation services to higher education. He began his library career in Dublin City Public Libraries in his native Ireland. Dempsey's thinking has influenced the evolution of libraries and library services around the world, and he has contributed to the language that describes those services. His career has coincided with the emergence of the web, and he is particularly interested in how networks influence library services and library organization. Recognizing this influence, the Open University (UK) conferred Lorcan with an honorary doctorate in 2014.

KENNETH J. VARNUM is the Web Systems Manager at the University of Michigan Library, where he manages the library's website and development of new features and functionality. His research has been focused on discovery systems and the use of personalized information systems in library settings. He is the author of *Drupal in Libraries* as well as numerous articles on library-related topics and a long-running blog, *RSS4Lib*. Varnum earned his master's degree in library science from the University of Michigan and graduated from Grinnell College.

© 2014 OCLC Online Computer Library Center, Inc. This work is licensed under a Creative Commons Attribution-NonCommercial 4.0 International License (CC BY-NC 4.0) http://creativecommons.org/licenses/by-nc/4.0

Printed in the United States of America

18 17 16 15 14   5 4 3 2 1

Extensive effort has gone into ensuring the reliability of the information in this book; however, the publisher makes no warranty, express or implied, with respect to the material contained herein.

ISBNs: 978-0-8389-1233-1 (paper); 978-0-8389-1997-2 (PDF); 978-0-8389-1998-9 (ePub); 978-0-8389-1999-6 (Kindle). For more information on digital formats, visit the ALA Store at alastore.ala.org and select eEditions.

Library of Congress Cataloging-in-Publication Data

Dempsey, Lorcan.
    The network reshapes the library : Lorcan Dempsey on libraries, services, and networks / by Lorcan Dempsey ; edited by Kenneth J. Varnum.
        pages   cm
    Includes bibliographical references and index.
    ISBN 978-0-8389-1233-1 (print : alk. paper) — ISBN 978-0-8389-1997-2 (pdf) — ISBN 978-0-8389-1998-9 (epub) — ISBN 978-0-8389-1999-6 (kindle) 1. Library information networks. 2. Libraries and the Internet. 3. Information resources. 4. Libraries—Communication systems. 5. Libraries—Information technology. 6. Dempsey, Lorcan—Blogs. I. Varnum, Kenneth J., 1967- II. Title.
Z674.7.D46 2014
025.042—dc23   2014020410

Book design by Kim Thornton in the Cardea OT, Vista Sans, and Miso typefaces.

♾ This paper meets the requirements of ANSI/NISO Z39.48-1992 (Permanence of Paper).

CONTENTS

──┤ FIGURES │

I BEGAN WRITING this blog as an internal resource in OCLC Research. Many early entries were in the form of pointers to noteworthy sites or developments. But gradually the platform encouraged greater expansiveness, and I began to write about things myself, not just to point to what others were writing about them. I soon decided to externalize it, and for almost ten years, I have been using it to write about things of interest—of interest to me, and, I hope, of interest to others.

The first thing to say is that I found it an extraordinarily liberating experience. I have written quite a bit in the professional literature over the years.[1] However, in such long-form publications, I usually write slowly. For me, there are two practical differences in the blog environment. One is that entries never get long enough to worry overmuch about structure. And the second is a continuing sense that this is a fugitive medium. This means that an entry can be dispatched relatively quickly. And I think it is fair to say that more of my thinking has gone into the blog and into presentations[2] during these years than into "the literature."

As it became a place for thinking as well as for linking, a variety of themes emerged and evolved over the years as technologies and practices changed. A particular trend was to try and fix those themes—to make them usable in more general discussion—by giving them a distinctive name. Examples include "discovery happens elsewhere," "the collective collection," "in the flow," "making data work harder," "sourcing and scaling," "moving to the network level."

This is perhaps an example of a writerly pleasure. Although I would demur at the "writer" label, the blog certainly affords other writerly pleasures also. The major one of these is a connection with readers. This is enormously rewarding, and its loss is a major regret as my blog writing has slowed down over the last couple of years. I regularly meet people who comment on what I have written, who tie it to their libraries or their working practices, or who comment more broadly on themes or topics. This is especially the case with posts that go beyond professional interests to talk about technology, social, or literary topics. I have enjoyed pulling in other interests, even though the focus has remained libraries and networks. One observation as I have been looking at the full range of blog entries: my interests have evolved from service and technology matters to organizations and the institutional forms through which they get work done. In particular, the systemwide organization of libraries and other services in a network environment is of great interest.

I mentioned that blogs have seemed a fugitive medium. This is only partly true. Entries are indexed by Google, cited in the literature, and discussed in meetings and retreats. However, encouraged by Jay Jordan, now OCLC President Emeritus, I thought it would be useful to pull together some entries into book form. This is that book. Ken and I have had to be selective as the blog accumulated over those years, and some of my personal favorites may have fallen by the wayside. However, we aimed for general representativeness and some current interest.

I am grateful to Jay for his encouragement over the years and for his support for this endeavor. I am also grateful to Patrick Hogan, of ALA Publishing, for taking on this project. And for suggesting that Ken Varnum undertake the editorial task. Ken has been patient, industrious, and creative, and he has made a book out of a mountain of text.

Lorcan Dempsey
Columbus, Ohio
1 March 2014

NOTES

1. http://www.oclc.org/research/people/dempsey/publications.html
2. http://www.oclc.org/research/people/dempsey/presentations.html

EDITOR'S INTRODUCTION

AS IS SURELY the case with many of those who peruse this book, I have been reading *Lorcan Dempsey's Weblog* as long as it has been available as a public resource. Thoroughly rereading the 1,869 posts in the near decade from October 2003 through August 2013 has been an eye-opening experience and a trip down memory lane.

In working on this project, I have had the opportunity to reflect on how closely intertwined the milestones of my career and Lorcan's weblog were. At every stage in my career, *Lorcan Dempsey's Weblog* has shone light on the emerging trends and the key areas of concern to our profession. The very first item, in October 2003 (the succinct "Hello . . .," in the "Lorcan's Picks" chapter), was posted to OCLC Research's staff just as I was beginning my library degree at the University of Michigan. A year later, as I was weeks away from graduation, the blog became public. As emerging digital technologies and digital affordances have roiled the profession—whether those are the challenges of metasearch, the rise of web-scale discovery interfaces, the creation of large full-text repositories, the need for tighter integration of document discovery and delivery, or the emergence of the collective collection—the blog has neatly presaged the projects and challenges that would next face me in my professional life. In fact, it seems my career has been an endless attempt to catch up with the trends and directions Lorcan has, often presciently, described.

This book contains, in our estimation, the most significant posts from the past decade. Significance is partly measured by their impact on the profession and partly by the degree to which they reflect Lorcan's thinking or show seeds of future ideas. We have tried to keep some items that feel dated now but, when viewed in the context of the time they were written, were of import.

Of course, time goes on, and some websites, services, tools, and links are undoubtedly gone. We have made no attempt to update details or refresh the content of posts. The items included here are largely as they appeared in the blog; we have occasionally omitted long quotes from other posts from the blog and made the occasional edit for clarity.

The book is organized into nine topical chapters. Within each of these topical chapters, items are organized chronologically by publication date. A few items have been assigned "tags" to indicate a particular kind of importance:

> **Noteworthy**—a post that has a particular influence above and beyond the norm
>
> **Coinage**—where a turn of phrase employed in the post has caught on in the larger profession

A number of fellow readers of the blog have been kind enough to contribute brief reminiscences and commentary on its importance to their thinking. These are included throughout.

Finally, thanks to those who helped produce this manuscript. Patrick Confer assisted with images. Brian Lavoie and Constance Malpas reviewed the entire manuscript at different stages. And Eloise Kinney, the copy editor, brought stylistic consistency to a work written over more than a decade.

Ken Varnum
Ann Arbor, Michigan
1 March 2014

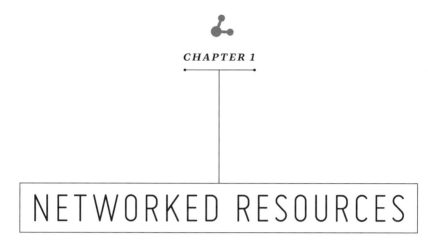

CHAPTER 1

NETWORKED RESOURCES

THIS SECTION IS connected with the "Network Organization" section that follows. Given Dempsey's vision for organizationally interconnected libraries, what do the resources themselves look like? How do libraries structure their systems, their data, and their access protocols to ensure that the promise of the network organization will be fulfilled?

The posts here focus on the resources, rather than the entities. As resources move into centralized, common, shared, or cloud-based services, how does that change the ways the resources function and people interact with them?

JANUARY 29, 2005

The sound of words: *Amazoogle* and *Googlezon*

http://orweblog.oclc.org/archives/000562.html   Tag: Noteworthy, Coinage

Amazon, Google, eBay: massive computational and data platforms which exercise strong gravitational web attraction.

I coined the expression *Amazoogle*[1] to have a handle to talk about this phenomenon in our space. It seems to me that *Amazoogle* has a slightly uplifting sense; it evokes a smile.

The Museum of Media History has produced a short video[2] about Googlezon, a merged Amazon and Google. Googlezon sounds more sinister?

1

The video has been noted in a variety of places, and I had expected to see more discussion of it in our space. It provides a dystopian (for some?) vision of the future of media, seen from the perspective of 2014. "2004 will be remembered as the year that everything began." Everybody is served by EPIC (Evolving Personalized Information Construct), which programmatically compiles person-specific views of the collaborative "mediascape." The *New York Times* is a print-only newsletter for the elite and elderly.

Of course, 2004 is 20 years, and 2014 is 30 years, after 1984, a point underscored in the video as an ID card for <u>Winston Smith</u>[3] is flashed up on the screen at one stage.

NOTES

1. http://www.google.com/search?q=amazoogle+dempsey
2. http://www.broom.org/epic
3. http://www.google.com/search?q=%22winston+smith%22+1984

APRIL 6, 2005

Systems in the network world

http://orweblog.oclc.org/archives/000622.html   Tag: Noteworthy

The last year has really made it clear that library systems sit in a broader network environment. The emerging integration challenge is integration with the systems environment of the user. This makes it more important to think about the broader network systems environment. As I look at that broader environment, I see four emphases.

1. **Public platforms.** The emergence of several massive data and computational network presences, which have become infrastructural platforms for a range of users and uses. Google, Amazon, and eBay have each become central to the behaviors of millions of users, have each moved beyond their founding service, have each opened up their services and data to other applications, have each developed revenue-sharing models with partners. Their "users" are still people, but they are also building out to an environment where a growing number of their "users" are programs, other applications which talk to their machine interfaces. The most recent example of this is Google's

announcement of its API for ad management. They are tied into the fabric of user behaviors and applications through an intrastuctural tissue[1] of lightweight, loosely coupled, webby approaches. They make data work[2] hard: they extract as much intelligence as possible from growing reservoirs of data, and their services adapt reflexively based on accumulated data about users. They are massive gravitational hubs for consumers.

2. **Personal and interpersonal spaces are major focuses.** People accumulate learning caches, and work caches, and opinion caches (blogs?), and photo caches, and . . . life caches[3]. The emerging ecology and economy of image and music management, where materials may be distributed and moved across personal, shared, and commercial spaces, indicate a direction. Blogs, wikis, RSS, podcasting: a range of lightweight applications is rapidly emerging to help manage and share personal content. Again, we have seen the emergence of major consolidation services—Flickr, Bloglines, and Blogger, for example—which are intrastucturally connected with each other and user environments through RSS. These resources may be moved across cell phones, hard drives, portable devices, as content flows between the various caches that comprise our personal and, for some, increasingly collective data spaces. Increasingly it is the *-flow which is the consumer of services, where the *-flow is supported by a systems environment: the workflow, the learnflow, the researchflow, the consumerflow, the musicflow . . .

3. **Service orientation and on-demand platforms.** Two related things here. First, service-oriented architectures have been widely promoted and discussed. Whatever about actual implementation, the advantages of moving from large monolithic business systems to systems composed from more fine-grained service chunks seem to be accepted. This approach is in line with service goals, which emphasize rapidly changing consumer needs, and design goals, which need to respond to this need flexibly and economically. Second, there is growing interest in software delivered as a service over the network, in the ability to buy "on demand" rather than build business functionality locally. These two are related in the sense that each seeks to reduce the cost

and complexity of system ownership, and to support more flexible management of changing system needs in recombinant service environments. That said, we are in early days.

4. **The web all the way.** There is a strong argument that simpler, web-based approaches are to be preferred to more heavyweight protocols and data formats. This is particularly the case for what I call intrastructure, the tissue that connects applications together and weaves them into user behavior.

It is interesting to think about what library systems development looks like in the light of these emphases. I will return to this in future posts.

NOTES

1. http://orweblog.oclc.org/archives/000505.html
2. http://orweblog.oclc.org/archives/000535.html
3. http://orweblog.oclc.org/archives/000390.html

JANUARY 5, 2007

Web scale

http://orweblog.oclc.org/archives/001238.html   Tag: Noteworthy, Coinage

I like the expression *web scale*. It is used heavily by Amazon and others in discussion of their "platform" services like S3 and EC2. Here is a description of EC2, Amazon's on-demand computing infrastructure:

> Call it "utility computing" or "Web-scale computing" or "on-demand infrastructure." Whatever the case, Amazon is hoping that its new EC2 (Elastic Compute Cloud—why not just S4?) Web service (in the larger

sense, as both an interface and an on demand platform) will turn into a big business. In effect, Amazon is leveraging its massive infrastructure investment, providing it as a publicly facing service for a variety of applications, first with S3 and now adding the server component. (*Inside Amazon's EC2 | Between the Lines | ZDNet.com*[1])

Here is an example from Amazon:

Amazon S3 is storage for the Internet. It is designed to make web-scale computing easier for developers. (*Amazon.com: Amazon S3, Amazon Simple Storage Service, Unlimited Online Storage: Amazon Web Services*)[2]

In an interesting analysis of the current position of Google, Rick Skrenta uses it:

Google has won both the online search and advertising markets. They hold a considerable technological lead, both with algorithms as well as their astonishing web-scale computing platform.[3] Beyond this, however, network effects around their industry position and brand will prevent any competitor from capturing market share from them—even if it were possible to match their technology platform. (*Skrentablog*)[4]

"Web scale" refers to how major web presences architect systems and services to scale as use grows. But it also seems evocative in a broader way of the general attributes of the large gravitational hubs which are such a feature of the current web (eBay, Amazon, Google, Wikipedia . . .).

Incidentally, Skrenta makes[5] the arresting claim that Google has become the web's "start page." He argues that Google is dominant in the third age of computing in the way that IBM and Microsoft were in the first two. Worth a read.

Most businesses on the net get 70% of their traffic[6] from Google. These business [*sic*] are not competitors with Google, they are its partners, and have an interest in driving Google's success. Google has made partners of us all. (*Winner-Take-All: Google and the Third Age of Computing (Skrentablog)*[7]

NOTES

1. http://blogs.zdnet.com/BTL/?p=3541
2. http://www.amazon.com/gp/browse.html?node=16427261
3. http://blog.topix.net/archives/000016.html
4. http://www.skrenta.com/
5. http://www.skrenta.com/2007/01/winnertakeall_google_and_the_t.html
6. http://www.skrenta.com/2006/12/googles_true_search_market_sha.html
7. http://www.skrenta.com/2007/01/winnertakeall_google_and_the_t.html

JUNE 6, 2007

Systemic change: CIC and Google

http://orweblog.oclc.org/archives/001366.html

Today Google and CIC announce[1] an agreement to digitize ten million volumes across the CIC libraries. Google has been adding new partners since the first announcement was made about the Google 5. Some folks have wondered what rationale has governed selection of partner opportunities. We do not know, but they sure are moving fast! Here are some early thoughts.

The CIC announcement is interesting for several reasons:

- It is a shared effort across a major group of libraries with significant collections. There appears to be strong CIC institutional commitment. Of course, CIC has a history of collaboratively sourced activities, and this "pooling" model makes increasing sense given the necessary policy and service challenges that need to be addressed. In this case, but also across a range of other issues that libraries face as they support changing research and learning behaviors in a reconfigured network environment. For some things, scale matters.
- The libraries have a shared approach to managing the digital copies based on shared infrastructure at the University of Michigan, and serving them up to their user communities. An example of collaborative sourcing.
- Google recently advertized for somebody to work on collection development, and we seem to be seeing a stronger focus in this area. Collecting areas of importance within each library (PDF[2]) have

been identified for attention. Presumably, these decisions have been influenced by the "collective collection" of the full Google partnership also.

This initiative in turn prompts some more general thoughts about access:

- One of the most valuable features of the Google initiative is that it digitizes book content, allowing fine-grained discovery over topics, people, places, and so on. Of course, this presents interesting questions about indexing, retrieval, ranking, and presentation, but the advantage of having this access seems clear. It drives use and sales, and it supports enquiry. Without it, the book literature is less accessible than the web literature.

- However, as we are beginning to see on Google Book Search, we are really going beyond "retrieval as we have known it" in significant ways. Google is mining its assembled resources—in Scholar, in web pages, in books—to create relationships between items and to identify people and places. So we are seeing related editions pulled together, items associated with reviews, items associated with items to which they refer, and so on. As the mass of material grows and as approaches are refined, this service will get better. And it will get better in ways that are very difficult for other parties to emulate.

- Currently, this material is made available within the Google destination site. Google is an advertizing engine, and its approach depends on aggregating attention for adverts. This approach may be difficult to deploy within a more "data services" approach where others—especially the partners—have remixable access to content and services. However, the "utility" value of this resource will be diminished if it is not made available in this way so that others can mobilize these resources within their own environments. How and if this gets done remains to be seen. (See the related discussion[3] about the search API.)

- This type of access seems especially important for the partner libraries. In the early days of this activity, there was some discussion of the types of services which would be built on top of the digitized books by the libraries. However, it is difficult, and maybe not very sensible, for the libraries to individually invest in some types of service development. An important factor here is that they cannot benefit from the network effects that arise in larger collections and so are limited in the range of service that they could individually develop. This points again to issues of collaborative sourcing.

For me, the CIC announcement moves the conversation about mass digitization to another level. The Google relationship with libraries has seemed like an interesting initiative. But it now seems plausible to think that we are looking at systemic change in how we engage with particular classes of material. Which in turn will cause us to look at the way in which the systemwide library resource is organized. It touches on so much:

Disclosure, discovery, delivery. This initiative highlights the changing dynamic of discovery and delivery in a network environment. As folks have richer discovery experiences on the network, it becomes more important for libraries to disclose what they have into those environments and to offer well-integrated fulfillment services. A library will want a user of Google Book Search to know what is available to him or her within his or her own institution. Of course, Google currently links through to library services, but this needs to get smoother.

Collective collection. As more materials are digitized, it promotes stronger thinking about collective approaches to collection management: from access, development, inventory management, and preservation perspectives. This direction is visible in emerging discussions about off-site storage and uses of library space. Over the next few years, I believe we will see major initiatives which address these issues in collective ways.

Copyright. Issues here are well-known and debated. For libraries—and others—it is important to be able to efficiently determine the copyright status of an item, at various stages in the life cycle. We cannot now do this, not efficiently, and certainly not in any way that can be automated and made available as a "data service" for easy checking by applications. There are several initiatives looking at this, among them OCLC, which is exploring the feasibility of a Registry of Copyright Evidence.

Knowledge organization. Libraries, archives, museums, and others have made major investments in structured data in the form of taxonomies, gazetteers, authority lists, and so on. The value of those resources needs to be released in web environments. As Google refines its approaches to text mining, or if others are able to do computational work over the resource, then there is an interesting opportunity to see how they might be mobilized to support identity identification (of personal names, place-names, and so on) in large amounts of text, and how those tools might themselves be enhanced in the process.

Preservation. Libraries and related organizations have collectively exercised a responsibility to the scholarly and cultural record. They have safeguarded rare materials. They have also managed the broad range of published output. And much of this has been as a benign consequence of the physical print-distribution model. Lots of copies keep stuff safe. Of course, the digital environment changes this dynamic also. So, we need to think about keeping the digital copies that emerge from this process. But it also highlights issues around the management of the collective print resource moving forward and how that responsibility is dispersed. And it raises interesting questions about what we expect from a digital version of the print record in terms of quality, coverage, specificity, and so on, which will keep us busy for some time.

Much of what I have said revolves around systemic issues: How does the systemwide library resource reconfigure in a network environment which is seeing this type of change? This requires collective responses, which is why I think that this CIC initiative is so interesting. For OCLC, and the other library organizations which operate at the systemic level, it underlines the importance of working with libraries to develop web-scale, or, in other words, responses which match what users now expect in a web environment.

NOTES

1. http://www.cic.uiuc.edu/programs/CenterForLibraryInitiatives/Archive/PressRelease/LibraryDigitization/index.shtml
2. http://www.cic.uiuc.edu/programs/CenterForLibraryInitiatives/Archive/PressRelease/LibraryDigitization/Collections6-5-07final.pdf
3. http://orweblog.oclc.org/archives/001258.html

OCTOBER 8, 2008

Stitching costs

http://orweblog.oclc.org/archives/001785.html   Tag: Coinage

We are familiar with "switching costs," the costs of changing a supplier. I may decide not to change my phone or e-mail arrangements, for example, because I do not want to incur the effort of notifying all my contacts. Libraries are very familiar with switching costs, given the range of data migration issues involved in changing library systems. Indeed, high switching costs are one reason that libraries often stay with the same vendor for long periods.

Libraries are also familiar with high "integration" costs: perhaps these might be called "stitching costs." This means that it may be costly developing higher-level services based on integration of various lower-level services.

Think, for example, of the website integration issues libraries have where they want to provide unified access to the catalog, to licensed resources, to repositories, and so on. The intermittent levels of integration we see are because the "stitching costs" are high.

This is largely because they are providing a thin layer over two sets of heterogeneous resources. One is the set of legacy and emerging systems, developed independently rather than as part of an overall library experience, with different fulfillment options, different metadata models, and so on (integrated library system, resolver, knowledge base, repositories . . .). Another is the set of legacy database and repository boundaries that map more to historically evolved publisher configurations and business decisions than to user needs or behaviors (for example, metadata, e-journals, e-books, and other types of content, which may be difficult to slice and dice in useful ways).

Or think of higher-level federation across library services. We have few compelling federated services, whether these are based on metadata harvesting, metasearch, or other approaches. Again, this is partly because of high stitching costs. I cited[1] Jerry McDonough's article[2] the other day about how abstraction and optionality in library standards design creates unhelpful variation in implementation, which in turn is a barrier to efficient interoperability.

Things are changing, as it becomes more important to effectively stitch library resources into other environments and as lighter-weight approaches get adopted. However, it is useful to bear stitching costs in mind when there is discussion of approaches based on federation and interoperability. These costs may be to do with technical issues (interfaces, metadata . . .), or policy issues (ILL policies in a resource-sharing system, for example), or higher-level organizational and resource allocation issues (who will run the federation service, etc.). And they are very real.

NOTES

1. http://orweblog.oclc.org/archives/001779.html
2. http://balisage.net/Proceedings/html/2008/McDonough01/
   Balisage2008-McDonough01.html

Network as a service . . .

http://orweblog.oclc.org/archives/002018.html

We have entered the era of "everything-as-a-service," where lowering transaction costs mean that a growing range of capacities can be sourced from the cloud.

It has become common to talk about a threefold model:

1. **Software or applications as a service.** A particular application may be used in the cloud (for example, Salesforce or Webex web meetings).
2. **Platform as a service.** A development environment is provided which supports application development (for example, Azure,[1] Microsoft's cloud operating system, or force.com,[2] from Salesforce).

3. **Infrastructure as a service.** Computing or storage or some other infrastructure component is provided (an example is the computing and storage services available from Amazon).

Recently, I have been wondering about "network as a service." Think of Facebook and eBay. In each case, a major part of their value for third-party developers is access to a "network" of other users. And this is an explicit part of the offer of Facebook and eBay. In the former case, a developer can "leverage the social graph;"[3] in the latter, developers have access to the "largest ecommerce opportunity on the web."[4] There are cases where access to a network is a useful feature of a service, even when network creation is not its primary purpose. Take, for example, firms which provide Employee Opinion Survey services. A firm which provides this service to many organizations will have benchmarking and comparison data which will make it an attractive option for some potential clients.

Business models vary in these examples, and in some cases, the "interconnectedness" of the network provided is important; in other cases, less so. Value may reside in access to the network, or access to intelligence generated by the network (analytics data).

I have been thinking about this in the context of WorldCat. WorldCat is a bibliographic database. A major part of its value, however, is in the holdings data: it associates bibliographic items with libraries which hold them. In other words, it creates a library network. OCLC leverages this network in other services—notably resource sharing. The WorldCat network is also leveraged by services provided by other organizations. For example, it provides a switch between other bibliographic services (Google Book Search, LibraryThing, OpenLibrary, Goodreads, etc.) and library collections.

It provides a network as a service . . .

NOTES

1. http://www.microsoft.com/windowsazure/windowsazure
2. http://www.salesforce.com/platform
3. http://developers.facebook.com/cases
4. http://developer.ebay.com/businessbenefits

Mobile . . . Top Tech Trends 1

http://orweblog.oclc.org/archives/002115.html

I was pleased to participate in LITA's Top Tech Trends panel at ALA this year (see the video[1] and live coverage[2]).

We were each asked to talk about three trends: current, a bit further out, and a bit further out again. In thinking about the exercise, it seemed to me that it would be interesting to talk about how services are being reconfigured in a network environment, and not just focus on technology as such. This is the first of three blog entries, one devoted to each of my trends. We had three minutes in which to discuss each trend.

The first trend I chose was somewhat broad: mobile. I discussed five ways in which mobile is impacting our services:

1. **Atomization**: get to relevance quickly. Mobile encourages designers to think of atomic services rather than complicated workflows or rich, multilayered experiences. And to think about services that are immediately relevant and convenient. Room or equipment booking or bus timetables may become more visible, for example.

2. **Localization**: where you are can matter. WolfWalk[3] is a nice example of a library application which is location aware. It associates materials from NCSU's special collections with historic buildings on campus. "The application supports a map view with geotagged place marks for 90 major sites of interest on the NCSU campus, and a browse view for quickly locating a known site by name."

3. **Imbrication**: our physical and digital spaces overlap. Andy Walsh, of Huddersfield University, for example, discusses how[4] QR Codes (and RFID tags) can be used to connect library places with network information services. And I was interested to see a QR code prominently displayed on one vendor booth at ALA providing a link to further information online.

4. **Socialization**: microcoordination and ad hoc rendezvous affect how we think about space. Mobile communications allow us to coordinate as we go: let's meet up in an hour in Starbuck's; I am in Target; will I buy

these ones? I thought you were going to be here 15 minutes ago! <u>I have written before</u>[5] about Starbucks as an "on-demand place" for the type of ad hoc rendezvous that we are now used to. William Mitchell has written about how this affects our need for different types of space, and we can see how this impacts library space:

> The fact that people are no longer tied to specific places for functions such as studying or learning, says Mr. Mitchell, means that there is "a huge drop in demand for traditional, private, enclosed spaces" such as offices or classrooms, and simultaneously "a huge rise in demand for semi-public spaces that can be informally appropriated to ad hoc workspaces." This shift, he thinks, amounts to the biggest change in architecture in this century.[6]

5. **Mobile and cloud go together.** We have multiple connection points which offer different grades of experience (the desktop, phone, Xbox or Wii, GPS system, smartphone, netbook, Internet radio/music streaming, and so on). While these converge in various ways, they are also optimized for different purposes. A natural accompaniment of this mesh of connection points is a move of many services to the cloud, available on the network across these multiple devices and environments when they are needed. This means that an exclusive focus on the institutional website as the primary delivery mechanism and the browser as the primary consumption environment is increasingly partial.

NOTES

1. http://litablog.org/2010/06/video-top-tech-trends-washington-dc-annual-2010
2. http://litablog.org/2010/06/top-tech-trends-liveblog-2
3. www.lib.ncsu.edu/wolfwalk
4. http://orweblog.oclc.org/archives/002087.html
5. http://orweblog.oclc.org/archives/001898.html
6. Economist, "The New Oases" (10 April, 2008). Quoted in http://firstmonday.org/htbin/cgiwrap/bin/ojs/index.php/fm/article/view/2291/2070

JANUARY 1, 2012

Linking not typing . . . knowledge organization at the network level

http://orweblog.oclc.org/archives/002195.html

Knowledge organization seems a slightly quaint term now, but we don't have a better in general use. Take the catalog. This has been a knowledge organization tool. When an item is added, the goal is that it is related to the network of knowledge that is represented in the catalog. In theory, this is achieved through "adjacency" and cross-reference, notably with reference to authors, subjects, and works. In practice this has worked variably well.

In parallel with bibliographic data, the library community, notably national libraries, has developed "authorities" for authors and subjects to facilitate this structure. From our current vantage point, I think we can see three stages in the development of these tools.

1. **Label.** In the first, subject and name authorities provide lists from which values for relevant fields were chosen. Effectively, they constrain the range and format of subject or name data, providing an agreed text label for a concept or name. Examples are LCSH, Dewey, and the Library of Congress Name Authority File. These provide some structuring devices for local catalogs, but those systems do not exploit the full structure of the authority systems from which the values are taken. Think of what is done, or not done, with classification, for example. The classification system may not be used to provide interesting navigation options in the local system, and more than likely is not connected back to the fuller structure of the source scheme. That said, having a consistent label is an advantage, and facilitates matching within and between systems.

2. **Data.** The second stage is that these authority systems are being considered as resources in themselves, and not just as sources of controlled values for bibliographic description. So, we are seeing the Library of Congress, for example, making LCSH and the name authority file available as linked data. OCLC is working with a group of national libraries to synthesize name authority files and make them available

as an integrated resource in the VIAF[1] service. FAST[2] has recently been made available in this way. The Digital Author Identifier,[3] a national Dutch system for identifying researchers, is interesting in this context. In this arrangement, there is collaboration between the apparatus for uniquely identifying researchers and the national authority file.

3. **Network.** In a third stage, as these network-level resources become more richly linkable and as local environments exploit that linking ability, it becomes possible to do more. This type of linking has only just begun, though, and it will be interesting to see how it develops. In this context, a URI is added to the label, making it actionable and globally unique. As an example, think again of the catalog. The structuring devices we employ are about structuring relationships *within* the catalog. This would be turned inside out if we not only imported values, but also linked those labels to those external resources. In this way, the item represented could be replaced in the broad network of knowledge established by the authority file from which it comes.

Of course, alongside this, they may also link to, or draw data from, other navigational, contextual, identifying, or structuring resources, such as DBpedia, MusicBrainz, or Geonames. These and other reference points are likely to be important web-scale identity and knowledge-organization services. In a sense, more generally, this has already happened, as people orient themselves by links to Wikipedia, MusicBrainz, IMDb, and other network-level resources.

As in other areas of our activity, we need to think about how activities whose natural level was once local are now moving up to the network level. And once they are at the network level, they have to live alongside other approaches.

If this were to become more common, there are some implications . . .

From records to entities . . . We ship data around in "records," bundles about individual items, and our systems are structured around managing these records. We do not tend to manage data about other things of interest to us to the same extent: authors, places, people, concepts, works, and so on, the types of things we have in authority files. What would happen if we more clearly described an item by linking it to these files? More generally, we can see stronger interest emerging in some of these other entities, personal names especially. Think, for example, of how Amazon has created people pages or the growing interest in researcher identification. Or of places, as geolocation services take hold. Freebase is creating an "entity graph"[4] giving IDs to millions of entities (people, places, and things).

Much of the library linked data discussion has been about making that local record-based data available in different ways. As interesting is the discussion about what key resources libraries will want to link to, and *how they might be sustained*. An important question for national libraries and others who manage some of the schemes mentioned above is how to move into this third phase. What would this mean for library systems or for library data of this type? What resources are important? How should they be sustained? To make this concrete, are the name authority files maintained by national libraries fit for purpose in a network world? Does it make sense to limit their scope to authors identified in a particular library workflow, cataloging, and exclude other authors (of articles, for example)? Does it make sense to limit their creation to a restricted group of specialist librarians? And so on . . .

Finally, as knowledge organization moves to the network level, how do library resources relate to others? Can other services leverage *the accumulated investment of the library community,* or does it fade? The organized relationship between the Deutsche Nationalbibliothek and Wikipedia in Germany is an interesting example here, where the German Wikipedia explicitly takes advantage of the structuring work done by the DNB. Wikipedia itself is very interesting in this regard, as it has effectively become an "addressable knowledge base." If I want to tell you about a new concept or movement, or refer you to a place, or mention a person, I can send you a Wikipedia link. What would be required for Wikipedia to take advantage of "knowledge organization" approaches developed in the library community?

NOTES

1. www.viaf.org
2. http://experimental.worldcat.org/fast

3. www.surffoundation.nl/en/themas/openonderzoek/infrastructuur/Pages/
digitalauthoridentifierdai.aspx
4. http://wiki.freebase.com/wiki/What_is_Freebase%3F

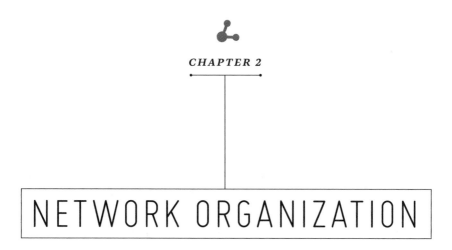

CHAPTER 2

NETWORK ORGANIZATION

THIS SECTION AND the "Networked Resources" section that precedes it are closely related. Dempsey's vision for the near future of libraries is one of seamless yet loose integration across a range of scales—integration within a library and across regional collectives, the nation, and the world. Data and items should flow speedily among libraries and users at all levels.

A lot of habits, systems, and functions will necessarily change for this vision to take root. This section includes posts describing the organizational and administrative characteristics of libraries in the context of large-scale networked resource availability.

OCTOBER 31, 2004

Externalizing the blog

http://orweblog.oclc.org/archives/000464.html   Tag: Noteworthy

I have maintained this blog for a year now, writing for colleagues internally at OCLC. We have decided to externalize it. I wonder will the dynamic change very much . . .

The focus is on libraries and network services, and on libraries more broadly. It is quite general, although readers will notice recurrent themes.

Library logistics

http://orweblog.oclc.org/archives/000487.html   Tag: Coinage

Logistics is everywhere. During the recent Olympics,[1] DHL and UPS were heavy advertisers. Recently, UPS has been advertising that its role is to "synchronize" companies.

It seems to me that *logistics* is a significant part of what libraries do; they *synchronize* the need for and the supply of research and learning materials.

Logistics is about moving information, materials, and services through a network cost-effectively. Resource sharing is supported by a library logistics apparatus. The emerging e-resource discovery-to-delivery chain, tied together with resolution services, is a logistics challenge. Many of the e-resource management issues are like supply-chain management issues.

In the library community, we tend to resist the vocabulary of business or other domains. That said, *library logistics* is growing on me!

NOTE

1. http://orweblog.oclc.org/archives/000399.html

READER COMMENT

John Wilkin
Juanita J. and Robert E. Simpson Dean of Libraries and University Librarian, University of Illinois at Urbana-Champaign

Dempsey's insights into the work of libraries and their place in society continue to be important guides in the continuing evolution of the profession. Of the several distinct threads in his blog, one stands out for me: Lorcan's thoughts about "Sourcing and scaling." This very helpful framing of the challenges we face and the approaches we take to addressing them shapes the discussions in which I participate on an almost daily basis.

MAY 6, 2005

Recombinance all the way up . . . remixing all the way down

http://orweblog.oclc.org/archives/000657.html

I have been using *recombinance* quite a lot in the last year or two to talk about how network flow affects structures. You can tell that I am generationally challenged: I should be saying *remixing,* which is cropping up in places in the same sense. This is happening to structures at all levels. Here is a compressed and reductive list:

- We are used to seeing *metadata* flow between repositories: libraries developed an early mechanism to share records between nodes and have an extensive bibliographic apparatus. More recently, OAI-PMH has provided a mechanism for publishing processable metadata for consumption by recombining services. We have also seen the emergence of RDF and XML schema, namespaces, and application profiles which extend this recombinant ability to "data *elements.*"
- We have always assembled collections of content objects, and seen them flow between collections. These flows are facilitated in a network environment, and resources may appear in a variety of aggregations. Again, *content* has become less "solid" also: think of what has happened with music. We can recombine tracks in various ways, on various devices, in various collections, for various purposes. The same is happening with other constructs, where we want to decompose and recombine differently. Taking images or figures from journal articles or chapters from textbooks, for example, and recombining and contextualizing them in courseware is an ambition. Related to this, we have seen the emergence of *"content packaging"* standards—METS, SCORM, MPEG DIDL—to bind particular resource combinations.
- With *network services,* recombination/remixing is very clear. There is a clear move toward more fine-grained services which can be recombined to meet application needs more flexibly. In fact, flexible

service recombination is the goal of the service-oriented approach. One reason that this is important for libraries[1] is because they want to be able to mix library services into the e-learning mix, or into the campus portal mix, as well as into the library mix. Related to service orientation are on-demand services and outsourcing, the move to source particular business processes from third parties.

- And this moves us to the organizational level, where increasingly we see that *organizations* themselves may articulate organizational components of different types to achieve particular ends. Think of an organization like Cisco, for example. In the library world, libraries already rely on a range of cooperative and other groups, of various sizes and scopes. My own view is that libraries will increasingly want to secure shared services, which will mean relying on other organizations, whether it is OhioLINK, OCLC, JISC, the California Digital Library, DEF, Ithaka . . .

What is happening is that at all these levels, structures are internalizing the network, and are adapting accordingly. At all levels, the need for complex interactions is driving interest in better facilitating decomposition of structures and flexible recombination to meet service needs. To package various materials into a learning object. To deliver various library "channels" into the enterprise portal. To add various databases to the metasearch. And this points to the importance of interoperability. Interoperability is the "recombinant ability" an object has, the ease with which it can be remixed in different combinations to create value. To caricature a long-term resident of the British Museum Reading Room: all that is solid melts into flows.

NOTE

1. www.oclc.org/research/staff/dempsey/recombinant_library/dempsey
_recombinant_library.htm

JUNE 20, 2005

The one-stop-shop that isn't

http://orweblog.oclc.org/archives/000691.html

When talking about a well-defined, discrete problem, maybe *one-stop-shop* expresses a useful notion. Or when the entry point is so wide as to seem comprehensive . . . as with Amazon or Google.

However, we are more often dealing with situations which fall between these poles.

And there, *one-stop-shop* more often seems to express a forlorn aspiration, sadly out of step with the realities of user behavior and expectation. In fact, sometimes its introduction seems to be a substitute for thinking about what is really needed.

One-shop-stop is probably a better way of characterizing what is provided. We are sometimes satisfied by one shop; many times we are not, and we want to create a plural shopping experience. (Look carefully—that is *one-shop-stop*.)

For many information applications, it is difficult to arrange all the resources that might be of use, or to anticipate possible needs, or to presume that they are the favored site of integration for the user. They are part, only, of a landscape of resources, which may be configured in different ways by the user.

Closely related to the *one-stop-shop* discussion is the YAP syndrome: the *yet another portal* syndrome. Put together the aspiration to meet all needs in one place, and the unlikelihood of achieving this aspiration, and you end up with several one-stop-shops. A proliferation of portals.

JUNE 27, 2005

Libraries, maps, and platforms

http://orweblog.oclc.org/archives/000713.html

Google Maps seems to have sparked a growing interest in location-based services, partly because it has opened its interface, allowing others to build applications on top of it. Here are a couple of links to discussions of libraries and locations.

- Peter Brantley draws attention[1] to the O'Reilly Where 2.0 conference, and speculates about location-based services in the information space.
- Paul Miller has been writing extensively about this in recent months. See here[2] and here[3] for examples.

What we are looking at here are "platform" services, using "platform" in a Web 2.0[4] sort of way. In this sense, a platform is a resource which makes services available through machine interfaces. Others build applications drawing on platform services through APIs/web services. Amazon, Google, and eBay are major platform service providers.

This suggests a rather simple model of "horizontal" platform providers whose services may be consumed by many "vertical" application builders.

Now, clearly, cataloging and resource sharing have some of the characteristics of "platform" services, even though they are not always consumed through machine interfaces. Indeed, one reason why libraries were very early developers[5] of protocols and exchange formats was that libraries, and their system vendors, were building applications on top of data and services from elsewhere. Structurally, union catalog organizations arose to provide an early form of shared service for libraries. In fact *utility* is a very platform-like word, and the motivation that is currently driving platform services is very similar to that which drove library resource-sharing organizations. This might be summarized as developing shared services to remove redundancy and build capacity.

And indeed, OCLC and other organizations in our space *are* considering what it means to be a "platform" provider. Experimental and trial services like xISBN[6] and terminology services[7] indicate a direction. As do the construction of registry services for library catalogs and OpenURL resolvers. As does the further development of machine interfaces to other service areas. The Talis Silkworm[8] initiative is explicitly positioned as a "horizontal" platform play in an environment of "vertical" ILS application builders. Interestingly, Talis began life[9] as a shared cataloging service in 1969 and continues to provide that service around its union catalog. And the work of Peter Brantley and colleagues at the California Digital Library also has a "platform" flavor about it, as they build "horizontal" infrastructure services for the UC libraries. Of course, CDL provides the union catalog Melvyl. Paul Miller works for the Common Information Environment,[10] one of whose aims is to ensure that UK public sector organizations that are developing information systems do so in ways which avoid unnecessarily redundant platform development through a common appreciation of shared services.

This alignment of "horizontal" and "vertical" services will be one of the most interesting things to watch over coming years in the library space. My view is that one of the major changes we will see is that more operations are moved into horizontal "shared services" so that libraries can concentrate on creating value in their vertical, user-oriented services. These "horizontal" services may not start out as "platform" services in the sense that they are made available through web services and can be stitched recombinantly[11] into other applications. However, they will move in that direction.

Libraries and the system vendors that serve them cannot afford to build the full range of services which will be needed to meet user expectations and service ambitions moving forward. Think of virtual reference, repository infrastructure, recommender systems, metadata creation, exposure to search engines, directory and registry services, knowledge bases, selective web harvesting and preservation, aggregated repositories of open access and other materials. The list could be extended considerably. This is one reason why I think that some of the most interesting questions facing libraries are organizational: What organizational frameworks will best secure these services, and what will be the balance between local and shared or third-party activity?

NOTES

1. http://ono.cdlib.org/archives/shimenawa/000153.html
2. www.common-info.org.uk/thoughts/archives/2005/06/archaeology_dat.html
3. www.common-info.org.uk/thoughts/archives/2005/05/more_thoughts_o_1 .html
4. www.itconversations.com/shows/detail329.html
5. www.worldcatlibraries.org/wcpa/ow/075e71ada9407c10a19afeb4da09e526.html
6. www.oclc.org/research/researchworks/xisbn/default.htm
7. http://orweblog.oclc.org/archives/000695.html
8. http://silkworm.talis.com
9. www.talis.com/about_talis/corporate.shtml
10. www.common-info.org.uk
11. http://orweblog.oclc.org/archives/000657.html

READER COMMENT

 John Naughton
Professor, Wolfson College, Cambridge

The key test of a blog, in an era of digital logorrhea, is whether it adds intellectual value to the public sphere. Does it add a new perspective, point to stuff one doesn't—but should—know, make one think again about something hitherto taken for granted? For as long as I have been reading Lorcan Dempsey's blog, it has been passing that test. Long may it continue.

Library logistics (again)

http://orweblog.oclc.org/archives/000746.html

I have suggested in these pages[1] that *logistics* is a central part of what we do. Logistics is about moving information, materials, and services through a network cost-effectively. Resource sharing is supported by a library logistics apparatus. The emerging e-resource discovery-to-delivery chain, tied together with resolution services, is a logistics challenge. Many of the e-resource management issues are like supply-chain management issues. Increasingly, as libraries look at shared solutions for off-site storage, e-resource management, digitization, and archiving, they run into logistics and supply-chain management questions. They are looking for efficiencies within the system, whether that system is a consortium, a network of suppliers, or some other grouping.

In the last year or two I have spoken to a variety of people about "library logistics"; I don't think that they have been entirely persuaded ;-). That may be about to change . . .

This is by way of introduction to the significant report "Public Libraries: Efficiency and Stock Supply Chain Review," written by PKF consultants and published by the Museums, Libraries and Archives Council and the Department of Culture, Media and Sport in the UK. Check the press release,[2] the report home page,[3] and the executive summary[4].

The report argues that English public libraries need to reorganize themselves to create more value for users in public-facing roles. This should be achieved by taking cost out of the back-office functions through the improvement of systemwide logistics and supply-management functions. There are 149 local authorities in England, each with a responsibility to provide the local public library service. Some sample recommendations:

- Standardize the processes through which library authorities meet their goals. For example, standardizing the purchase of books would lead to economies of technical processing and higher discounts.

- Reduce redundancy of effort in stock selection through supplier selection.
- Move to a single cataloging system.

One might argue with some recommendations, or suggest that some are missing. However, the main import of this report is the strong statement that libraries can remove costs from back-office processing by mobilizing their collective resources at the national level. The standardization and consolidation of processes across authorities should deliver savings.

The minister for culture comments:

> For libraries to be able to provide the best possible selection of books they need to purchase them at the most economical cost, and for this they need to adapt their ways of buying. By working together on joint orders and shared systems they could save between £7m and £20m that could be spent on more books or on other improvements such as longer opening hours. (*Independent report supports single library purchasing agency / eGov monitor*[5])

NOTES

1. http://orweblog.oclc.org/archives/000487.html
2. www.mla.gov.uk/news/press_article.asp?articleid=834
3. www.mla.gov.uk/action/framework/framework_04b.asp
4. www.mla.gov.uk/documents/fff_efficiency_01execsum.pdf
5. www.egovmonitor.com/node/2162

FEBRUARY 8, 2006

The preservation turn

http://orweblog.oclc.org/archives/000942.html

We have become used to thinking about digital preservation as an issue. We don't tend to think of print preservation in quite the same way. Several things have come over the horizon recently which have made me think about this issue a little differently:

I have been involved in several discussions around the mass-digitization projects—OCA and G5. I have also participated in some discussion about appropriate disposition of off-site storage facilities and how those might be better articulated within some overall pattern of provision. In this context, there has been some discussion of the cost of managing print collections over time.

Chris Rusbridge has a provocative short article[1] on digital preservation in the current issue of *Ariadne* where he wonders how we can suggest that the putative costs of digital preservation are high when compared with the actual cost of preserving print collections.

I noted the useful UK report a while ago which looks at models of shared repositories: "Optimising Storage and Access in UK Research Libraries."[2] A report for CURL and the British Library, September 2005.

The historic library model has been physical distribution of materials to multiple locations so that they can be close to the point of need. In the network environment, of course, this model changes. Resources do not need to be distributed in advance of need; they can be held in consolidated stores, which, even with replication, do not require the physical buildings we now have. As we move forward, and as more materials are available electronically, we will see more interest in managing the print collection in a less costly way. This discussion is starting, as I note above, in relation to the mass-digitization projects and the heightened interest in off-site storage solutions: in developing a set of consolidated stores. In each case, there is a growing interest in being able to make investment choices which maximize impact—based, for example, on a better understanding of what is rare or common within the system as a whole, on what levels of use are made of materials, and so on. In fact, again looking forward some time, it would be good to have management support systems in place which make recommendations for moving to storage or digitization based on patterns of use, distribution across libraries, and an agreed policy framework.

There are two medium term questions that are of great interest here. First, what future patterns of storage and delivery are optimum within a system (where a system may be a state, a consortium, a country)? Think of arranging a system of repositories so that they are adjacent to good transport links, for example, collectively contracting with a delivery provider, and having better system support for selection for moving to the repositories, and monitoring traffic between the repository and libraries. And managing this alongside growing digitization activity.

Second, think of preservation. Currently, we worry about the unknown long-term costs of digital preservation. However, what about the long-term costs of print preservation? I contend that for many libraries, they will become unsustainable in the current model. If the use of large just-in-case collections declines, if the use of digital resources continues to rise, if mass-digitization projects continue, then it becomes increasingly hard to justify the massive expense of maintaining redundant collections. Long term we may see a shift of cost from print to digital, but this can only be done if the costs of managing print can be reduced, which in turn means some consolidation of print collections, and a shared approach to their preservation.

In this way, the management and preservation of the collective print collection becomes more of an issue. In time, even, it may become an overwhelming issue in the way that preserving the digital record now seems.

NOTES
1. www.ariadne.ac.uk/issue46/rusbridge/
2. www.curl.ac.uk/about/documents/CURL_BLStorageReportFinal-endSept2005.pdf

Ranganathan and the long tail

http://orweblog.oclc.org/archives/000954.html

Ranganathan's[1] five "laws" have classic status in the library community. I am using "classic" in the Frank Kermode[2] sense of being "patient of interpretation" over time: they express something which remains relevant as contexts change.

I wrote[3] about the long tail in terms of aggregation of supply and aggregation of demand.

In this context, aggregation of supply is about improving discovery and reducing transaction costs. It is about making it much easier to allow a reader to *find it* and *get it*, whatever *it* is. Or, in other words, every reader his or her book.

Aggregation of demand is about mobilizing a community of users so that the chances of rendezvous between a resource and an interested user are increased. Or, in other words, every book its reader.

Incidentally, for those who need to be reminded about the full five laws, check out the stylish *Quædam cuiusdam*[4].

NOTES

1. http://en.wikipedia.org/wiki/S._R._Ranganathan
2. www.bartleby.com/65/ke/Kermode.html
3. http://orweblog.oclc.org/archives/000949.html
4. www.wallandbinkley.com/quaedam/?p=56

NOVEMBER 28, 2006

Discovery, delivery, distributed inventory management

http://orweblog.oclc.org/archives/001215.html

Resource *discovery* has been a focus of much attention in recent years.

Once discovery opportunities are provided, a focus on delivery is inevitable. Folks want to have what was *discovered delivered*, to *get* as well as *find*. And delivery, broadly understood, has indeed been a major focus of recent activity. For licensed resources, this has led to an explosion of interest in resolution, to get people from metadata about a discovered item to services on that item, including delivery.

However, I want to focus on the print collections in this post. For print materials, we have seen growing interest in patron-initiated ILL and more sophisticated group and consortial arrangements. This is not universal, but many libraries now participate in consortial, state, or national systems. For example, as I have commented before, in Ohio we are well placed to observe the good work of our neighbors, OhioLINK, in providing an integrated discovery-to-delivery experience across library collections in the state.

Now, just as better discovery drives the need for better delivery, so will the need for better delivery encourage further thinking about how the collective book stock is managed across libraries or groups of libraries. Especially where there are strong consortial or collaborative structures in place that can be leveraged. Libraries have been optimized for local operation. Collections are local and are driven by local requirements. However, where libraries operate in collective systems of delivery and those systems become more important, then issues of how to optimize collections for delivery on a systemwide basis become more important also. Interlibrary lending is an expensive practice, involving multiple transactions and extensive round-trip shipping of materials. So, a natural extension of OhioLINK services, for example, would be to think about shared inventory management across the libraries it serves, maybe supporting its delivery service with consolidated storage of less used materials. Or working with its libraries to coordinate some acquisitions to better match supply and demand at the state level. Or thinking about how to cut down round-tripping by having materials returned to, and "carried by," a library local to the user, until they are requested again. And so on.

Clearly, this connects strongly to discussions of off-site storage, use of library space, collective collection development, mass digitization, preservation, and other "collective collection" issues. Some of these are new issues; some have been long-discussed but remain marginal or peripheral to the mainstream. Of course, one of the more interesting things about the growth in importance of the network is how network activity reconfigures physical activity. In coming years, one interesting manifestation of this will be the selective reconfiguration of print collections—inventory management—in shared settings, to support better delivery, allocation of resources, and preservation.

MARCH 2, 2008

The two ways of Web 2.0

http://orweblog.oclc.org/archives/001556.html

I find Web 2.0 increasingly confusing as a label; no surprise there. This is not just because of its essential vagueness, but because I think it tends to be used in a couple of very different ways. Where this happens, there is bound to be some confusion. Schematically, I will use the labels "diffusion" and "concentration" for these two ways.

Diffusion is probably the more dominant of the two. Here it covers a range of tools and techniques which create richer connectivity between people, applications, and data; which support writers as well as readers; which provide richer presentation environments. What tends to get discussed here are blogs and wikis; RSS; social networking; crowdsourcing of content; websites made programmable through web services and simple APIs; simple service composition environments; AJAX, flex, Silverlight; and so on.

Concentration is a major characteristic of our network experience, which often involves major gravitational hubs (Google, Amazon, Flickr, Facebook, propertyfinder.com). These concentrate data, users (as providers and consumers), and communications and computational capacity. They build value by collaboratively sourcing the creation of powerful data assets with their users. The value grows with the reinforcing property of network effects: the more people who participate, the more valuable they become. And opening up these platforms through web services creates more network effects. These sites also mobilize usage data to reflexively adapt their services, to better target particular users, or to identify design directions. Of course, these platforms are very closely controlled, and there is an interesting balance of interests between openness and control at various levels in how they manage resources (see, for example, my discussion[1] of the Amazon and Google APIs).

Interestingly, if you trace Tim O'Reilly's writings on Web 2.0 since the publication of his major defining article, you see an emphasis on what I have called "concentration" come through. (See my note on an interview[2] with Tim O'Reilly by David Weinberger, on which I draw above, and also see O'Reilly blog posts here[3] and here[4].)

Now, of course, "concentration" and "diffusion" are often complementary approaches. The major Internet hubs "diffuse" their benefits through service and data syndication, APIs, participation, etc., but their value often derives from successfully driving network effects through wide participation and consolidation of data. In fact, many of the "diffusion" techniques work best when associated with concentrating applications. Think of tagging, for example. People have incentives to tag their resources in Flickr or LibraryThing in ways that may not obtain in the library catalog. Scale matters in the context of the social value created in these services (of course, in these examples, folks are also tagging *their own* resources). You cannot simply add social networking to a site and expect it to work well. Think of all those empty forums.

Much of the library discussion of Web 2.0 is about "diffusion," about a set of techniques for richer interaction. It is appropriate that libraries should offer an experience that is continuous with how people experience the web.

However, there is a very important way in which the library experience is not continuous with the web. It remains fragmented: it does not have the characteristics of the concentrating, gravitational hubs which characterize so much web use, and are so much a part of O'Reilly's Web 2.0. Fragmented by database boundary, by service boundary (e.g., connecting a discovery experience gracefully to a fulfillment experience through resolution), by library boundary. We are now familiar with the comparison between this fragmented experience and discovery on the web. And we are also familiar with discussion of how the library presence is weakly represented in the major network presences.

However, think also of the library management environment. Think, for example, of places where data needs to be concentrated to create value: aggregating user data across sites (e.g., COUNTER data), or aggregating user-created data (tags, reviews), or aggregating transactions (e.g., circulations, resolver click-throughs). Motivations here are to drive business intelligence which allows services to be refined (e.g., how does my database usage compare to that of my peer group), to develop targeted services (people who like this also liked that), to improve local services (e.g., add tags or reviews). These are examples where scale matters, where data may need to be concentrated above the individual library level.

And we are seeing for-fee services emerge which address this need. LibraryThing, for example, syndicates its user-generated tagging to libraries. I am not sure that ScholarlyStats[5] provides a service which compares usage across libraries; it would be interesting to know if there were demand for such a thing.

This then touches on larger questions about sourcing decisions (in what combination of local, collaborative, and third party do libraries acquire their service capacities) and about concentration of library presence (in what combination of library or library and third party are services offered).

For example, I discussed[6] Georgia Pines and OhioLINK the other day as examples of groups of libraries collaboratively sourcing a concentrated library presence which increases their gravitational pull.

And libraries are beginning to think more seriously about sourcing services with central web presences. Think, for example, of the decisions made by the National Library of Australia[7] and the Library of Congress[8] when they chose to use Flickr for significant image projects. NLA is seeking to expand the coverage of PictureAustralia; LC is seeking to collect tags from viewers. In each case, the library wants to benefit from the concentration of users and data that Flickr has created on the web. And to suggest another example, Andy Powell has been raising some intriguing questions about how repository services should be sourced in ways that, again, map onto peoples' experience of the web: would a consolidated network-level service be more motivating than a series of institutional presences? (See here[9] and here[10].) Social networking or other services, he suggests, might flourish at this network level in ways that are not feasible at the institutional level.

When we discuss Web 2.0, there is a temptation to think about blogs and wikis, RSS and a Facebook application, and to stop there. There is also some useful thinking about how to expose web services or data in ways that they can be remixed into other applications. However, Web 2.0 is also about concentration: concentration of data, of users, and of communications. We need also to think about how libraries reconfigure services in an environment of network-level gravitational hubs, driven by network effects. This will involve greater concentration of library resources in various ways, and also—probably?—greater reliance on other web presences to deliver their services.

NOTES

1. http://orweblog.oclc.org/archives/001258.html
2. http://orweblog.oclc.org/archives/001266.html
3. http://radar.oreilly.com/archives/2007/08/programming_col.html
4. http://radar.oreilly.com/archives/2007/03/web_20_goes_mai_1.html
5. http://www2.ebsco.com/en-us/ProductsServices/scholarlystats/Pages/index.aspx
6. http://orweblog.oclc.org/archives/001564.html
7. www.nla.gov.au/pub/gateways/issues/80/story01.html
8. www.flickr.com/commons
9. http://efoundations.typepad.com/efoundations/2008/02/repositories-th.html
10. http://efoundations.typepad.com/efoundations/2008/02/repositories-fo.html

READER COMMENT

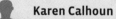 **Karen Calhoun**
Associate University Librarian for Organizational Development and Strategic Initiatives, University Library System, University of Pittsburgh

In his blog, Lorcan has consistently offered a clear line of sight to the opportunities for integrating traditional knowledge organization practices, metadata silos like catalogs, and other fragmented information systems with the new networked environment. In retrospect, my favorite post may be the one he wrote a day or two after Tim O'Reilly's famous one on Web 2.0. One word can sum it up: *prescient*. And we (the library profession) are still not where Lorcan has known we needed to be with our data those many years ago.

Community is the new content

http://orweblog.oclc.org/archives/002013.html

We are now very used to interacting with resources in a social context. The application of community to content, in terms of discussion, recommendation, reviews, ratings, and so on, is evident in many of the services we use, and in some form in most of the major network services we use (Amazon, iTunes, Netflix . . .). Indeed, this is now so much a part of our experience that sites without this experience can seem bleached somehow, like black-and-white TV in a color world.

In a reductive view, here are three types of social experience, which may be present singly or in combination in these sites.

1. Conversation
2. Connection
3. Context

We explicitly talk about resources (conversation). And the traces that we leave intentionally or unintentionally can be mined to create connections between people and to add context to resources (relating, ranking, recommending), based on patterns of association between them. What I am calling "context" here may not be explicitly social, but as it is often mined from aggregate behaviors, it does not seem too much of a stretch to include it.

Conversation. Conversation about services is a natural part of our experience of them. I bought a <u>Zune HD</u>[1] recently; it was not clear to me how to turn it off. A search threw up an answer on one of the several Zune forums. It also showed that others had the same issue, so we can expect that this particular feature will change in future releases. In fact, the detailed instructions we might once have seen with a device like this seem to be a thing of the past; in this case, even the online documentation is not very full. Maybe their decision to not be exhaustive is influenced by the knowledge that a rich documentation base will be collaboratively sourced across multiple conversational forums? Forums may have dominant contributors, and employees of the product provider may participate. Such signed network presences are common: we are used to seeing "signed" reviews, recommendations, comments, and ongoing interactions on music, movie, book, and general consumer and social sites. And online conversation clearly influences online behavior. I have been interested to receive letters from vendors of items I have acquired through Amazon asking that I give them the highest satisfaction rating, and urging that if I am unhappy in any way to contact them first so that they can rectify issues and preserve their rankings.

Connection. I like this quote from Hugh MacLeod:

> 14. The most important word on the internet is not "Search." The most important word on the internet is "Share." Sharing is the driver. Sharing is the DNA. We use Social Objects to share ourselves with other people. We're primates. we like to groom each other. It's in our nature. (*gapingvoid: cartoons drawn on the back of business cards: more thoughts on social objects*[2])

We connect with others by sharing information about ourselves. Networks form around "social objects," the focus of these shared interests. Think of social bookmarking, picture sharing, and social bibliography sites, for example, where we connect around shared interests, in, respectively, interesting resources, pictures, and collecting/reading interests. Facebook and LinkedIn connect people—or their online signed identities—based on the networks of connections they have already made. Users of services—the Zune, for example—who sign up are offered the opportunity to connect with users of like interests, and can prospect the interests of those who chose to disclose them.

Context. We leave traces everywhere. We click, buy, rate, follow pathways, add to playlists. We also create collections, lists, and playlists, which disclose our interests and can be compared to make connections or to generate recommendations, or to seed other lists. Services use this subterranean data not only to make connections with other users, but to create context, to configure resources by patterns of relations created by shared user interests and choices, and to use these patterns to broaden the experience of their users. Google mobilized linking behaviors; Amazon made "people who bought this, also bought this" types of association popular. Such context is now a central part of music, movie, and other sites. Think of the rich recommendation apparatus of Netflix, or the generation of channels, playlists, and recommendations in iTunes, Last.fm, or other music sites. This approach has spread to more academic contexts. Mendeley, a research management and social networking site for researchers, is explicitly modeled after Last.fm (and some Last.fm veterans are among its investors). One of its aspirations is to generate impact rankings and relationships based on patterns of collecting and use of research literature.

Here are some random observations that occur in this context . . . Thoughts about libraries may follow . . .

- Residents and visitors.
- Managing scale and guided navigation.
- Customer relationship management.
- Real-time tracking of trends and analytics.
- Social experiences around content.

Residents and visitors. This is a useful distinction introduced[3] by Dave White. The residents live a part of their lives online; their web selves have become an important projection of identity, and they maintain online networks of friends and colleagues. "They are likely to see the web as a worthwhile place to put forward an opinion." The visitors use the web to get their work done. "They are skeptical of services that offer them the ability to put their identity online as they don't feel the need to express themselves by participating in online culture in the same manner as a Resident." In the schematic advanced above, the resident is interested in conversation and connection as an active participant—his or her traces are visible. Everybody leaves the subterranean traces which contribute to context.

Managing scale and guided navigation. The social provides a layer of interpretation, connection, context, direction, filtering which valuably orients us in large information resources. Services mobilize "intentional data," data about usage and choices, and crowdsourced data to manage abundance where "professional" approaches may not scale. Of course, this can be managed. Nicholas Carr recently remarked[4] of Netflix: "What I've noticed is that the company has deliberately geared its search, filtering, and recommendation tools to lead customers away from newly released hits."

Customer relationship management. Services use the data generated by the activities described above to develop customized engagement with customers, personalizing communications, providing recommendations, and so on. Such data-driven communication is often useful, sometimes intrusive, but is clearly a priority, where scale, again, makes other approaches difficult.

Real-time tracking of trends and analytics. Where there is a critical mass of participation, conversation and context can reveal emerging trends and behaviors. Twitter may be an obvious case, but consider, for example, what the real-time usage data coming from a service like Mendeley might tell us about academic interests.

Social experiences around content. I was struck by some remarks by Trip Hawkins, the CEO of Digital Chocolate and the founder of leading games publisher Electronic Arts, in an interview at the Web 2.0 Summit in 2007. He was talking about games in a mobile environment, where Digital Chocolate is active. "In my opinion traditional content is dead," he said, and he went on to characterize traditional content as "about a playback and immersive experience and which involve a business model where you pay a fee for the privilege of escapism and checking out." These traditional forms include reading and cinema experiences, and he suggests that participation in those media has leveled out. He contrasts this with a new type of content and associated experience, which is growing: "Where the consumer is increasingly going to spend their money is on social value which is enabled by content where the content isn't for sale for its own sake—the content is there to enable improvements in your social life."[5] Depending on your point of view or cultural formation, this characterization might be plausible or startling ;-).

NOTES

1. A couple of eyebrows were raised at work when I mentioned that I had bought a Zune HD, the recently released third-generation Zune. I just wanted a media device and this is very nice. It is growing on me. David Pogue notes that "the software design is fluid, beautiful and incredibly responsive." www.nytimes .com/2009/09/17/technology/personaltech/17pogue.html

2. www.gapingvoid.com/Moveable_Type/archives/004265.html

3. http://tallblog.conted.ox.ac.uk/index.php/2008/07/23/not-natives-immigrants -but-visitors-residents

4. www.roughtype.com/archives/2009/09/netflixs_tail_m.php
5. "Edge: Gaming Moderated," by Morgan Webb with Trip Hawkins and Robert Kotick, from Web 2.0 Summit, San Francisco, October 18, 2007, at http://blip.tv/file/441160 [http://blip.tv/file/441160]

Sourcing and scaling

http://orweblog.oclc.org/archives/002058.html

One of the major issues facing libraries as the network reconfigures processes is how appropriately to source and scale activities. What does it make sense to do at institutional level, what does it make sense to source elsewhere (repository services in the cloud, for example, or institutional e-mail services from Google), and what should be left entirely to other providers?

I discussed[1] "scaling" from the supply side—what libraries do and how—a while ago when discussing a NISO report on resource management. (See "Untangling the library systems environment"[2] in chapter 5, "Library Systems.")

Such decisions are going to become more important, as externalization becomes more feasible and more attractive. There at least two dimensions which may be interesting to spell out.

Following from the note above, I label the first *scalar emphasis:* at what level is it appropriate to get things done. For simplicity here are three scales:

1. **Institution-scale.** Activity is managed within an institution with a local target audience.
2. **Group-scale.** Activity is managed within a supra-institutional domain whether this is a region, a consortium, or a state or a country. The audience is correspondingly grouped. In educational terms, think of the activities of JISC in the UK or SurfNet in the Netherlands. In library terms, think of the HathiTrust, or of Georgia Pines, or of OhioLINK.
3. **Web-scale.** Activity is managed at the network level where we are now used to services like Amazon, Flickr, Google, and YouTube providing

e-commerce, collection, discovery, and other functions. Here, the audience is potentially all web users.

We have seen more activity in 2 and 3 in recent years. There has been stronger consortial activity, and libraries have been looking at how to exploit web-scale services more (think of knowledge-base data in Google Scholar, for example, or links to special collections materials added to Wikipedia).

This then raises a sourcing decision. Again, consider three possible ways in which a product or service might be sourced:

1. **Institutional.** Activity is developed locally.
2. **Collaborative.** Activity is developed in concert with partners (e.g., purchasing consortium, shared off-site storage, open source software . . .).
3. **Third party.** Activity is secured from a third-party service (e.g., e-journal access). A third party might be a commercial or not-for-profit supplier, or it might be a public provider, as a part of state or national provision. The latter is especially important in those jurisdictions where some library infrastructure may be provided as part of educational or cultural funding (see Rachel Bruce's presentation,[3] for example).

As the network reduces transaction costs, it is now simpler to externalize in this way. The reduced cost and effort of collaboration and of transacting with third parties for services have made these approaches more attractive and feasible. There are also scale advantages. Although it has become common to talk about moving services to the cloud, it is important to remember that important choices still have to be made. And there may not always yet be good options as the environment continues to evolve. Decisions about scaling and sourcing will be interesting for several years to come.

NOTES

1. http://orweblog.oclc.org/archives/002015.html
2. http://orweblog.oclc.org/archives/002015.html
3. www.niso.org/apps/group_public/download.php/2888/bruce_siteversion _lrms09niso.ppt

SEPTEMBER 12, 2010

Emerging network-level management of the collective print collection

http://orweblog.oclc.org/archives/002135.html

One of the recurrent themes in these pages is that systemwide coordination of print materials is necessary as libraries begin to retire collections—to off-site storage or removing them altogether. There are various drivers here: the demands on space, the emergence of a digital corpus, the cost of managing a resource that releases progressively less value in research and learning. Print runs of journals have been an early focus, but interest is extending to books also. I believe we are moving to a situation where network-level management of the collective collection becomes the norm, but it will take some years for service, policy, and infrastructure frameworks to be worked out, and evolution will be uneven. The network may be at the level of a consortium, a state or region, or a country. At the moment, this trend is manifesting itself in a variety of local or group mass-storage initiatives, as well as in several regional and national initiatives.

Last week, I came across interesting discussions of two of the more high-profile initiatives in this area. These are WEST: Toward a Western Regional Storage Trust,[1] a US consortium of institutions, and the UK Research Reserve (UKRR),[2] a national approach.

Karen Schneider discusses WEST, placing it in the context of her own library's needs to reclaim space to meet local needs.

But the most significant infrastructure issue faced by the library facility is that the bulk of the space is occupied by very-low-use materials: books and journals.

In the mid-1950s, it made sense that the bulk of the library's space needs were occupied by then-state-of-the-art information tools. But the only way our library can maintain relevance is to reclaim the bulk of this space for 21st-century services such as information literacy instruction, faculty technology development, group study, and cultural events. We are not a museum for obsolete information technologies; to again quote our beloved Ranganathan, "The library is a living organism." (*Free Range Librarian*[3])

The UKRR was a central topic at the Dare to Share conference[4] organized by the British Library's Preservation Advisory Centre and Research Libraries UK to consider preservation as a part of collective approaches to print management. I was not at this event, but it generated very interesting twitterage; the presentations[5] are now available online, and University of Huddersfield archivist, Sarah Wickham, has written a brief report[6] of the day's discussions.

A presentation[7] by Deborah Shorley describes the UK Research Reserve: "UKRR is a HEFCE-sponsored scheme which helps UK university libraries dispose of their low use research journals, safe in the knowledge that one copy will be kept in BLDSC, with two backup copies in other UKRR libraries" (HEFCE—Higher Education Funding Council for England. BLDSC— British Library Document Supply Centre). The local rationale is raised to the national level: "We must manage our national research information infrastructure responsibly; print material is becoming less important to researchers; UK universities urgently need more space to do their work; we can no longer cope with the ever-expanding collections in our university libraries."

Each of these discussions notes the importance of data: to make sensible decisions you need to have good intelligence about the collective collection of which individual libraries are part. Holdings and circulation data, especially, come to mind. This point is also raised in the very interesting presentation[8] by Brian Clifford, which focuses on the management of books at

Leeds University. He introduces an interesting collections typology, as a way of framing different dynamics at work across the collection:

> *Heritage:* Significant and distinctive collections which continue to be developed
>
> *Legacy:* Significant and distinctive collections: historic strengths but no longer added to

One of Lorcan Dempsey's significant contributions to libraries over the past decade has been to identify important but amorphous developments and codifying them into well-coined phrases. Through this work, Lorcan has made it possible for librarians to debate issues more concretely and advance service development more strategically.

Perhaps my favorite such phrase is "the collective collection," which has proven to be a remarkably durable and valuable concept. Lorcan has used this term to help us navigate from the comparatively simple idea of analyzing library collections collectively (early work on which I was privileged to conduct with Brian Lavoie) to boundary-pushing efforts in more recent years to develop or manage a single collection across institutions "at the network level." Whether different futures are emerging for different components of the collective collection—for journals as compared with books and for print materials as compared with digital—is a key question before us today.

Another example is "discovery happens elsewhere," which Lorcan has conceptualized as having implications for the discovery environments a library should offer as well as the design of its disclosure and fulfillment mechanisms. If discovery happens elsewhere, where does it, in fact, happen? Since libraries no longer control discovery, many will be rethinking how to assist the development of user skills to find and evaluate information resources and connect this up with their own discovery strategy.

Lorcan's work to codify these themes has helped our community identify some of the most pressing issues we face. Even when we cannot play a role in controlling change wrought from outside, taking hold of these key issues has helped libraries effectively with how best to adapt their strategic posture.

Self-renewing: Supporting current research and teaching

Finite: No longer relevant—can be considered for withdrawal

[Heritage or legacy?[9]]

Brian goes on to discuss action at local, regional, and national levels if the library's responsibility to its own users and to the scholarly print record are to be met.

As can be seen, the move to shared responsibility for print raises major service and policy issues, as well as very practical management issues.

An effective and efficient approach will depend on good intelligence in the form of aggregate data about collections (and Karen discusses OCLC in this context). Brian notes the balance between metrics and local knowledge in making judgments. Local knowledge will always be important, but it does seem that to scale across many institutions, some shared decision criteria which can be operationalized through available data resources will be required.

NOTES

1. www.cdlib.org/services/collections/sharedprint/westinitiative.html
2. www.ukrr.ac.uk
3. http://freerangelibrarian.com/2010/09/04/the-west-project-the-first-shoe-drops-for-the-big-shift
4. www.bl.uk/blpac/dare.html
5. www.bl.uk/blpac/dare.html
6. http://msarahwickham.wordpress.com/2010/09/06/dare-to-share-new-approaches-to-long-term-collections-management
7. www.bl.uk/blpac/pdf/dareshorley.pdf
8. www.bl.uk/blpac/pdf/dareclifford.pdf
9. www.bl.uk/blpac/pdf/dareclifford.pdf

FEBRUARY 13, 2011

The library network and the scholarly record

http://orweblog.oclc.org/archives/002154.html

The library community is a highly interconnected one. Networks are motivated both by library mission and effective management of resources. This trend will accelerate as the Internet favors shared services, and libraries will see more benefit in building such shared services. The HathiTrust is an important example. The growth of interest in sharing library systems infrastructure is another (see the <u>Orbis Cascade Alliance RFI</u>[1] for a current example, or the Canadian <u>TriUniversity Group</u>[2] of Guelph, Waterloo, and Laurier).

Any library is likely to belong to a variety of networks: for resource sharing, for cataloging, for acquisition of licensed materials, and so on. These have a variety of governance mechanisms and operate at different scales. In some, a group of libraries explicitly connect around a shared purpose: think of OhioLINK, for example, or the TriUniversity Group mentioned above. At a much broader scale, one might talk about the "public library network" or the "university library network" in a particular country.

OCLC has an interesting role here. It provides infrastructure, or a platform, which supports a large network, or networks, of libraries. This shared capacity removes the need for multiple explicit bilateral or group arrangements: libraries benefit from the network OCLC facilitates as they participate in its services. So libraries participate to share the effort of cataloging, or to make other libraries' collections available to their users, or to share question-answering capacity. Because of the number of libraries participating, OCLC, libraries, and others can leverage the power of this network for discovery, collection analysis, and other services. For example, OCLC can provide access to the library network for users of Google Book Search. It provides access to the network as a <u>service</u>[3].

I have been reading *Networks, Crowds and Markets*,[4] by David Easley and Jon Kleinberg. (OK, to be honest, I have read the first chapter.) I was interested early on to come across this characterization of a network:

> When people talk about the "connectedness" of a complex system, in general they are really talking about two related issues. One is connectedness at the level of structure—who is linked to whom—and the other is connectedness at the level of *behavior*—the fact that each individual's actions have implicit consequences for the outcomes of everyone in the system. (p. 4)

So—a small "behavioral" example—if you think about the shared cataloging network, we are familiar with the phenomenon whereby some libraries wait for others to catalog an unavailable item, thereby reducing the overall effectiveness of the system.

I wrote the other day about how libraries were beginning to <u>manage down their print collections</u>[5]. As this trend becomes more pronounced, it will highlight the way in which libraries see themselves as belonging to a network which has a collective responsibility to the print scholarly record. At the moment, this responsibility is weakly defined and variably accepted. Some libraries may discard materials without regard to the collective collection of the library network as a whole. Others may check WorldCat to get a quick measure of "rareness." Others may have particular responsibilities defined within a consortium, state, or other group to which they belong.

Easley and Kleinberg define *institution* as follows:

> Our notion of institution here is very broad. It can be any set of rules,
> conventions, or mechanisms that serve to synthesize individual
> actions into a pattern of aggregate behavior. (p. 15)

In this sense OCLC has helped institutionalize shared cataloging. Over the next few years, we will see some institutionalization of the shared responsibility to the print collections across the library network. Patterns of aggregate behavior will emerge which will need to be supported by a variety of evolving arrangements:

1. **Policy and service frameworks.** <u>The WEST initiative</u>[6] is an example of a venue in which policy and service frameworks are developing. An important aspect of WEST is that it provides a framework within which libraries of multiple sizes can affiliate to coordinate their print management activities or to support the overall mission. The HathiTrust is also important here, as the management of the print scholarly record will co-evolve with the management of its emerging digital surrogate. These and other initiatives are also developing sustainability models which aim to secure the shared resource.

2. **Inventory infrastructure.** Many institutions have developed off-site and shared storage initiatives in recent years. Digital stores are emerging. Attention is turning to how these might be managed as nodes in a network, rather than as stand-alone activities.

3. **Registry.** It is unlikely that this activity will be centralized within a particular governance structure. However, the actions of particular initiatives have consequences for others across the network, and it will be useful to have access to some "intelligence" about them. It will be important to know how many copies of an item exist, who owns them, or once owned them, where they are stored, whether they are digitized, what archival commitments have been made about them, and so on. This is a potential role for WorldCat, the registry that is already central to much library network activity.

In a library meeting I attended last year, there was a discussion about the number of libraries whose missions included a responsibility to the long-term curation of the print scholarly record. There seemed to be some consensus that the number was about twenty-five. I think the number is bigger although the burden will be variably spread through a network of affiliations yet to be institutionalized.

NOTES

1. www.orbiscascade.org/RFI_2011_02.pdf
2. http://trellis3.tug-libraries.on.ca
3. http://orweblog.oclc.org/archives/002018.html
4. www.worldcat.org/title/networks-crowds-and-markets-reasoning-about-a-highly-connected-world/oclc/495616815
5. http://orweblog.oclc.org/archives/002151.html
6. www.cdlib.org/services/collections/sharedprint/westinitiative.html

MAY 19, 2011

Sourcing and scaling: The University of California

http://orweblog.oclc.org/archives/002175.html

I was interested to see Heather Christenson describe the HathiTrust as a collaboratively sourced web-scale research library in a recent article ("HathiTrust: A Research Library at Web Scale"[1]).

This reminded me of an entry I wrote a while ago about sourcing and scaling[2] (which is referenced in the article). In a shared network environment, one of the most interesting issues facing libraries is how appropriately to source and scale activities.

A few years ago, this activity would have been sourced within the institution: each library would have developed its own infrastructure, user interface, local community outreach, and so on. Now, such an impulse is questioned. It makes sense to source something like this collaboratively. And it is provided at the level of the network: its target user population is the population of web users.

Questions about sourcing and scaling are becoming much more common as the logic of the network reconfigures patterns of information production and use. What does it make sense to do at institutional level? What does it make sense to source elsewhere (repository services in the cloud, for example, or institutional e-mail services from Google)? And what should be left entirely to other providers? At what level, or scale, is it best to do things? Locally, or within a consortium, or . . . ?

Think of four sourcing options: Self (provide it locally), collaborative (provide it within a group), public (provided through state or national activity), or third party (provided by another commercial or noncommercial entity).

Think of three scaling options: local or institutional, group, and web scale.

These can be put together to give a variety of options. So, for example, Tripod, the shared catalog of Swarthmore, Haverford College, and Bryn Mawr, is a collaboratively sourced group solution. PubMed is a web-scale public offering. And, as already noted, HathiTrust is a collaboratively sourced web-scale service.

An interesting contrast between the US and many other parts of the world is that often what is done collaboratively in the US may be done through a public agency elsewhere. For example, Christenson contrasts the HathiTrust as a collaborative activity with something that the JISC, an activity of the public higher-education funding councils, might provide in the UK. It is also common in many countries outside the US to have publicly supported union catalog and related activities.

We can observe two trends. First, there is a trend toward externalization: libraries are looking to collaboratively source activities or to outsource them to third parties. Think of collaborative activities around managing down print collections here, the WEST project for example, or the growth of shared library systems (the Orbis Cascade Alliance, for example, recently issued an RFI[3] about a shared integrated library system). Think of the growing interest in cloud-based sourcing of systems and services.

Second, there is a trend to "move up" in the network, by doing more things at group level within consortia or public contexts (think of Ohio-LINK or Summit), or by leveraging network-level services (think of social networking sites, for example).

The current economic environment further encourages these trends. Institutions look for economies of scale through collaboration. And they also want to focus attention on high-value areas, and outsource routine or shared activities.

I was reminded of these issues while reading a very interesting internal report of the University of California on library services. This is the interim report of the systemwide Library Planning Task Force, convened under the auspices of the Systemwide Library and Scholarly Information Advisory Committee[4] (report and related material[5]).

A stark environmental picture is presented:

The libraries will experience budget reductions of as much as $52M, or 21% of their current budget base, over the next six years. "To put this into perspective, this cut is greater than the total library budget of any single UC campus, and roughly equivalent to the budgets of three of our mid-sized campuses, all AAU members."

The libraries will likely lose the equivalent of $17M in buying power in the same period given publisher price increases. "This is equivalent to the current library materials budgets of two mid-sized campuses, and means a reduction in the systemwide acquisition rate of about 200,000 items per year."

Existing facilities will run out of space for new materials over the next five to seven years, at the same time as "demand increases for extended hours and services and technologically well-equipped and flexible learning environments in the libraries' prime campus locations."

They go on to observe that the impact of these factors can be mitigated through collaboration. They propose four strategies:

1. Expand and collectively manage shared library services.
2. Support faculty efforts to change the system of scholarly communication.
3. Explore new sources of revenue.
4. Improve the existing framework for systemwide planning, consultation, and decision-making.

Of course, the University of California is an unusual institution, bringing together some of the world's major universities in a shared organizational framework. One result of this shared framework has been the <u>California Digital Library</u>,[6] which concentrates operational and innovation capacity for the whole system. CDL has been responsible for some major services, and is an active partner in the HathiTrust. Another is the Regional Library Facilities, north and south, for managing print collections. A major recommendation is that the range of such shared services should grow, whether sourced within the UC universities or externally.

Cooperation is difficult. Especially where money flows, and impact needs to be seen, at the institutional level. However, given the existing level of shared services, the organizational framework, and the pressures described in this report, it will be interesting to watch what services the UC libraries move to a shared environment over the next few years.

P.S. The report describes the WorldCat Local–based Next Generation Melvyl in these terms:

> The Next-Generation Melvyl (NGM) initiative moves the discovery of information for researchers and students to the highest networked level. The initiative takes access to the highest level of aggregation and is vital for the most effective provision of information access and services. Strategically, NGM also positions the UC Libraries to provide aggregated access to a significantly increasing array of full-text information resources: e.g., the millions of digitized books in the Google Books Project and the HathiTrust.

NOTES

1. www.hathitrust.org/documents/christenson-lrts-201104.pdf
2. http://orweblog.oclc.org/archives/002058.html

3. www.orbiscascade.org/index/shared-integrated-library-system-team-2011
4. http://libraries.universityofcalifornia.edu/planning/taskforce
5. http://libraries.universityofcalifornia.edu/planning/taskforce/interim_report
   _package_2011-05-09.pdf
6. www.cdlib.org

CHAPTER 3

IN THE FLOW

IF LIBRARIES WERE once the reservoir of accumulated knowledge that a scholar would visit to conduct his research, they are now part of the research flow: more flexible, agile, and omnipresent. For better or worse, libraries are just one more source of information. How are they adapting to this tectonic shift in the information landscape? And, more important, how could they adapt differently? The posts in this section include the seminal "In the flow" and begin to explore how the research process, and libraries' role in it, is evolving.

APRIL 24, 2005

Which environment?

http://orweblog.oclc.org/archives/000638.html

We are used to thinking about the user in the library environment. This will continue to be important.

A major part of our challenge moving forward is thinking about the library in the user environment.

The user is increasingly a network person, who may move through several environments.

In the flow

http://orweblog.oclc.org/archives/000688.html   Tag: Noteworthy, Coinage

Workflow is important. We often think of the network as multiple individual opportunities: a mass of websites. However, just as we increasingly work, learn, research, and play in a network environment, so will services evolve to reduce effort and improve effectiveness. These services will support flow construction and resource integration—tying together tasks and the resources needed to address them.

Libraries have always been eager to "fit in" to their users' lives. In a network environment, this increasingly means "fitting in" with evolving network workflows.

Think reductively of two workflow endpoints.

The first is demand-side: we are constructing flows and integrating resources in our own personal spaces. We are drawing on social networking sites, blogs, RSS aggregators, bookmarklets, toolbars, extensions, plug-ins. These are variably configured, stitched together by what I have called the _intrastructure_[1] of RSS, bookmarklets, tags, and simple web services. Participation is also variable. Some are developing elaborate digital identities, a

---

READER COMMENT

Wendy Lougee
University Librarian and McKnight Presidential Professor, University of Minnesota

Lorcan's blog has become a destination in my online "following" for two distinct reasons. There have been specific themes that have resonated with critical issues we have been grappling with locally–e.g., his analysis of "discovery." Equally important, however, have been his insights (and turn of a phrase) at a more conceptual level. We've exploited his notion of "getting in the flow" of users as an accessible mantra in our planning. More recently, his spin on "engaging, rightscaling, and innovating" surfaced immensely important trends for libraries. That dual ability to explore an issue and to reveal the higher-order trends is spot-on for understanding our volatile environment.

personal bricolage of network services. Others are less actively constructive, working with what comes straight out of the box. However, whether they are built into our browser or available from a growing number of network services, we will increasingly have rich demand-side flow construction and resource integration facilities "straight out of the box." The advance of RSS and its integration with new Apple and Microsoft operating systems is interesting in this regard.

The second is supply-side, where workflow and integration have been prefabricated to support particular tasks. Think of a course management system, or a customer relationship management system. We will also see growth here, as <u>processes are standardized</u>[2] and supported in applications.

One reason that supply-side customization and personalization services have not been more actively taken up is that it may be less important to me to be able to manipulate flows and resources within a supply-side environment than to be able to integrate them into my self-constructed demand-side environment. So, for example, the most important thing for me may not be to manipulate components within some user interface, or to have e-mail alerts sent to me; it may be to have an RSS feed so that I can interact with a range of resources in a uniform way. The value may be in playing well with my aggregator, a central part of my workflow, of how I engage with network services.

What does this mean for libraries? We have begun to realize more keenly that the library needs to co-evolve with user behaviors. This means that understanding the way in which research, learning, and consumer behaviors are changing is key to understanding how libraries must respond. And as network behavior is increasingly supported by workflow and resource integration services, the library must think about how to make its services available to those workflows. Many of our recent discussions have in fact been about this very issue, about putting the library *in* the flow. Think of the course management system. If this helps structure the "learnflow" then the library needs to think about how to be in that flow. Think of Google. It has reached into the browser and the cell phone. It is firmly in the flow of user behavior, and as libraries and information providers want to be in that flow also, they are discussing how best to expose their data to Google and other search engines. Think of the iPod. If this is the preferred place to manage my liquid content, what does this mean for library content?

Here are some examples I have come across recently which may make this more real.

The first is a general one. In the past month or two, I have heard two presentations from public librarians talking about digital audiobooks, and suggesting that they will be popular. The reason given is clear: in an iPod world, digital audio fits nicely into the "commuteflow" or, indeed, the "lifeflow."

The second is from the very interesting work at the University of Rochester which seeks to understand research work practices in the context of the evolution of institutional repository services.

> In the long run, we envision a system that, first and foremost, supports our faculty members' efforts to "do their own work"—that is, to organize their resources, do their writing, work with co-authors, and so on. Such a system will include the self-publishing and self-archiving features that the DSpace code already supports, and will rely heavily on preservation, metadata, persistent URLs, and other existing features of DSpace. When we build this system, we will include a simple mechanism for converting works in progress into self-published or self-archived works, that is, moving documents from an in-progress folder into the IR. We believe that if we support the research process as a whole, and if faculty members find that the product meets their needs and fits their way of work, they will use it, and "naturally" put more of their work into the IR.[3]

I hope that it is reasonable to read this work in this way: based on their investigations, Rochester staff recognize that they need to describe and deliver the service in such a way that faculty see it supporting their workflow. The library has identified a flow construction gap, to do with the writing and sharing of papers, which they hope to fill by providing workflow support through augmentations to DSpace. Looking forward, we might surmise that future success will be more assured to the extent to which the new support is a natural extension of current workflows.

The final one comes from a presentation[4] by David Tosh[5] and Ben Werdmuller[6] which draws on their work modeling "learning landscapes" in the context of the evolution of e-portfolios. They see the e-portfolio as a place where the student constructs a digital identity, which connects resources, experiences, and tutors. *Connection* is important, because *learning* happens in contexts of communication and exchange beyond the formal course structures. The VLE (*virtual learning environment* aka course management system), which in the terms presented above is a supply-side workflow manager, is one part of this landscape. A focus of this work appears to be to develop capacity for richer demand-side integration. Now, I do not have the context to assess this work in terms of its own discipline, but I think it has nice illustrative value and is interesting here for a couple of reasons. One, the "library" is not present in this iteration of the landscape. But, more important, how would one represent the library if it were to be dropped in? As "the library"? As a set of services (catalog, virtual reference . . .)? If as a set of services, which services? And, if a particular set of services, how well would they "play" in this environment? What would need to be done for them to be in the flow?

The importance of flow underlines recurrent themes:

> The library needs to be in the user environment and not expect the user to find his or her way to the library environment.
> Integration of library resources should not be seen as an end in itself but as a means to better integration with the user environment, with workflow.

Increasingly, the user environment will be organized around various work-flows. In fact, in a growing number of cases, a workflow application may be the consumer of library services.

The message for libraries is clear: *be in the flow.*

NOTES

1. http://orweblog.oclc.org/archives/000505.html
2. http://orweblog.oclc.org/archives/000693.html
3. Nancy Fried Foster and Susan Gibbons, "Understanding Faculty to Improve Content Recruitment for Institutional Repositories," *D-Lib Magazine* 11 (January 2005), at www.dlib.org/dlib/january05/foster/01foster.html
4. http://elgg.net/dtosh/files/260/568/creation_of_a_learning_landscape.ppt
5. http://elgg.net/dtosh
6. http://elgg.net/bwerdmuller

JULY 1, 2005

The network and the library

http://orweblog.oclc.org/archives/000716.html

Libraries have always been nodes in networks. They have managed flows of materials into those nodes from a range of suppliers, and between nodes in resource-sharing initiatives. These flows are supported by variably config-ured networks—of supply and use.

In the print world, library services were concentrated in those nodes. The library was vertically organized around the management of its collec-tions. Distribution networks grew up to support this model, supported by various agents, jobbers, and others.

Over time, more was given from the local node to the "network cloud" of consortia, shared services, commercial third-party services, and so on. Digital networks reduced the friction in organizational networks and pro-vided more opportunities for interaction with suppliers and users.

This emerged gradually. Think of shared cataloging. Of remote access to abstracting and indexing services. But the pace is accelerating. Think of developments in consortial resource sharing. Of licensed full-text content. Of virtual reference. Of third-party archiving services. Of the emergence of hosted services (see RefWorks, for example). A growing part of library

services are secured within horizontal networks where the library partic-
ipates with suppliers or other libraries. There is a similar trend in the way
that the library interacts with its users. More of that is *moving*[1] into the
network also.

This phenomenon is not unusual. And anybody who has read Thomas
Friedman's *The World Is Flat*[2] or the more academic *The Rise of the Network
Society,*[3] by Manuel Castells, will be familiar with its various manifestations.

Castells talks about how a growing proportion of our personal, social, and
business activity is moving into the "space of flows" supported by digital
networks. Flows of information transform relationships, and allow a general
reshaping of organizations, work, and behavior according to a networking
logic, a logic based on addition at the edges, decentralization, and horizontal integration around processes. He talks of the emergence of the "network enterprise" where firms organize in networks with multiple sourcing
dependencies. Think of how a company like Cisco, for example, draws on
services from many other companies to develop and deliver its own.

Friedman tells a similar story albeit in different terms. The pervasive-
ness of the digital environment, the emergence of workflow technologies
around web services, and the growth of capacity in India, China, and Rus-
sia have led to a "flattening" of business activity. Supply chains and logistics networks are becoming more streamlined, and communication and
standardization support outsourcing of business processes. These developments allow organizations to meet their goals by assembling processes
from horizontal networks of suppliers, rather than by vertically assembling processes within their own organizations. Friedman gives the example of how Toshiba will tell you to drop off your computer with UPS to be
repaired. However, it is UPS which repairs the computer. He goes so far as
to say that there are some companies that never touch their own products
anymore. Horizontal deep collaborations are becoming common, as organizations look for efficiencies in their operations.

So libraries, like the rest of the world, are getting flatter. They are giving
more to the network cloud. They are entering the space of flows.

The incentives for libraries are the same as for other organizations. By
reducing the friction in interactions, the network creates potential efficiencies and improved service. An example is the ability to do deeper

resource sharing more efficiently because you can tie together the various steps—discovery, location, fulfillment—quickly and conveniently, joining up previously separate processes. So, once an ILL request would have to be written out and passed vertically up the organization to be sent to another organization where it would travel down to the appropriate place for processing. Now, in some resource-sharing environments, the user can discover what he or she wants, initiate a request, and horizontal communication between systems steps in to do fulfillment and manage the transaction. Similarly, in some virtual reference environments, processes in different libraries communicate horizontally with others to satisfy requests.

Because of what they do, libraries have been early adopters of such networks of mutual dependence. They have recognized the value of shared resources, which build capacity and remove redundant operations. As libraries work to create and demonstrate value in the age of Amazoogle, it is likely that this trend will continue as they seek further efficiencies so that they can develop new services.

Again, think of digital preservation, virtual reference, shared acquisitions and collection building, cooperative digitization, metadata aggregation.... These lend themselves to new network arrangements, to the development of shared services. What will be most interesting is to see how the balance between the library and the network continues to develop in the next few years.

NOTES

1. http://orweblog.oclc.org/archives/000688.html
2. www.worldcatlibraries.org/wcpa/ow/d3d28d7123bb69cda19afeb4da09e526.html
3. www.worldcatlibraries.org/wcpa/ow/58aa259f13cdb8e0a19afeb4da09e526.html

MARCH 30, 2006

An addressable knowledge base

http://orweblog.oclc.org/archives/000984.html

There has been a lot of discussion about Wikipedia of late. Much of this has been about "authority." There is another major issue at play here as well, which is really quite interesting for libraries.

Let me step back a moment to talk about the URL. The URL is the currency of the web. For something to be referenced, to be talked about, to be shared in the web environment, it needs to have a URL. Those things that are referenceable are more likely to enter the web conversation; those that are not referenceable in this way are off-web and much less visible.

Wikipedia is an addressable knowledge base. It allows me to incorporate additional "knowledge" in my communications by simply including a URL. The economy and convenience of doing this is enormous, and it is only possible because the resource is on-web.

MARCH 28, 2007

Our digital identities: Bricolage, prefabrication, and disclosure

http://orweblog.oclc.org/archives/001309.html

In recent presentations[1] I talk about *workflow* in quite general terms. I suggest that we have seen the focus of our attention shift from the database, to the website, to workflow as the web environment becomes richer. We want to get things done on the network, not just find things.

Workflow, in this general sense, may be self-assembled from the range of resources available to us as network services (Flickr, for example); as widgets, extensions, and toolbars; as bookmarks and RSS feeds; and so on. Some folks may have elaborate apparatuses; others less so. However, there are also important prefabrications that may support workflow, course management systems or campus portals, for example. And in between, there are environments which allow us to compose resources to support what we want to do, My Yahoo! or the personalized Google home page, for example. We do not currently share a "composition" environment, although we are seeing a richer shared-browser environment emerge, RSS support, for example.

In this context, I was interested to read a post by Tony Hirst, of the Open University. He is talking about "personal learning environments," or PLEs (Wikipedia entry on PLE[2]).

Anyway, I think I've worked out what PLEs are—they're the set of web services we each use for our own purposes; and they're personal because the combination we use is unique to each of us. (*oh, you use Google docs do you—I use Zoho; GTalk? I'm on MSN; Flickr? no, Photobucket; Typepad? WordPress . . .*)[3]

These remarks are part of a more general discussion about *network-level personal resource-sharing services* (that's my phrase) such as YouTube, Slide-Share, Scribd, Flickr, and so on. As part of our personal digital identity, we disclose and share traces and works on the network, and we have various ways of doing that. Hirst wonders why JISC in the UK does not support a national-level version of a service like Scribd for academic materials. Many institutions, including his own,[4] have institutional repositories, but these are "independently hosted," and he is not aware of a discovery service across them. There is a national service, Jorum, for sharing learning materials, but it co-exists with institutional resources such as the OU's Open-Learn,[5] without, again, an obvious shared discovery service across them.

And he observes:

> The problem is, there are just sooooooooooooo many places to share content now. And I'm not sure what the solution is? Maybe it's that I keep all my stuff where I want it, and then share it into the communities I want to, and let search engines/harvesters pull it into other communities where it's relevant (maybe letting me know when they do, and giving me the option of stopping them).[6]

I thought that this was a really interesting post. For several reasons. First, it highlights how folks are in fact assembling personal digital identities from a variety of tools on the network, piecing them together in ways that make sense to get things done. Second, for me, and this may not be the intention of the post, it underlines some issues of institutional fragmentation. Scale and brand matter, and are connected, and in turn relate to incentives. If I want to manage stuff, I may put it one place. If I want to share it with a broad community, I may put it another. If I want it to be universally discoverable, it needs to be in the right place. A national resource may be more compelling than an institutional one; a network-level one more compelling again. Consolidation has its uses as new network services show. Consolidated discovery is very important, whether or not the underlying resources are consolidated. And finally, it provides some interesting use cases for thinking about how to put institutional—library and other—services "in the flow"⁷ of research and learning behaviors.

NOTES

1. www.oclc.org/research/staff/dempsey/presentations.htm
2. http://en.wikipedia.org/wiki/Personal_Learning_Environment
3. http://ouseful.open.ac.uk/blogarchive/010073.html
4. http://oro.open.ac.uk
5. www.open.ac.uk/openlearn/home.php
6. http://blogs.open.ac.uk/Maths/ajh59/010073.html
7. www.cic.uiuc.edu/programs/CenterForLibraryInitiatives/Archive/Conference Presentation/Conference2007/home.shtml

APRIL 6, 2008

Some thoughts about egos, objects, and social networks . . .

http://orweblog.oclc.org/archives/001601.html

More of a linked list of other people's thoughts . . . about egos and objects. I quote some pieces below: all of the posts are suggestive and worth reading. The linking theme is that people connect and share themselves through "social objects," pictures, books, or other shared interests, and that successful social networks are those which form around such social objects.

Here is Fred Stutzman in a post which contrasts *ego-centric* and *object-centric* social networks. Flickr or LibraryThing are object-centric networks, while Facebook is an ego-centric one.

> In a post I wrote exploring the network effect multiplier,[1] the value proposition of object-centric social networks is described. Object-centric social networks offer core value, which is multiplied by network value. A great photo-hosting service like Flickr stands alone without the network, making it less susceptible to migration. An ego-centic network, on the other hand, has limited core-value—its value is largely

in the network—making it highly susceptible to migration. We see this with Myspace: individuals lose little in terms of affordances when they migrate from Myspace to Facebook, making the main chore of migration network-reestablishment, a chore made ever-simpler as the migration cascade continues.[2]

In a much-discussed post, Jyri Engeström of Jaiku talks about the importance of objects in mediating connections between people. He talks about the "'social just means people' fallacy," suggesting that FOAF, for example, will not work because it tries to connect people to people without representing the objects around which they connect.

> Russell's disappointment in LinkedIn implies that the term "social networking" makes little sense if we leave out the objects that mediate the ties between people. Think about the object as the reason why people affiliate with each specific other and not just anyone. For instance, if the object is a job, it will connect me to one set of people whereas a date will link me to a radically different group. This is common sense but unfortunately it's not included in the image of the network diagram that most people imagine when they hear the term "social network." The fallacy is to think that social networks are just made up of people. They're not; *social networks consist of people who are connected by a shared object.*[3]

Here is a report of a talk by Engeström where he talks about five key principles involved in a successful social network built around objects.

1. You should be able to define the social object your service is built around.
2. Define your verbs that your users perform on the objects. For instance, eBay has buy and sell buttons. It's clear what the site is for.
3. How can people share the objects?
4. Turn invitations into gifts.
5. Charge the publishers, not the spectators. He learned this from Joi Ito. There will be a day when people don't pay to download or consume music but [have] the opportunity to publish their playlists online.[4]

These thoughts <u>are picked up interestingly</u>[5] by Hugh MacLeod (of gapingvoid fame). He suggests that sometimes he will use "sharing device" rather than "social object" in conversation. Social networks are built around social objects, he suggests, not the other way around; the objects are nodes which appear before the network, and around which it forms.

> 5. Yesterday at <u>the Darden talk</u>[6] I explained why geeks have become so important to marketing. My definition of a geek is, *"Somebody who socializes via objects."* When you think about it, we're all geeks. Because we're all enthusiastic about something outside ourselves. For me, it's marketing and cartooning. For others, it could be cell phones or Scotch Whisky or Apple computers or NASCAR or the Boston Red Sox or Buddhism. All these act as Social Objects within a social network of people who care passionately about the stuff. Whatever industry you are in, there's somebody who is geeked out about your product category. They are using your product [or a competitor's product] as a Social Object. If you don't understand how the geeks are socializing—connecting to other people—via your product, then you don't actually have a marketing plan. Heck, you probably don't have a viable business plan.[7]

John Breslin picks up the theme in practical terms and has some pictures which try to show this "decentralized me."

> I've extended my <u>previous picture showing a person being linked across communities</u>[8] to this idea of people (via their user profiles) being connected by the content they create together, co-annotate, or for which they use similar annotations. Bob and Carol are connected via bookmarked URLs that they both have annotated and also through events that they are both attending, and Alice and Bob are using similar tags and are subscribed to the same blogs.[9]

And a final quote from Hugh MacLeod.

> 14. The most important word on the internet is not "Search." The most important word on the internet is "Share." Sharing is the driver. Sharing is the DNA. We use Social Objects to share ourselves with other people. We're primates. We like to groom each other. It's in our nature.[10]

NOTES

1. http://chimprawk.blogspot.com/2006/07/network-effect-multiplier-or-metcalfes
.html
2. Fred Stutzman, "Unit Structures: Social Network Transitions," November 2011,
at http://chimprawk.blogspot.com/2007/11/social-network-transitions.html
3. Jyri Engeström, "Why some social network services work and others don't; or,
The case for object-centered sociality," April 13, 2005, at www.zengestrom.com/
blog/2005/04/why-some-social-network-services-work-and-others-dont-or-the
-case-for-object-centered-sociality.html
4. Kevin Anderson, "NMKForum07: Jyri of Jaiku," June 13, 2007, at http://strange
.corante.com/2007/06/13/nmkforum07-jyri-of-jaiku
5. www.gapingvoid.com/Moveable_Type/archives/004265.html
6. www.darden.virginia.edu/html/standard.aspx?menu_id=68&styleid=2&id=10724
7. www.gapingvoid.com/Moveable_Type/archives/004265.html
8. www.johnbreslin.com/blog/2007/03/01/linking-personal-posted-content
-across-communities
9. www.johnbreslin.com/blog/2007/04/23/t-sioc-object-centred-sociality
10. www.gapingvoid.com/Moveable_Type/archives/004265.html

MAY 31, 2008

Workflow is an intermediate consumer

http://orweblog.oclc.org/archives/001646.html

I have been using the following contrast in presentations for a while. This is to make a distinction between library services—or any other service for that matter—in a pre-network age, and such services now.

Then: people were prepared to build their workflows around library services.

Now: the library must be prepared to build its services around people's workflows.

This is to try to capture succinctly a recurrent theme in these pages. This shift is because people are increasingly building their workflows—or learnflows, or researchflows . . .—on the network. In some cases through a bricolage of desktop and network tools (e.g., toolbars, RSS feeds, social networking sites, search engines, etc.); in some cases through prefabricated workflow environments (e.g., course management systems . . .). Where resources are not easily available to those workflows, they may not be used.

Of course, putting library services in those flows is not straightforward. . . . It does mean that the library needs to think about "intermediate consumers"[1]—those workflows and applications that may sit between the library and its users (search engines, RSS aggregators, course management systems, search engines, social networking sites, cell phones, etc.).

NOTE

1. www.libraryjournal.com/article/CA609689.html

Amplification around a tag

http://orweblog.oclc.org/archives/001804.html   Tag: Coinage

My former colleague and network resident,[1] Andy Powell,[2] advocates strongly that public events should publish a conference tag, a virtual venue to which event-amplifying[3] network activity like blog posts, tweets, images, and so on can cluster.

> It's easy to forget, but I'd go as far as saying that the tag is almost as important as the venue. In fact, in a sense, the tag becomes the virtual venue for the event's digital legacy.[4]

For a network resident this may make complete sense; to others, it may seem overstated.

I raise this in the context of the 2008 Libraries Australia Forum[5]. They have gone the extra step of pulling that network amplification into a single page[6].

> This is what people have posted about the 2008 Libraries Australia Forum. If you are posting about the forum, please tag your blog posts, presentations or Flickr photos *laf2008*. If you are using Twitter, use the tag *#laf2008* in your tweets.[7]

Now, at the time of writing, the network amplification seems largely to be the work of one person. I don't think this is a particular issue: whatever the level of participation, the organizers are to be commended for taking this extra step, I think.

However, it does raise for me an interesting question about the relative balance in conference audiences between "network residents" and "network visitors," or, more broadly, the relative balance between these categories in the general use of our network services. (For those that are not familiar with this helpful distinction, see Dave White's discussion[8] and my comments[9] made after I read about it in Andy's post[10].)

I know from my own experience that the balance is very different in different audiences. In some audiences, there are likely to be bloggers; in others, it is very unlikely. In some audiences, there may be people who will take pictures and post them; in others, it is very unlikely. And from a service point of view, I think that it would be very interesting to get a sense of how the users of a library catalog, for example, break down along a resident/visitor spectrum.

NOTES

1. http://orweblog.oclc.org/archives/001773.html
2. www.eduserv.org.uk/foundation/people/andypowell
3. http://en.wikipedia.org/wiki/Amplified_conference
4. Andy Powell, "Tags as virtual venues," September 14, 2007, at http://efoundations .typepad.com/efoundations/2007/09/tags-as-virtual.html
5. www.nla.gov.au/librariesaustralia/aum/laf08
6. www.nla.gov.au/librariesaustralia/aum/laf08/web.html
7. "2008 Libraries Australia Forum—From the Web," at www.nla.gov.au/libraries australia/aum/laf08/web.html
8. http://tallblog.conted.ox.ac.uk/index.php/2008/07/23/not-natives-immigrants -but-visitors-residents
9. http://orweblog.oclc.org/archives/001773.html
10. http://efoundations.typepad.com/efoundations/2008/09/residents-and-v.html

FEBRUARY 4, 2009

A signed network presence: People as entry points again

http://orweblog.oclc.org/archives/001873.html

The phrase "People are entry points" has stayed in my mind since I heard Dan Chudnov use it at a meeting a while ago. It tends to occur to me also when I read, as I just have, documents which talk about "providers" and "users" of information, as in many of our more interesting services, these roles mingle. Here is something I wrote a while ago on this:

> People connect and share themselves through "social objects" (music, photos, video, links, or other shared interests), and it has been argued that successful social networks are those which form around such social objects. We are becoming used to selective disclosure and selective socialization through affinity groups within different social networks. Together, these experiences have created an interesting expectation: many network resources are "signed" in the sense that they are attached to online personas that we may or may not know, whose judgment and network presence we may come to know. Think of social bookmarking sites or Amazon reviews, for example. People are resources on the network, and have become entry points and connectors for others.[1]

Now, clearly, services are increasingly capturing usage and other data invisibly to refine what they do. Some services solicit explicit participation, in the form of tags, reviews, and so on. And some services are structurally built around people's interests, where social value enhances the practical value they provide, as with social bookmarking services, for example.

We have become used to this, as part of the "weather" of our web lives, and it is interesting to think about how much of what we learn and discover is shared with us by other people in network environments.

However, I have been struck recently by how I will intentionally seek out more directly personal entry points where before I might have done a more general topical search. Of course, we are now used to following particular blogs in particular contexts. So, for example, I have come to value

PersonaNonData[2] for publishing and book trade context. I am not currently on Twitter, but I subscribe to several folk's Twitter pages via RSS, because it is often the best way of understanding what is important in particular areas. Delicious provides another example. I don't tend to follow what is happening with Second Life. But if I want a quick update, my starting point is Andy Powell's[3] Second Life Delicious bookmarks[4]. In each case, I recognize the value and economy of a personal entry point.

In the *First Monday* piece I quote from above, I went on to talk about how this may change expectations . . .

> *A "signed" network presence:* As I noted above, we are used to seeing "signed" resources: reviews, ratings, social networking profiles, bookmarks. People have become entry points on the network, and signature is important. Think of library websites. They tend to be anonymous. Often, it is not straightforward finding appropriate contact points: there may not be photographs, or communication options are limited (office hours, IM, texting, e-mail, phone). Library services are not always associated with people. How often do subject pages, for example, carry a name and contact information who can be consulted?
>
> Connaway and Radford (2007) (PDF[5]) note how students are sometimes reluctant to use virtual reference because they do not want to interact with somebody who remains anonymous or who they do not know, even if it is a library service.[6]

In this context I was very taken with a presentation[7] I saw a while ago by Cody Hanson[8] which I tend to associate with Dan's comment about people being entry points. I have referred to this before in these pages. Cody discusses the importance of signature in social networking sites and goes on to recommend that librarians be more personally visible on the network and . . .

> Make personal and public recommendations of sources and articles
> Expose our selection processes
> Expose our expertise

NOTES

1. http://firstmonday.org/htbin/cgiwrap/bin/ojs/index.php/fm/article/view/2291/2070
2. http://personanondata.blogspot.com
3. http://claimid.com/andypowell
4. http://delicious.com/andypowell/secondlife
5. www.oclc.org/research/publications/archive/2007/connaway-acrl.pdf
6. http://firstmonday.org/htbin/cgiwrap/bin/ojs/index.php/fm/article/view/2291/2070
7. http://codyhanson.com/CodyHansonCIC032007.ppt
8. http://codyhanson.com/blog

JUNE 14, 2009

An identity incompletely centered . . .

http://orweblog.oclc.org/archives/001975.html

The Facebook user name landgrab created a flurry of excitement over the weekend. Individuals "claimed" their piece of network real estate in the form of a Facebook URL, and organizations had an opportunity to protect registered marks. I am now

www.facebook.com/lorcand

which chimes with my recently established Twitter presence

www.twitter.com/lorcand

I decided to consolidate on *lorcand* a little while ago, when I switched from the more opaque *lisld* on Twitter. Of course, this was late in my online life, meaning that—as most others do—I have a fractured online identity: it is pretty decentralized. I feel that I ought to more actively adopt some centering strategies (see below) but it never gets to the top of the list.

I am prompted by this experience to incorporate here a post of last year—"Centering the decentralized identity"[1]—which is still relevant . . .

Andy Powell, network resident,[2] has an interesting post about his "fractured" network identity. How does he define identity?

Digital identity is the online representation of an individual within a community, as adopted by that individual and/or projected by others.

An individual may have multiple digital identities in multiple communities.[3]

He describes how his digital identity is "fractured" across many environments (Facebook, Flickr, various home pages and blogs, Second Life, Twitter, etc.). Various professional or personal affiliations are explicitly visible in several "friendspaces" (my word), on Facebook and Twitter for example. Andy even confesses to an "identity crisis" around his Second Life identity, Art Fossett.

> I also have something of an identity crisis around Art Fossett—specifically concerning how closely the digital identities of Andy Powell and Art Fossett should be related.[4]

Reading the entry, it seemed to me that Andy is talking about "centering" this "decentralized identity" in various ways: he talks about wanting to "consolidate" his network presence.

(John Breslin schematically represents decentralized identity in a blog entry[5] of some time ago.)

There are various centering or consolidating strategies . . .

Andy talks about limiting the number of "handles" his identity has—e-mail addresses and user names, although he is not in a position where his personal identities can override his current work identity (at Eduserv).

He is working to center his network presence at http://andypowell.net/ and has some interesting comments about steps taken or to be taken. These include the suggestion that his former place of work put redirects from historically superseded network presences to his current one so that he can capture their "Google juice," which raises interesting questions about our view of the historical record on the web.

He also has some advice about the use of third-party services, about control of domain names, and about where you build up "Google juice" as moving it may be outside of your control.

Several things struck me reading this post . . .

Andy's concerns here are probably in advance of most people's, but it seems clear that managing our network presences and the relationships between them is becoming of more interest. And this cuts across previous boundaries—between work, family, and friends, for example—in different ways.

My network identity is less decentralized than Andy's: overall, I am less residential ;-). Until recently, I would have seen this "fracture" as simply a part of an ongoing transition into new ways of doing things. And I wouldn't have had the patience or the inclination to adopt various centering strategies. That said, I have been more conscious recently of where I want my network presence to be "signed" and where I don't. To take an example close to home, I wrote some longish reviews on items in World-Cat; recently, I realized that I would like the system to be able to support in some way my assertion that I was their author, and now it does by linking to a profile page. I have tended to use *lisld* as a handle in a variety of places. Now, I would probably more consistently use something like Lorcan Dempsey where I was more concerned about "signature," although I am quite attached to lisld ;-).

Of course, Google is a strong bottom-up centering service (see Tony Hirst's interesting suggestion[6] that an institution's de facto home page is the first page of Google results in a search for that institution). My first-page Google results tend to be dominated by this blog, but there are also current and previous work pages, some articles come and go, and more recently, Wikipedia and Facebook make a showing. None of these is at a domain name controlled by me. This blog was established as an internal OCLC communications tool for a year before it was externalized so it is "located" at OCLC (in several ways). Now, I am sure that it gets a ranking "lift" from the OCLC domain name, but it also means that I cannot bring it with me as it now stands if I ever leave. In a sense, I lose some of that network capital. Of course, this is quite reasonable from another view, but it does raise interestingly the balance between individual and institution.

My name is not unique. However, it is not very common. Andy notes his "Google nemesis," Andy Powell of Wishbone Ash. It would be interesting to know more[7] about what the impact of findability in Google has been on the naming of children.

Now, I know that there are various initiatives under way which may make our identities more portable. I assume—hope—that we will end up with the ability to port our identities flexibly, but that we also retain the ability to support decentralized identities which may not know very much, or anything, about each other ;-).

NOTES

1. http://orweblog.oclc.org/archives/001809.html
2. http://orweblog.oclc.org/archives/001773.html
3. http://efoundations.typepad.com/
4. http://efoundations.typepad.com/efoundations/2008/11/definedigital-identity .html
5. www.johnbreslin.com/blog/2007/03/01/linking-personal-posted-content -across-communities/
6. http://ouseful.wordpress.com/2008/11/20/where-is-the-open-university -homepage/
7. http://orweblog.oclc.org/archives/001385.html

Interstitial reading

http://orweblog.oclc.org/archives/002081.html   *Tag: Coinage*

Evan Schnittman of OUP has an interesting post[1] in which he discusses three types of digital reading: extractive, immersive, and pedagogic. It is worth a read.

Looking at his post, I was reminded of a phrase I used for a while: *interstitial reading*. We do quite a bit of reading in the interstices of our lives. The bathroom comes to mind, but I am in particular thinking about reading and travel.

Wolfgang Schivelbusch[2] devotes some interesting passages to the interconnection of reading and trains in his wonderful monograph, *The Railway Journey: The Industrialization of Time and Space in the 19th Century*. He notes how reading became popular as an alternative at once to the fast-disappearing view out of the window and to interaction with other passengers. He describes the emergence of book-selling and -lending operations in train stations. He quotes from the minutes of an 1860 French medical congress:

Practically everybody passes the time reading while traveling on the train. This is so common that one rarely sees members of a certain social class embark on a journey without first purchasing the means by which they can enjoy this pastime. (p. 64)[3]

He quotes an advert from John Murray: "Literature for the rail—works of information and innocent amusement." And he provides a reference to how Hachette aimed to turn the "enforced leisure and boredom of a long trip to the enjoyment and instruction of all" through the introduction of stores in railway stations.

The story of how Allen Lane conceived of Penguin Books while on a railway platform is also well known (whether it is true or not) (Wikipedia[4]).

Reading is now an integral part of travel, and we are very familiar with the "opportunities" provided in the seat pocket on an airplane, the readers on the subway or tube, and the inevitable magazine stand or bookshop at stations and airports.

More recently, mobile communications have introduced a new dimension to the "enforced leisure" of those interstitial times in the airport or while waiting for a train, as people catch up on e-mail, Facebook, Twitter, news, sports results, and so on.

Now, this is by way of introduction to a note about the iPad. The iPad seems an ideal device for interstitial reading, supporting social networking, immersive reading, extractive interaction with the web, and so on. However, it does not have the portability of the magazine, newspaper, or paperback. For this reason, rumors about the smaller iPad seem to make a lot of sense. The Kindle, on the other hand is eminently portable, and, importantly, can be held with one hand. But it is less well able to support the full variety of interstitial reading and network interactions. For this reason, it is not surprising to see it open up as a platform to other apps, although one imagines its niche will continue to be the immersive reader, albeit one that fits such reading into the various interstices of his or her daily routine.

NOTES

1. www.blackplasticglasses.com/2010/03/23/digital-reading/#more-445
2. www.worldcat.org/wcidentities/lccn-n81-5225

3. Wolfgang Schivelbusch, *The Railway Journey: The Industrialization of Time and Space in the 19th Century* (Berkeley, CA: University of California Press, 1986).
4. http://en.wikipedia.org/wiki/Allen_Lane

JUNE 13, 2010

Three switches

http://orweblog.oclc.org/archives/002104.html

I have been using these three "switches" as contextual background in presentations for a while:

CONSUMER SWITCH

Then: More investment in business/education environments.
Now: More investment in consumer environments.

It used to be the case that the computer and communications capacities we had at work or in college exceeded those available to us in personal or family settings. Now this is no longer the case. Consumer sites like Amazon or Etsy set expectations for services, and we have multiple computing and communications devices. Indeed, educational and work settings now often lag behind the consumer space (look no further than the library website). This is a significant change and will continue, given the level of investment in the consumer space.

WORKFLOW SWITCH

Then: Expect workflows to be built around my service.
Now: Build services around workflows.

Much of our information creation and use is now carried out on the network. This may be assisted by the prefabricated workflow supported by a course management system, a lab notebook, or a pre-print archive, for example. Or it may be assisted by the bricolage of tools we use to find and organize information resources: citation management services, bookmarks, RSS readers, Twitter clients, and so on. People have varying levels of sophistication of support within an overall trend toward adopting research and learning workflows on the network. What this means is that while users may once have built their workflows around the library, now, the library needs to consider how to build its services around the user workflow, to be available where its readers are doing their work. Think, for example, of Netflix, which works hard to make itself available in as many ways as make sense for its users. We can get a DVD. We can also stream to a PC, an Xbox, an app on the iPad, and so on.

ATTENTION SWITCH

Then: Resources scarce; attention abundant.
Now: Attention scarce; resources abundant.

Library users now have many opportunities to meet their information needs, and they have many demands on their attention. No single site is the sole focus of attention, and convenience is important.

JUNE 13, 2010

Indirect discovery

http://orweblog.oclc.org/archives/002105.html

I have found that the phrase *discovery happens elsewhere*[1] has quite a bit of resonance in discussion.

Increasingly people discover websites, or encounter content from them, in a variety of places. Most clearly, this happens through network-level services like Google or Twitter, but also happens in personal services (my RSS aggregator), or services which allow me to traverse from personal to network (social networking, bookmarking . . .). The library may also want to "place" resources in various ways in other environments, course management systems, for example.

If *discovery happens elsewhere,* then there are several important consequences for libraries. Most important is the recognition that a library's own, locally managed or provided discovery environments—the catalog, metasearch service, or discovery layer—are only a part of the picture, that there are other areas of discovery which would benefit from attention.

Libraries will also want to support *indirect discovery.* By this, I mean they will want to connect the discovery experience, whenever it happens outside of the library environment, to the possibility of fulfillment in the library.

This may happen in several ways. Importantly, it makes sense that libraries will want to *disclose* the existence of their resources into other discovery environments. Think of a library's unique resources, for example, its digitized special collections or the institutional assets it manages in an institutional repository. As with other information providers on the web, the library will want to make sure that these are exposed in ways that optimize crawling, indexing, and finding by search engines. Other approaches may be sensible, adding relevant links to Wikipedia pages for example, or selectively putting images from the collection on Flickr.

For non-unique resources, a library may want to disclose the fact that it holds a particular item. Think here, for example, of making sure that Google Scholar knows how to resolve article metadata to your particular library (see the Library Links[2] program). Or of being represented in one of the several union catalogs (including WorldCat) that Google uses to direct the "find in a library" link on Google Book Search.

Another approach is to "leverage" a discovery environment which is outside of your control to bring people back to your environment. Here I am thinking of the use of tools like LibX[3] which may mobilize metadata found "elsewhere" in a variety of ways to connect to a particular library resource. The developers report that LibX has been customized for over 700 different use environments.

Other approaches could also be discussed. We don't yet have a routine way of supporting "indirect discovery" or a shared inventory of use cases. This will be one of the more interesting development areas in coming years.

NOTES

1. http://orweblog.oclc.org/archives/001430.html
2. http://scholar.google.com/intl/en/scholar/libraries.html
3. http://libx.org/

AUGUST 22, 2010

Three stages of library websites . . .

http://orweblog.oclc.org/archives/002129.html

While writing about <u>subject pages and library websites</u>[1] the other day, it occurred to me that we might think of library websites in three stages—which emerged successively and continue to exist together. Always mindful of the <u>rule of three</u>[2] ;-).

We might clumsily call these stages (1) fragmentary, (2) integrated supply, and (3) demand influenced.

Fragmentary. Libraries have to manage a variety of resources which are outside their control and present them to their users as best they can. This has meant that the library website has often been a thin wrapper around two sets of heterogeneous resources.

> One is the set of legacy and emerging systems, developed independently rather than as part of an overall library experience, with different fulfillment options, different metadata models, and so on (integrated library system, resolver, knowledge base, repositories . . .). Another is the set of legacy database and repository boundaries that map more to historically evolved publisher configurations and business decisions than to user needs or behaviors (for example, metadata, e-journals, e-books, books, A&I databases, and other types of content, which may be difficult to slice and dice in useful ways).[3]

Integrated supply. Recently, libraries have been focusing on the website in a more holistic way, as a unified service. There are several developments which have supported this. One is the move to the single, or tabbed, search box as a focal point of the website. This may sit over a metasearch product, or, more recently, over a <u>discovery layer</u>[4] product. Another is the adoption of a consistent content management framework which gives a similar look and feel across the website, extending to linked services (the catalog for example) where possible (I was interested to note that SOPAC[5] and Ting[6] both advertise the integration between the catalog and the rest of the website). Others include the integration of staff-interaction capabilities (making relevant staff visible[7] in appropriate places, including various ways of contacting staff or asking questions . . .), and a consistent approach[8] to developing subject or course pages. I discussed some examples of unified service provision in this post[9] a while ago.

Given the fragmentation they face, it is easy for libraries to see integration—the consolidation of supply—as an end in itself. However, the real end is less the integration of information resources *with each other* than the integration of relevant information resources *with the working patterns of their users.* For this reason, we will begin to see more emphasis on sorting out demand as well as sorting out supply.

Demand influenced. I gave some examples recently[10] of how sorting out demand is becoming more important. This, of course, touches on core library values, connecting users to appropriate resources in convenient ways. A specific example might be the Bookspace[11] section of the Hennepin County Library website.

Looking at the North Carolina State University Libraries website[12] the other day, it also seemed to me that it provided a nice example of a site trying better to predict, meet, and guide demand. As well as continuing to integrate the various sources of information supply. Here are a few things that occurred to me. As always, it is sensible to note that my impressions are those of an interested tourist rather than somebody who regularly uses the site . . .

Legible. The tabbed search box is centrally visible. Underneath this are three labels: "Computing," "Learning," and "Courses." The first and second provide access to computing resources and learning spaces, respectively. The third provides information resources specialized to individual courses. The site is not cluttered with uncontextualized information resources, library administrivia, or brochureware.

Relation of virtual to physical. This is an interesting emphasis. It is possible to book a room, to borrow computing equipment, to find out how many computers are in use. There is a service, Groupfinder,[13] which allows you to alert others to your physical location in the library. Another is called, nicely, Tripsaver,[14] and offers requesting/delivery options while allowing you to check status of request. There is a clock icon which links to a page of library opening times. A calendar of events is also published.

Library staff and expertise are very visible, and users are encouraged to make contact. "Get Help" and "Ask Us" links are visible at the top of the page. Alongside help, there is a link to an "expert" in your area of study. Chat options are very visible. And users can offer feedback on the site in general. Help with creating digital media is offered. There are links to the relevant library experts on course and resource pages.

The website is not the only destination. There is a row of familiar icons at the foot of the page: Twitter, Facebook, RSS, YouTube, and Flickr. And there is a stream of news and tweets on the page. Of course, NCSU has also been a leader in mobile apps, and there are several available.

NOTES

1. http://orweblog.oclc.org/archives/002128.html
2. http://en.wikipedia.org/wiki/Rule_of_three_(writing)
3. http://orweblog.oclc.org/archives/001785.html
4. http://orweblog.oclc.org/archives/002116.html
5. http://thesocialopac.net/about
6. http://orweblog.oclc.org/archives/002065.html
7. http://orweblog.oclc.org/archives/001873.html
8. http://orweblog.oclc.org/archives/002128.html
9. http://orweblog.oclc.org/archives/002007.html
10. http://orweblog.oclc.org/archives/002124.html
11. www.hclib.org/pub/bookspace
12. www.lib.ncsu.edu
13. www.lib.ncsu.edu/groupfinder
14. www.lib.ncsu.edu/tripsaver

AUGUST 31, 2012

Two things prompted by a new website: Space as a service and full library discovery

http://orweblog.oclc.org/archives/002202.html

Drawn by a tweet, I looked at <u>Stanford's very nice new library website</u>[1] just now. I only spent a few minutes there, but I was immediately and strongly struck by two things. Each makes so much sense that I imagine they will become routine.

The first was the foregrounding of *library space as a service*. The second was what I might call *full library discovery*, the ability to *discover the full capacity of the library*, not just the collections, with a single search.

LIBRARY SPACE AS A SERVICE

A shift is under way in library space, from being configured around collections to being configured around research, learning, and related social behaviors. In this way, space is an important aspect of how a library engages with its users; it is a service in itself, not only part of the infrastructure to manage collections.

This is recognized here in that two of the elements in the nice central navigation strip are about space, "Library Hours" and "Places to Study." If you look at "Library Hours," it tells you what is open *now*, as you look at it. It is not just a static list of times and locations.

If you look at the "Places to Study" tab, it opens out interestingly to allow you to filter by your requirement—for individual study, for quiet, for group study, for particular facilities, and so on.

FROM "FULL COLLECTION" TO "FULL LIBRARY" DISCOVERY

There has been a major focus on integrated discovery services in recent years, with the model of a cloud-based, central index over catalog, article, and related data becoming common. The goal has been "full collection discovery" delivered in a single search box.

We are now seeing an extension of this ambition to cover "full library" discovery where services, staff profiles and expertise, or other aspects of library provision are made discoverable alongside, and in the same search environment, as the collections.

I have written before[2] about the University of Michigan site, which is a good example. It works well to project the library on the web as a unified service. A central part of this is the integrated search over collections, library website, LibGuides, and library staff profiles. The return of relevant subject specialists which match the query in a separate results pane is particularly interesting. And is in line with my view[3] that if libraries wish to be seen as expert, then their expertise must be visible.

The Stanford site offers a "Search Everything" tab, with this amplifying tagline: *"Not sure where to start? Try this."* What I like about it is that the examples searches shown emphasize the "full library" aspect of what is on offer here: they are very deliberately pitching this at a broader level than books and articles. The example searches are *"renew books, dissertations, feminist studies, WorldCat"*: they are about questions people may have when they come to the library website, not only about items they might find in the collection.

Now, in practice, results work better sometimes than others, but the general principle is good, and you can see how it can be improved over time. In an accompanying blog description,[4] Chris Bourg repeats feminist studies[5] as an example. Note the staff profile pages returned in the library website search (see figure 3.1).

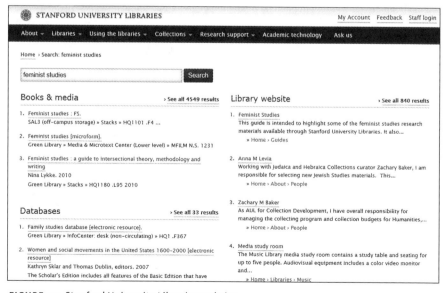

FIGURE 3.1 Stanford University Libraries website

As libraries move in this direction, several trends are apparent. One is the use of Drupal, Blacklight, and other "container" frameworks to deliver unified services. A second is a rethinking of how services, staff profiles and expertise, and other library activities are represented and indexed. The increased use of resource guides—in many cases LibGuides—is one aspect of this, in particular as they are used as a simple content management framework for various type of information about the library, and not only for lists of information resources. Another is the "Bento box"[6] style results, as not only may it be difficult or confusing to rank results across different types of resources, but a tabular presentation like this may make more sense to users.

For more information about Stanford design decisions and ambitions, see the justifiably proud blog entries[7] by Chris Bourg.

NOTES

1. http://library.stanford.edu
2. http://orweblog.oclc.org/archives/002007.html
3. http://orweblog.oclc.org/archives/002086.html
4. http://chrisbourg.wordpress.com/2012/08/28/awesome-library-website-pt-3 -lift-off
5. http://library.stanford.edu/search/all?search=feminist%20studies
6. www.twylah.com/lorcanD/topics/bento
7. http://chrisbourg.wordpress.com/2012/08/28/awesome-library-website-pt -3-lift-off

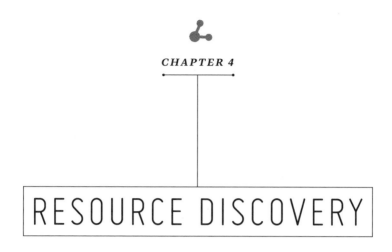

CHAPTER 4

RESOURCE DISCOVERY

RESOURCE DISCOVERY IS, of course, the very heart of the research process. It is what researchers hope to achieve and what libraries strive to offer. What is remarkable about the posts in this section is that, although the terminology and technology have evolved, Dempsey has been able to capture in the earliest posts the core characteristics of the systems we view as state of the art today. Metasearch is passé (and was recognized as suboptimal in the earliest mention of it here, in early 2005), but connecting the user with the resource in the most efficient way, regardless of the geographical location of either, never goes out of style.

Posts in this section describe the evolution of resource discovery from sequentially searched silos to cross-silo federated search to web-scale single-index discovery systems.

MARCH 20, 2005

Metasearch, Google, and the rest

http://orweblog.oclc.org/archives/000615.html

How quickly things can change! Last year there were discussions about the Google-busting potential of metasearch. How naive. This year there are discussions about the metasearch-busting potential of Google Scholar. Let us wait and see.

Clearly, there are various issues with metasearch: the variety of data and interfaces that has to be managed means that it will always be a difficult process. It is also difficult to build out services on top of a federated resource. (I write briefly about "<u>portals</u>"[1] here, and about library search <u>here</u>[2].)

But to think about the question in terms of metasearch and Google obscures a potentially more interesting longer-term question. This is a question about consolidation: at what level does it make most sense for resources to be aggregated for more effective use?

Think of two poles: the fractured resource available to a library user, and Google.

Libraries struggle because they manage a resource which is fragmented and "off-web." It is fragmented by user interface, by title, by subject division, by vocabulary. It is a resource very much organized by publisher interest, rather than by user need, and the user may struggle to know which databases are of potential value. By off-web, I mean that a resource hides its content behind its user interface and is not available to open web approaches. Increasingly, to be on-web is to be available in Google or other open web approaches.

These factors mean that library resources exercise a weak gravitational pull. They impose high transaction costs on a potential user. They also make it difficult to build services out on top of an integrated resource, to make it more interesting to users than a collection of databases.

A couple of recent examples emphasized for me the issues that fragmentation raises. First, see the following statement in the KB article I mention <u>below</u>[3]:

> It is recommended to index all metadata in a single index, and use as few different databases as possible for storage. There are hardly any databases or collections for which the use of a specific database package is justified. When there is a choice between indexing distributed databases in a central index or performing federated searching in distributed databases, it is best to choose the central indexing. There are several reasons for this, but it should be sufficient to compare Google as a central index with a theoretical Google that would distribute every user search to all websites all over the world. A combination with fed-

erated searching remains needed for databases that do not allow harvesting into a central index or for focusing a search into a specific area. (*Renewing the Information Infrastructure of the Koninklijke Bibliotheek*[4])

Second, I recently visited the Research Library in Los Alamos National Laboratories where they have a tradition of locally loading data where possible. (PDF[5]—scroll down to page 6.) This is partly because of some of the particularities of their environment, but also because it is possible to build services out on top of this consolidated resource much more readily than on top of a federated resource. And the LANL Research Library has indeed created a very impressive set of recommender and other personalized services for its users, much richer in fact than most other libraries. It adds significant value to the underlying collection of data, in large part because it has the data in-house in a consolidated form.

The other pole is the centralized index of Google with an array of much-discussed advantages, and a stated aim of consolidating all interesting data.

So, metasearch is one response to fragmentation, albeit one with limited effectiveness. Another approach is to consolidate data resources into larger reservoirs. This has the advantage of reducing the burden of integration, and enhancing the ability to create value-added services. But how and at what level could this be done? What are the sensible and possible consolidations in between the universal Google and the current debilitating fragmentation?

We have some existing consolidations: WorldCat for library materials, books especially; CrossRef for journal articles; Artstor aspires to provide the benefits of consolidation for art images. I expect that over the next while we will see some more.

NOTES

1. www.cilip.org.uk/publications/updatemagazine/archive/archive2004/october/lorcan.htm
2. www.cilip.org.uk/publications/updatemagazine/archive/archive2004/november/lorcan.htm
3. http://orweblog.oclc.org/archives/000614.html
4. www.dlib.org/dlib/march05/vanveen/03vanveen.html
5. www.springeronline.com/sgw/cda/pageitems/document/cda_download document/0,11996,0-0-45-135576-0,00.pdf

Metasearch: A boundary case

http://orweblog.oclc.org/archives/000768.html

A couple of metasearch reports have been recently released. One, carried out as part of an NSDL project at the California Digital Library, proposes "approaches, principles and practices" which might be applied by anybody evaluating integrated search options (PDF[1]). The second, the RLG Metasearch Survey Report,[2] discusses member experiences and expectations with metasearch. Roy Tennant, one of the authors of the former, comments in the latter on hangingtogether.org[3].

The reports raise many issues, especially when laid alongside a more general discussion about how library services are presented to users. To this I will return; in the interim, a few remarks on metasearch:

ADVANCES?

Metasearch has come onstage in a big way in the last couple of years: there are now a variety of products available, and many libraries are implementing them. However, the concepts, technologies, and approaches that they adopt have been in currency for many years. Index Data and Fretwell Downing, among others, for example, or indeed OCLC with SiteSearch, have many years of experience deploying metasearch approaches. There is also quite a record of discussion of some potential features: creating an individualized "landscape" based on some match between a representation of user interests and a representation of collections and services available, alerting, metadata schema and terminology merging, deduplication, forward knowledge based on collection description or an index, and so on. What has changed most over the years is the emergence of the Amazoogle search experience[4] and the recognition that fragmentation reduces the gravitational pull of library resources. The renewed emphasis on metasearch is one response to this—and the NISO Metasearch Initiative[5] responds to a recognition that despite several years of deployment, it needs to work better. How do you avoid some of the current inefficiencies of interaction which make life difficult for the data provider and the metasearch application supplier?

INCENTIVES?

How to explain this lack of progress over the years? There seem to be social or business factors delaying forward progress: what incentives are there for parties to change or improve the situation? One major incentive for the library is clear, and was mentioned above: to reduce fragmentation and increase gravitational pull for the user. At the same time, Ben Toth points to a countertrend in a comment on another post.

> I know it's a bit of a generalisation, but professionally we've had little incentive to simplify search experience for users and quite a lot of incentive to emphasise the complexity and mystery surrounding search.

Various library activities are indeed bound up with that complexity. And he goes on to touch on data-provider incentives:

> It's not just the fault of librarians—the industry is locked into a business model—creating and maintaining large sets of metadata—that is increasingly irrelevant to connecting users with the content they need. (*Comment to "Simpler search"*[6])

A major issue that metasearch is trying to address is that boundaries may fall in different places on the demand and supply sides. On the demand side, one wants to present data in terms of user interest, for which purpose database or technical boundaries may be unhelpful. On the supply side, databases are provided by many providers, some of whom may be concerned about their distinctiveness disappearing behind somebody else's interface. They may want the user to be very aware of the boundary between their data and other people's. (I refer to this as the "brandscape"[7] factor elsewhere, where the interests of individual providers may overcome the interests of the overall user experience.) It is also interesting to wonder about the distinctiveness of current metasearch providers and what impact more streamlined metasearch would have on their position in the value chain. How does that play into incentives for change? So, while there may be general assent to the benefits of more streamlined metasearch capacity, incentives for librarians, data providers, and metasearch application providers may not all be clearly aligned around this direction.

ONE BRICK IN THE WALL

Metasearch is not an end in itself, although we sometimes talk about it as if it were. The aim is to provide search services at the level of database combination that makes sense for the user, to provide guidance on those combinations, and to present the services in ways which make sense in user environments. This last point is important; one may want to present a metasearch service as a web page, as a box in a reading list or course page, as a machine interface which other applications talk to, and so on. Metasearch, like all other library services, will be part of an ecosystem of services. One can talk of its place in the discover-locate-request-deliver[8] chain, and we have seen much work of late providing integration with resolution and fulfillment services of various kinds, so that the user can move from discovery to fulfillment in a more streamlined way. Increasingly, we may want data to flow more easily (to work with reference/citation managers), or to mix metasearch capacity into particular environments (a course apparatus is an example). In some cases, a search may bring back updated results against a particular stored query. Some users might like the ability to set up searches whose results can be viewed in their RSS aggregator. And so on. Search—and metasearch—is a part only of what a library user wants to do—it needs to be integrated into a variety of workflows.

ALTERNATIVES?

Now, in the last section, I may have been a touch heavy on the qualification. This is because of the difficulties involved in providing some of these services effectively, and the lack of progress I noted over recent years. It is for this reason that I wondered a while ago[9] if it might make more sense to attack the boundary issue differently, by working on business and technical approaches which would result in fewer, larger resources to search. This would reduce the complexity of boundary spanning by pushing data integration and other issues upstream. At the cost of putting more burden on the search system to make discriminations that have been lost. It does also raise the question of how much difference is useful. This would require significant change in how we currently manage the data supply side, but we are living in a time of significant change.

NOTES

1. www.cdlib.org/inside/projects/metasearch/nsdl/nsdl_report2.pdf
2. www.rlg.org/en/page.php?Page_ID=20750
3. http://hangingtogether.org/?p=24#comment-20
4. http://orweblog.oclc.org/archives/000667.html
5. www.lib.ncsu.edu/niso-mi/index.php/Main_Page
6. Comment to http://orweblog.oclc.org/archives/000778.html
7. http://orweblog.oclc.org/archives/000636.html
8. www.google.com/search?q=%22discover%2C+locate%2C+request%2C+deliver
9. http://orweblog.oclc.org/archives/000615.html

NOVEMBER 20, 2005

Discover, locate . . . vertical and horizontal integration

http://orweblog.oclc.org/archives/000865.html

I was involved in some work years ago which developed the discover-locate-request-deliver[1] string of verbs to talk about integrating library services. One emphasis of the work was that discovery was one part only of a whole chain (discovery2delivery—D2D) through which requirements were met. Requiring the user to complete the D2D chain by manual interactions dampened library use: writing down the results from an A&I search and then looking in the catalog to see if the journals were held, for example. As we look at resource-sharing environments, we still see that we have imperfectly integrated the D2D verbs. In fact, the integration has been greater with journals as a major focus of the OpenURL resolver is to join up the D2D chain. One wonders whether it will make sense to put the catalog behind the resolver also, and it is certainly interesting to see the importance of resolution in some of the examples below. I now think of the verbs in this way:

- **Discover.** *Discover that a resource exists.* Typically, one may have to iterate to complete the discovery experience: search or browse candidate A&I databases, for example, and then search selected ones. The publish/subscribe model is increasingly important to discovery, as users subscribe to syndicated feeds. One of the major issues facing library users is knowing where to search or subscribe to facilitate relevant discovery.

- **Locate.** *Discover services on found resources.* A service may be as simple as notifying somebody of a shelf location. Resolvers are important here: an OpenURL resolver will return services decided to be available on the resource indicated in the OpenURL.
- **Request.** *Request a service.* A user may select and initiate a found service.
- **Deliver.** *The service is executed.* A book is delivered, a document downloaded, or whatever.

Of course, other services will be deployed along the way: authorization, authentication, tracking, billing, etc.

What the web does is give us an integrated discover-locate-request-deliver experience. Some sophisticated infrastructure supports this concatenation: crawling and indexing by search engines, DNS resolution . . .

In library services, the joins are more visible, and many of the places where one wants integration are precisely at the seams between these processes. Think horizontal and vertical as in the picture. The joins are horizontal where one wants to move between the processes, to traverse process boundaries. Having discovered that an article exists, one wants to find services that will make it available, and select one (or maybe have all of this done for you in the background, just as it does with a web page). The horizontal joins are most likely to be achieved within monolithic systems: the library catalog for example, which may allow you to discover, locate, request, and have delivered items. Living in Ohio, one is very aware of the value to faculty and others of OhioLINK. OhioLINK closely integrates the D2D process for books on a systemwide level within Ohio higher education, and creates great value for its participants and users in so doing.

The joins are vertical where one wants to integrate activities within processes: metasearch is a topical example, where one is trying to integrate discovery across many resources. One may want to locate an item or service in several places—Amazon, the local catalog, a group of catalogs within a consortium—and present back to the user options for purchase or borrowing with indications of cost and/or likely delivery times. A request may be initiated through interlibrary lending or through a purchase order, and so on.

Much of the complexity of constructing distributed library systems arises from traversing the boundaries between these processes (horizontal integration) or from having unified interaction with services within a particular process (vertical integration). An example of the former is the difficulty of interrogating local circulation systems for status information; an example of the latter is differences in metadata schema or vocabularies across database boundaries.

I was reminded of the discover-locate-request-deliver string as I have been looking at various publicly available union/group activities recently, and these words crop up from time to time:

- RedLightGreen[2] offers a rich discovery experience, based on aggregate data from the RLG union catalog. It also has a marvelous name ;-)—one of the few library initiatives to have a name worthy of the Internet times we live in. I speculate that it has not had the traction that one might have expected because it does not integrate the *locate-request-deliver* verbs so well into the discover experience.
- The recently visible Talis Whisper demonstration site[3] gives a nice indication of how one might tie these things together, although not all the joins appear to be working in the available site. Interestingly, it offers the user tabbed access to *discover, locate,* and *borrow* processes.
- The European Library (TEL) has a facility to search across European national libraries. This somewhat confuses the discovery experience as results are not rolled up into a single set for you. There is little integration of the other services. One can configure it with an OpenURL resolver of choice, but otherwise, it does not offer much integration.
- CURL[4] (which appears to have drifted clear of its acronymic mooring to become the Consortium of Research Libraries in the British Isles) lists as part of its vision to allow researchers, "wherever in the world," to "search, locate and request all resources, whatever their format, easily and quickly from the desktop." Some of those verbs

again. One vehicle for achieving this vision is COPAC,[5] a union catalog of the national libraries in the UK and twenty-four research
libraries in the UK and Ireland. COPAC offers discovery over its
constituent catalogs. Again, it allows outward OpenURL linking through an experimental user interface,[6] using the OpenURL
Router[7] to land in the appropriate institutional resolver. (The
OpenURL Router is a UK service which provides a central registry of OpenURL Resolvers. It is similar to, and preceded, OCLC's
OpenURL Resolver Registry[8].)

- OCLC's OpenWorldCat does not currently have a destination site;
rather, entries may be discovered in Yahoo! or Google, or be directly
linked to. Where we recognize a user's IP address, we offer services
(deep link to OPAC, user-initiated ILL, resolver) which we know
they are authorized to use.

This cursory overview shows that we have intermittently and imperfectly
managed to integrate location, request, and delivery into systems whose
focus is still largely discovery. However, discovery without fulfillment is of
limited interest to an audience which wants D2D services which are quick
and convenient, and which hide the system boundaries which need to be
traversed in the background. I am also surprised, especially given the linking of discover services to locate services through the resolver in the journals arena, that we have not seen more linking of general discover services
(e.g., Amazon) to library locate services (e.g., catalog/circ).

To complete the D2D chain efficiently in open, loosely coupled environments (that is, not within closed communities with tightly integrated
systems environments) will require quite a bit of infrastructure development. Much of this relies on better metadata about institutions (libraries,
branches), collections (databases, library collections . . .), and services (how
to connect to catalogs, ILL systems, resolvers, e-commerce sites . . .), as
well as about policies (for example, who can borrow from us and under
what conditions) and terms. It is for this reason that we are seeing greater
interest in registries and directories which will provide the ability to discover, locate, request, and have delivered resources more effectively.

NOTES

1. www.google.com/search?q=%22discover%2C+locate%2C+request%2C+deliver
2. http://redlightgreen.com/ucwprod/web/workspace.jsp
3. http://research.talis.com/2005/whisper
4. www.curl.ac.uk
5. www.copac.ac.uk
6. http://copac.ac.uk/msgw
7. http://openurl.ac.uk/doc
8. www.oclc.org/productworks/urlresolver.htm

NOVEMBER 27, 2005

Circulating intentional data

http://orweblog.oclc.org/archives/000875.html

I have posted a couple[1] of times[2] recently about intentional data, data that records choices and behaviors. I mentioned holdings data, ILL records, circulation records, and database usage records. One could extend this list to any data which records an interaction or choice. We are used to looking at transaction logs of various sorts, and new forms of data are emerging, for example, in the form of questions asked in virtual reference. What types of intelligence could be mined from a comparison of the subject profiles of virtual reference questions to the subject profile of collections? Would it expose gaps in the collection, for example?

In that context I was interested to read a post on the Gordian knot[3] pointing to some work[4] by David Pattern at the University of Huddersfield which shows a "people who borrowed this also borrowed . . ." feature. And it does look like a good enhancement. (It does not seem to be available on the "publicly visible" catalog[5].)

Circulation is interesting in this context. We run into a long tail sort of a thing. Amazon is the primary exemplar of this type of "recommender" service. Amazon aggregates supply (it has a very big database of potential hits in the context of any query, increasing the chances that a person will find something of interest), and it aggregates demand (it is a major gravitational hub on the network, so it assembles lots of eyeballs, increasing the chances that any one book will be found by an interested person). The result of this—the aggregation of supply and the aggregation of demand—is that use is driven down the long tail. More materials are aggregated, and more of them find an audience.

Now, we know that, typically, the smaller part of a library collection circulates (maybe less than 20% in a research library). We also know that, typically, interlibrary lending traffic is very, very much smaller than circulation.

What does this suggest? Well, the former suggests that we have an excess of supply over demand in any library, and we have indeed built "just in case" collections. However, aggregating demand should make those collections more used, and this appears to be the case in services like OhioLINK, for example, which have aggregated demand for institutional collections at the statewide level, increasing the chances that an item will be found by an interested reader. The latter suggests that we have not aggregated supply across libraries in a systemwide way very efficiently, as library users do not very often go beyond their local collection. There are various reasons for this, including library policy in what is made available, but in general one might say that the transaction costs of discovering, locating, requesting, and having delivered resources are high enough to inhibit use. Again, this suggests that we have not aggregated supply as effectively as we might in systemwide situations (this was the focus of another post[6]).

Coming back to recommendations based on circulation, two things occur to me:

1. One might imagine a complement to a circulation-based recommender service which recommends other books in the collection which have not circulated, or have not circulated as much. In other words, which ties circulating books to the noncirculating ones. And we know about various "books like this" measures: by subject, by author, by series. In fact, catalogs were originally designed to make these types of connections. However, there is other data which shares the "intentional" element which makes circulation interesting, and which represents aggregate choices: things that have appeared on the same reading list, that have been recommended by the same faculty member, and, importantly, things that cite or have been cited by the

selected item. Now, in some of these cases, the benefits resulting may not be worth the effort of collecting and manipulating the data; we do not know. In others, citation for example, there clearly are benefits.

2. For many of these examples, it may be difficult for a library to generate the data and build services on top of it without better support—in their systems or in services available to them. Furthermore, in many cases, the results may be improved by aggregating data across libraries, or across other service environments. The Gordian knot suggests there may be scope, for example, for services based on aggregated circulation data. (This is not to ignore the real policy questions surrounding the sharing of circulation data. Of course, there are also technical issues of exporting and exchanging in common ways.) Amazon has introduced very useful services based on citation and also associates books based on shared distinctive word patterns. One could imagine those connections being leveraged in a catalog, and Amazon is well placed to do this based on the volume of data it has. In fact, one of the benefits of the mass-digitization projects currently under way would be to allow more of that type of connection to be made. Clearly, services based on holdings data depend on aggregations. In World-Cat-based services, OCLC ranks results by volume of holdings, the most widely held first. And there has been interest from time to time from libraries and others in having access to holdings counts to allow them to rank results in their own environments by this measure, on the assumption that the more widely held an item is the more likely it is to meet a need. We do not offer a service like this at the moment, but you can imagine one. We are also experimenting with generating audience levels based on the pattern of holdings (something that lots of high schools hold is likely to be different to something that only a few research libraries hold). And we are seeing growing interest in the sharing of database-usage data, based on pooling of COUNTER-compliant data. One reason that aggregation is potentially beneficial is that it addresses the demand-side issue discussed above: by aggregating data, one may make connections that do not get made in the data generated by a smaller group of users.

It is clear that we will see services emerge in the library space which are based on the standardization, consolidation, and syndication of "intentional" data. We may also see greater systems support for the collection and mining of particular forms of local data. These will supply "intelligence" to support richer user experiences and better management decisions. Compare how services can already access Amazon's data in this way (see, for example, the liveplasma[7] service build on top of Amazon data).

As we extend the ways in which users can discover materials, it puts additional emphasis on the need to improve our systemwide apparatus for delivering those materials.

Making data work harder is an integral part of the Web 2.0 discussions, and we certainly have a lot of data to do things with!

NOTES

1. http://orweblog.oclc.org/archives/000822.html
2. http://orweblog.oclc.org/archives/000869.html
3. www.gordian-knot.org/index.php/2005/11/20/people-who-borrowed-this-also-borrowed
4. www.daveyp.com/blog/index.php/archives/49/using-circ_tran-to-show-borrowing-suggestions-in-hip
5. www.hud.ac.uk/cls-bin/cls.pl?c=98/24/18/19
6. http://orweblog.oclc.org/archives/000865.html
7. www.musicplasma.com

MARCH 6, 2006

Search, share, and subscribe

http://orweblog.oclc.org/archives/000964.html

We seem to have turned a corner with library search. For example, one of the strategic priorities for the British Library is to "transform search and navigation"[1] in support of access to their collections, although there is little detail about what will be attempted. There has been significant recent discussion about catalog search and the deficiencies of current approaches, with some recent emphasis on the UC study and on the NCSU catalog[2]. There has also been a growing interest in placing search at the point of need, reaching into user environments in various ways (for example, by placing subject-specific metasearch bundles in course pages), or by open-ing up search APIs. And, we are beginning to discuss how to mobilize the edge with collaborative bookmarking, tagging and so on. The original long tail discussion noted that "navigation" would be increasingly important in large databases, and I touched on this when talking[3] about the long tail and libraries.

Here are some directions in library *search* (is this the right word?) we are likely to see over the next while. And remember this is about "and" not "or." New value will emerge from the combination of a variety of approaches to create more engaging, functional, or effective services. What is also clear is that our historic notion of "search" as discovery will shift to something more like a search, share, and subscribe model. New ways of searching; new ways of sharing and recommending; new ways of syndicating data and service.

RANKING AND RECOMMENDING BASED ON INTENTIONAL DATA

The innovation of Google—ranking based on linking—has had a major impact on our thinking. We have a range of intentional data which can help ranking. By *intentional* I mean data which reflects choices and behaviors: it captures intentions. Examples are holdings data (collection development choices), circulation data, download counts, database usage counts, resolu-tion counts. Our experience with holdings suggests that such ranking can be very effective in large retrieval sets.

We can also do more recommendation based on intentional data (people who borrowed x also borrowed y; people who downloaded x also down-loaded y; these items appeared on the same reading list as that item; and so on). See Dave Pattern's work with circulation[4] as an example. And we can build on this. For example, we are experimenting with holdings data to see what we can say about likely audience: the pattern of holdings says some-thing about the audience that might find something interesting. We can infer something about audience where something is largely held by school libraries, or by ARLs . . .

MAKING BIBLIOGRAPHIC STRUCTURE WORK HARDER

Libraries are realizing that we should work harder to release the value of the historic investment in bibliographic data. Examples are the interest in FRBR (Functional Requirements of Bibliographic Records), faceted browsing, place-based access. The data in our catalogs can support rich and engaging experiences, as the NCSU catalog, RedLightGreen, and Fiction-Finder (a new version of which will soon be released) show.

MOBILIZING THE EDGE

Books and cultural memory materials encourage conversations. Sharing and recommending are natural learning and research behaviors. We need to mobilize such conversational and sharing behaviors to enrich the experience of those who use our services. Reviews, tagging, recommendations. There has been some early discussion about formal resource description and taxonomies versus tagging and other approaches. I don't see these as oppositional, as services can be built which exploit both the current structured and the textured conversational space. For example, tagging has a potentially valuable role in bringing together materials for a course, or a particular argument, or . . . (See the nice example cited[5] by Stu Weibel.) By the same token, one wants to make library resources easily citable and sharable in other environments—social bookmarking services, for example. We are in early days here.

SYNDICATING DATA AND SERVICES TO WHERE THE USERS ARE

We are used to the idea of searching a database or visiting a website. I think that we are seeing a move from database to website to workflow as the main focus of activity. Services need to be delivered into emergent personal digital environments (e.g., RSS aggregators) or prefabricated workflow managers (e.g., course management systems). This means that we are seeing growing interest in remixing data and services in environments outside the library website. Data flows into reading lists, citation managers, social bookmarking sites, search engines, RSS aggregators. . . . Services will be exposed through linkable URLs, APIs, and simple web services, which facilitate recomposition by user environments (see the experiments by John Blyberg[6] and Dave Pattern,[7] for example).

I find it interesting the way we talk about "technology." Often we imagine it as something additive, or something that changes one of the pieces in an existing frame; however, much of the import of the current Web 2.0 discussion is that the way we organize ourselves to achieve certain goals will change in the network environment also. This comes through in some of the examples I mention above.

NOTES

1. www.bl.uk/about/strategic/transsearchnav.html
2. http://orweblog.oclc.org/archives/000919.html
3. http://orweblog.oclc.org/archives/000949.html
4. www.daveyp.com/blog/index.php/archives/69
5. http://weibel-lines.typepad.com/weibelines/2006/03/hybrid_vigor.html
6. www.blyberg.net/2006/01/26/major-enhancements-for-patron-rest
7. www.daveyp.com/blog/index.php/archives/date/2006/03

MARCH 12, 2006

The simple search box and the rich texture of suggestion

http://orweblog.oclc.org/archives/000966.html

I have been in a couple of meetings recently where people have been talking about the attraction of the simple, single box search as the ultimate goal. To this, my response is "yes, and what else?" In Google's case, PageRank has been the principal "what else." Going forward, it has interesting questions to face about how to rank materials which do not fit the web-page model. The improvement of search, and the improvement of ad placement, is a major focus for them, as indicated in the much-discussed Google analyst day presentation[1]. A simple box is one part only of Google's formula: good results and good ads are necessary for it.

Interestingly, in Amazon's case, its results *are* its advertising. Each result represents a potential purchase. This is one reason that it is useful for Amazon to make APIs to its results available. And it is one reason that its presentation strategy is to offer a rich texture of suggestion on its results pages. You are hit with many hints about potential items of interest, and this data is created in multiple ways (mobilizing the edge of reader contributions, mining the "intentional" data from user purchase and browse patterns, mining the text of books). An Amazon page has many "suggestions," using a variety of approaches.

I think we will see more "simple search" but supported by smart results and rich browse. Whenever somebody says that people need a simple single box to search, try asking "yes, and what else?"

NOTE

1. http://investor.google.com/pdf/20060302_analyst_day.pdf

MARCH 21, 2006

Conversations and evidence

http://orweblog.oclc.org/archives/000971.html

The Reading 2.0 conference has had some nice coverage[1].

One of the interesting takeaways for me was the variety of requirements or use cases that drive service, and the dangers of substituting *either-or* discussion for *and* discussions.

I kept thinking of two nonexclusive emphases: conversation and evidence.

Major network presences are interested in providing "good enough" responses to queries and in enhancing the network experience of users. They will automate as much as possible. This is useful in many contexts and creates real value. However, in some cases libraries need to do other things. For example, some group of libraries are interested in the scholarly record, in the integrity and authenticity of documents, in the integrity over time of citation (ensuring that the cited item is available in its cited form). Clearly, these issues are very much alive in the archival community.

These discussions move one toward evidential integrity as a value, and the need for processes and structures to maintain it. This is a potentially costly activity over time, and it is variably exercised by libraries. It imposes requirements that not all services need to meet. Indeed, it is not entirely clear from here how we will secure the scholarly record in coming years as it diversifies into many digital forms that pose curation challenges.

We are seeing interesting developments around information services and "conversation." Again think of the major web presences: they are mobilizing the edge of user contribution. They have embraced tagging, reviews, recommendations, and a variety of other ways of enhancing the "conversation" about resources. Conversation is a good way of finding things out, and we make judgments all the time in our conversations about what to believe, or what to act on. This type of activity is a welcome addition to our services, and one that we need to pursue.

Think of something like FRBR in this context. In some contexts, one wants to know something about *Huck Finn*—something general about the "work," or to find any copy of it. One may be interested in a conversation about it. In other contexts, one may need to have access to a particular copy with a certain provenance, or to one which has been annotated, or access to a particular version of a critical edition. Needs vary. Use cases are plural. (I mention *Huck Finn* just because I was asked to speak about it at the conference.)

We need to support conversations *and* evidential integrity: *and* not *either-or.*

NOTE

1. http://radar.oreilly.com/archives/2006/03/link_list_reading_20_1.html

MAY 14, 2006

Lifting out the catalog discovery experience

http://orweblog.oclc.org/archives/001021.html

I have been talking to a variety of groups in recent weeks, and the future of the catalog has risen to the top of the list in discussion and questions.

The catalog is a topic of major debate. However, this discussion is really raising a set of broader issues about discovery and about the continued evolution of library systems, including the catalog, in a changing network environment.

Several things seem to be going on. Here are some thoughts.

The discovery experience does not have to be tied to the inventory management system. In some ways, we have end-to-end integrated library systems where the ends are in the wrong places. At one end, the discovery experience is embedded in a catalog interface. And, as we now realize, it is often a somewhat flat experience with low gravitational pull when compared to some other discovery environments. At the other end, the "fulfillment" options open out onto only a part of the universe of materials which is available to the user: the local cataloged collection. And there is a growing gap between the cataloged *collection* and the *available* collection.

Elsewhere, I have suggested[1] that we can think about some distinct processes—discover, locate, request, deliver—in the chain of use of library materials. Increasingly, we will see these sourced as part of separate systems which may be articulated in various combinations, and across material types.

Resolution, for example, is now used to *locate* instances of discovered items, usually articles. In the future, resolution seems likely to develop into more of a service router: given some metadata, what services are available to me on the resource referred to by the metadata (borrow it, buy it, send it to a colleague . . .), or which relate to the metadata itself (export in a particular citation format, for example). It is a way of connecting potentially multiple discovery experiences to multiple fulfillment (request/deliver) services, or multiple other services.

So, discovery of the cataloged collection will be increasingly disembedded, or lifted out, from the ILS system, and re-embedded in a variety of other contexts. And potentially changed in the process. And, of course, those contexts themselves are evolving in a network environment.

What are some of those other discovery contexts? Here are some current examples:

- **Local catalog discovery environments.** There has been a recent emphasis on the creation of an external catalog discovery system, which takes ILS data and makes it work harder in a richer user interface. The NCSU catalog[2] has been much discussed and admired in this context. Ex Libris has announced its Primo[3] product which will import data from locally managed collections and re-present it. And we have just seen announcements about the eXtensible Catalog[4] project at the University of Rochester.
- **Shared catalog discovery environments.** We also observe a greater trend to shared catalogs, often associated with resource-sharing arrangements. It has not been unusual to see a tiered offering, with resources at progressively broader levels (for example: local catalog, regional/consortial, WorldCat). The level of integration between these has been small. However, in recent times, we have seen growing interest in moving more strongly to the shared level. This may be to strengthen resource-sharing arrangements, to better match supply and demand of materials (the "long tail" discussion[5]), to save resources. And once one moves in this direction, the question of scoping the collective resource in different ways emerges: moving from local to some larger grouping or back.
- **Syndicated catalog discovery environments.** Increasingly, the library wants to project a discovery experience into other contexts. I use "syndication" to cover several ways of doing this. Typically, one might syndicate a *service* or *data.* In the former case, a machine interface is made available which can be consumed by other applications. We are used to this model in the context of Z39.50, but additional approaches may become more common (OpenSearch, RSS feeds . . .). How to project library resources into campus portals or course management systems has heightened interest here. The syndication of data is becoming of more interest also, as libraries discuss making catalog data available to search engines and others. And OCLC has been very active in this area with Open WorldCat.
- **The leveraged discovery environment.** This is a clumsy expression for a phenomenon that is increasingly important, where one leverages a

discovery environment which is outside your control to bring people back into your catalog environment. Think of Amazon or Google Scholar. Now this may be done using fragile scraping or scripting environments, as, for example, with library lookup or our FRBR bookmarklets. Here, a browser tool may, for example, recognize an ISBN in a web page and use that to search a library resource. The broader ability to deploy, capture, and act on structured data may make this approach more common: the potential use of COinS (Context Object in Spans) is a specific example here.

Here are some questions which arise whatever the discovery context.

- **The user experience—ranking, relating, and recommending.** There is a general recognition that discovery environments need to do more to help the user. Developers are looking at ranking (using well-known retrieval techniques with the bibliographic data, or, probably more important, using holdings, usage, or other data which gives an indication of popularity); relating (bring together materials which are in the same work, about the same thing, or related in other ways); and recommending (making suggestions based on various inputs—reviews or circulation data, for example). Users of Amazon and other consumer sites are becoming used to a "rich texture of suggestion," and we have data to do a better job here. And this leads naturally into the mobilization of user contribution—tagging, reviews—something that may best happen at a shared level.
- **The back end—an ILS service layer.**[6] If discovery is separated from the ILS, there needs to be a way for the two to communicate. Again, this is currently done through a variety of proprietary scripting and linking approaches. It would be useful to agree upon a set of appropriate functionality and some agreed ways of implementing it.
- **The discovery deficit—the cataloged collection is a part only of the available collection.** I am thinking of two related things here. The first is that there will be a growing desire to hide boundaries between databases (A&I, catalog, repositories, etc.) in some cases—especially where those boundaries are seen more to reflect the historical con-

tingencies of library organization or the business decisions of suppliers than the actual discovery needs of users. We will see greater integration of the catalog with these other resources, whether this happens at the applications level (where the catalog sits behind the resolver, or is a metasearch target) or at the data level (where catalog data, article-level data, repository data, and so on, are consolidated in merged resources). This then poses an issue about the data itself. Our catalogs are crated in a MARC/AACR world, with established practices for controlling names, subjects, and so on. However, as the catalog plays in a wider resource space, issues arise in meshing this data with data created in different regimes, and accordingly in leveraging the investment in controlled data. Think about personal names, for example, where authority control practices apply only to the "cataloged collection." What does it mean when that data is mixed with other data?

- **Routing.** As we separate functions—discovery from location and fulfillment—we need good ways of tying them back together. This was addressed above, when talking about resolution. In the longer term, it also is an example of the broad interest converging on directories and registries. In the type of environment I have sketched here, we need registries which manage the "intelligence" that applications need to tie things together. Registries of services (resolvers, deep OPAC links, Z39.50/SRW/SRU targets . . .), institutions (complex things ;-), and so on. One wants to be able to tie IP addresses to services (so that you know which services to present to a user), or institutional service points to geographic coordinates (so as to be able to place locations on a map), and so on.

- **Sourcing.** This is an interesting area which is not yet widely explored in the ILS area. The typical current model is a licensed software model where an instance of a vendor application is run locally. The examples above show some other models: local development, collaborative sourcing, and an on-demand model where the catalog is provided as a network service. Here, as in other areas of library systems work, we are likely to see a much more plural approach to sourcing system requirements in coming years.

The catalog discussion is often presented as just that, *the catalog discussion*. However, it belongs in a wider context. We may be lifting out the catalog discovery experience, but we are then re-embedding it in potentially multiple discovery contexts, and those discovery contexts are being changed as we re-architect systems in the network environment. These systems include discovery systems for other collection types (the institutional repository, or digital asset repository, or . . .); the emergence of a general search/resolution layer within the library; external environments as different as Google and Amazon, the RSS aggregator, or the course management system. It also includes a variety of supply chains: resource sharing, e-commerce, local.

The catalog question is a part of how we re-architect the discovery-to-delivery apparatus for the available collection.

(Lifting out, disembedding, re-embedding: I borrow language from Anthony Giddens, who uses it in a somewhat loftier context.)

NOTES

1. http://orweblog.oclc.org/archives/000865.html
2. www.lib.ncsu.edu/catalog
3. www.exlibrisgroup.com/webinar_1144862525.htm
4. www.rochester.edu/news/show.php?id=2518
5. www.dlib.org/dlib/april06/dempsey/04dempsey.html
6. http://orweblog.oclc.org/archives/000927.html

AUGUST 8, 2006

Discovery and disclosure

http://orweblog.oclc.org/archives/001084.html   Tag: Coinage

Science Library Pad has a couple[1] of posts[2] about libraries and the long tail. He makes the following interesting point contrasting "availability" with "discoverability":

> For example, PhotoBucket is in the availability business. You get a bucket of storage; you dump your photos in. It is mostly not in the discoverability business. That's up to the users, as they post the photos in various places on the net. I would also consider Amazon S3 and Open Access repositories to be mainly in the availability business.
>
> Google, of course, is a classic example of a discoverability business. And I think it's really in understanding the differences between availability and discoverability that we can learn a lot about our businesses.
>
> Libraries are mainly about availability, as far as I'm concerned. I think one of the big conflicts has been that some libraries thought they were in the discoverability business; this is why they perceive Google to be a competitor or a threat. One of the big areas of confusion, I think, is that physical availability is about providing the container. If I can find the book in its one-and-only-one possible shelf location, then I can provide you with the service. In the online world, availability is about providing the content. This is also a business that libraries thought they were in, but again I would argue, they really weren't. (*Science Library Pad*[3])

Now, you can make up your own mind about this argument. It highlights for me, though, a slightly different distinction, one between *disclosure* and *discovery,* and maybe one comes to a similar conclusion via a different route.

If you want something to be discovered, it has to be disclosed to a discovery environment. And techniques for effective disclosure are now big business, given the steps folks take to have their stuff found in the search engines. If I want people to know that I am a plumber available for hire,

I do not simply put a note on my door. I disclose my availability through the yellow pages, the local newspaper, Google ads: all those places where I know that I am going to be discovered. If I am a repository, I disclose what I have available by making metadata available for harvesting under OAI or other approaches, or for crawling by the search engines.

So, if I want the stuff in my library to be discovered by those to whom it will be useful, I have to disclose its existence in those discovery environments that people actually use. Now, yes, it is true. I can expect some of them to find their way to my door—the library catalog or website—but if people are having discovery experiences elsewhere, what should I do?

Think about the catalog. Schematically, we can see at least two broad directions as we look at disclosing the existence of library materials by mobilizing more general discovery environments:

- **Inside out: syndicating services and data.** The library wants to project a discovery experience into other contexts. I use "syndication" to cover several ways of doing this. Typically, one might syndicate services or data. In the former case, a machine interface is made available which can be consumed by other applications. We are used to this model in the context of Z39.50, but additional approaches may become more common (OpenSearch, RSS feeds, web services . . .). How to project library resources into campus portals, or course management systems, has heightened interest here, as has the interest in metasearch. A service might provide a search of the collection, but other services may also be interesting, providing a list of new items, for example. The syndication of data is of growing interest also, as libraries discuss making catalog data available to search engines and others, with links back to the library environment. Several libraries and library organizations are exposing data in this way. And, of course, OCLC has been very active in this area with Open WorldCat, where member data is exposed to several search engines. Another variation here is where libraries participate in shared initiatives which generate gravitational pull, OhioLINK or WorldCat.org, for example.

- **Outside in: the leveraged discovery environment.** This is a clumsy expression for a phenomenon that is increasingly important, where one leverages a discovery environment which is outside your control to bring people back into your catalog environment. Think of Amazon or Google Scholar. Now this may be done using fragile scraping or scripting environments, as, for example, with library lookup or our FRBR bookmarklets. Here, a browser tool may, for example, recognize an ISBN in a web page and use that to search a library resource. The broader ability to deploy, capture, and act on structured data may make this approach more common: the potential use of COinS is a specific example here. Basically, an application needs a hook which can connect to the local environment. How this will happen more smoothly is an intriguing question for discussion elsewhere.

As we move forward, disclosure becomes a more important concern. This may not be the best word. But we have to do a better job of "disclosing" what is "available" in the "discovery" environments where people look for things. Hanging a note on the door may not be good enough.

NOTES

1. http://scilib.typepad.com/science_library_pad/2006/08/my_review_of_th.html
2. http://scilib.typepad.com/science_library_pad/2006/08/academic_conten.html
3. http://scilib.typepad.com/science_library_pad/2006/08/academic_conten.html

SEPTEMBER 16, 2007

Discovery happens elsewhere

http://orweblog.oclc.org/archives/001430.html

I have been using the phrase "discovery happens elsewhere" in recent presentations. I think it captures quite nicely an increasingly important part of how we think about our services.

No single website is the sole focus of a user's attention. Increasingly, people discover websites, or encounter content from them, in a variety of places. These may be network-level services (Google . . .), or personal services (my RSS aggregator or "webtop"), or services which allow me to traverse from personal to network (Delicious, LibraryThing . . .).

This means thinking about services in different ways. About how we disclose stuff to other discovery environments; about where our metadata is; about URL structures, RSS feeds, and so on.

I have suggested before that it would be an interesting experiment to think about our services as if they had no user interface. Here maybe it would be interesting to think about services as if they could only be reached from some other place. It makes you think about the variety of other places that discovery happens.

Credits. "Discovery happens elsewhere" is influenced by Steve Rubel's use of the phrase "traffic happens elsewhere" in his discussion of what he calls the "cut and paste" web[1].

NOTE

1. www.micropersuasion.com/2007/08/the-cut-and-pas.html

JULY 27, 2008

SEO is part of our business

http://orweblog.oclc.org/archives/001733.html

John Wilkin has another nice post, talking about making resources available in such a way as to make them more likely to be crawled by Google and hence more generally discoverable and, importantly, useful and used.

> We often go wrong, however, when we try to share our love of complexity with the consumers. We've come to understand that success in building our systems involves making complicated *uses* possible without at the same time requiring the user to have a complicated *understanding* of the resource. What we must also learn is that a simplified rendering of the content, so that it can be easily found by the search engines, is not an unfortunate compromise, but rather a necessary part of our work. (*John Wilkin's blog » Our hidden digital libraries[1]*)

Roy Tennant has been talking[2] about this issue also.

This is clearly less straightforward than many imagine. Google can make choices about what to crawl, what to index, and what to present in results. At play for larger sites also is the danger of falling foul of the search engines' spam protection measures.

I participate in a JISC advisory committee on repository issues in the UK. I spent some time arguing earlier this year that search engine optimization should be a higher priority for repository managers, for institutions, and for both the capacity-building systemwide infrastructure and advisory structures that JISC is capable of providing. We now recognize that simply having stuff on the web is often not enough. It is increasingly necessary to think about how well it is being crawled, indexed, and discovered.

This is why I have emphasized[3] *disclosure* as a new word in our service lexicon. We may not control the discovery process in many cases, so we should be increasingly concerned about effective disclosure to those discovery services. Effective disclosure has to be managed, whether it is about APIs, RSS feeds, support for inbound linking, exposure to search engines . . .

NOTES

1. http://scholarlypublishing.org/jpwilkin/archives/14
2. http://hangingtogether.org/?p=475
3. www.google.com/search?q=%22lorcan+dempsey%22+disclosure

DECEMBER 14, 2008

SEO

http://orweblog.oclc.org/archives/001838.html

I have mentioned SEO (search engine optimization) a few times as an increasingly important area of interest for librarians. However, as I have suggested,[1] I come across resistance on the grounds that this is some sort of base or mendacious activity. We are very interested in interoperability, however, and for this reason it may be that *search engine interoperability* is a more palatable expression. In this case, interoperability means managing resources in ways which promote effective crawling, indexing, and ranking by search engines. A reasonable goal, given the importance of search engines in the lives of library users.

Anyway, I repeat these points prompted by a post by Tony Hirst on the topic.

> What does information literacy mean in the age of web search engines? I've been arguing for some time (e.g., in _The Library Flip_[2]) that one of the core skills going forward for those information professionals who "help people find stuff" is going to be SEO—search engine optimisation. Why? Because increasingly people are attuned to searching for "stuff" using a web search engine (you know who I'm talking about . . . ;-); and if your "stuff" doesn't appear near the top of the organic results listing (or in the paid for links) for a particular query, it might as well not exist . . . (_Revisiting the Library Flip—Why Librarians Need to Know About SEO « OUseful.Info, the blog_ . . .[3])

It is useful to think about the library website in this context. It is also important for materials which are unique to an institution/library: archival collections, institutional repositories, etc. It is also interesting to think about subject or other liaisons, or specialist library services, or advisory/reference materials. As libraries turn to assisted reputation management for their institutions (thinking about how faculty members, their expertise, and their outputs are effectively disclosed on the network for example), it is an important area for investigation. This is a topic which deserves quite a bit more attention . . .

NOTES

1. http://orweblog.oclc.org/archives/001810.html
2. http://ouseful.open.ac.uk/blogarchive/011081.html
3. http://ouseful.wordpress.com/2008/12/13/revisiting-the-library-flip-why-librarians-need-to-know-about-seo/

FEBRUARY 13, 2009

The centrality of the catalog?

http://orweblog.oclc.org/archives/001879.html

In listening to discussions about the library catalog, I am surprised not to hear more about how the type of library affects our assessment of how central the catalog is to library services or user behaviors.

For simplicity's sake, think reductively of three categories of library material: bought, licensed, and digital.

Bought materials (books, DVDs, CDs . . .) are typically managed within the integrated library system workflow, are cataloged, and appear in the library catalog.

Licensed materials (e-journals, databases . . .) are typically managed within an emerging knowledge base/ERM/custom workflow, and appear to the user in a variety of databases, maybe consolidated through metasearch and resolver systems.

Digitized/digital materials (digitized collections, research and learning materials in repositories . . .) are typically managed within a repository environment, and appear to the user through a user interface to that environment.

Newer discovery layers may try to provide access across these three strands (as well as others), and sometimes data or services will be syndicated to other environments (e.g., Google Scholar, toolbar/widget, etc.).

The systems to provide access to these three collection types probably account for the vast majority of access traffic to library collections.

However, volume of access breaks down differently across types of libraries. Digital is probably a minority in most. The catalog may get more traffic than access mechanisms for licensed materials in many public libraries, quite a bit more in many cases. And access mechanisms for licensed materials may get more traffic than the catalog in many academic environments, quite a bit more in many cases.

It would be interesting to synthesize recent research findings to quantify this . . .

JANUARY 11, 2010

Outside-in and inside-out

http://orweblog.oclc.org/archives/002047.html   Tag: Coinage

An "industry" pattern appears to have emerged which builds a discovery layer over resources available from the library (or from a group library service, at the level of a state or a consortium, for example).

Three characteristics come to mind. First, there is an attempt to provide an integrated discovery experience over multiple resource types/ workflows: bought materials (books, CDs, etc.), licensed materials (A&I databases, e-journals, etc.), and institutional digital materials (digitized special collections, for example, or repositories of learning and research materials). Second, this "horizontal" discovery layer is separated from the "vertical" management systems which may manage those resources: the "integrated" library system, the variety of systems which manage licensed resources, repository infrastructure, and so on. And, third, API access may be provided.

Various issues are being addressed as this model becomes more common. One that is interesting, I think, is that it will show how the three categories of resource I mention above—bought, licensed, and digital—have quite different dynamics in our systems and services.

Think, for example, of a distinction between "outside-in" resources, where the library is buying or licensing materials from external providers and making them accessible to a local audience (e.g., books and journals), and "inside-out" resources which may be unique to an institution (e.g., digitized images, research materials), where the audience is both local and external. Thinking about an external noninstitutional audience, and how to reach it, poses some new questions for the library.

Or think about the relationship between the "locally available" collection and the "universal" collection in each case.

- For bought materials (books, CDs . . .) the library provides access to the locally available collection—the materials acquired for local use—and then may provide access to a broader "universal" collection through WorldCat or another resource.
- For licensed materials, access is first through the broader "universal" level (in various databases) before checking for the subset of locally available materials.
- For institutional digital materials, access is provided to local repositories, but this will not typically be backed up by access to a "universal" source for such materials (although, one can see attempts to do this, as, for example, where an institutional repository expands a search to Scirus).

Of course, if one thinks about other discovery/disclosure channels (Google, for example), these three collection types also behave differently. That is a topic for another blog entry though.

Data wells: One big index

http://orweblog.oclc.org/archives/002068.html

I was interested to hear the concept of a "data well" discussed when I was in Sweden the other week.

It seems to be used in the sense of an infrastructure to ingest, normalize, and provide integrated access to multiple streams of data. In this way, library services can be built on a consolidated data resource, rather than having to actively manage the integration as a part of those services (as happens now in the metasearch model).

The idea of a data well is integral to the Ting project[1] (mentioned in these pages[2] the other day), collaboratively sourced data and systems infrastructure for Danish public libraries. It was also the subject of a tender[3] from DEFF, the Danish Electronic Research Library, earlier this year. In the latter case, the starting point was metadata for journal articles and e-books.

This is clearly in line with the trend we have seen recently toward consolidation of the fragmented database infrastructure to support a better user experience. Google Scholar was an important stimulus for this activity.

In thinking about this direction a few years ago, I asked a question about where this was going to happen . . .

> Another approach is to consolidate data resources into larger reservoirs. This has the advantage of reducing the burden of integration, and enhancing the ability to create value-added services. But how and at what level could this be done? (*Metasearch, Google, and the rest*[4])

The Danish examples are of national infrastructures (although the actual creation could be sourced with other suppliers). "Data wells" of the type discussed here are also under construction by OCLC, Serials Solutions

(Summon), EBSCO, Elsevier, and Ex Libris, among others. And Google Scholar continues to operate.

Two thoughts. One: the focus now is on integration; it will have to shift to creating value-added service over those integrated resources. Such added value may be created by the integrators, libraries, and others. And two: how many such data wells are required?

NOTES

1. http://gnit.dk/
2. http://orweblog.oclc.org/archives/002065.html
3. www.deff.dk/content.aspx?catguid={61D333DB-11A7-4029-AAED-9CDC6203 6E01}
4. http://orweblog.oclc.org/archives/000615.html

JULY 4, 2010

Discovery layers—Top Tech Trends 2

http://orweblog.oclc.org/archives/002116.html

I was pleased to participate in LITA's Top Tech Trends panel at ALA this year (see the video[1] and live coverage[2]).

We were each asked to talk about three trends: current, a bit further out, and a bit further out again. In thinking about the exercise, it seemed to me that it would be interesting to talk about how services are being reconfigured in a network environment, and not just focus on technology as such. This is the second of three blog entries, one devoted to each of my trends. We had three minutes in which to discuss each trend.

I really only decided to talk about my second trend the day before the event. I was influenced by discussions with several people as I wandered around the exhibits hall. Opinions varied as to how important this trend is, but I chose to talk about "discovery layers" because it seems to me that if these become successfully and commonly deployed they have quite far-reaching implications.

What do I mean by discovery layer? A discovery layer provides a single point of access to the full library collection across bought, licensed, and digital materials. Typically, a single search box is offered alongside a range of other navigation features. Products which support this approach include WorldCat Local, Summon, Primo Central, and the EBSCO Discovery Service, as well as a range of institutional, national, or other initiatives.

Working with hindsight ;-), these are the points I meant to make . . .

1. **The full library collection.** If they develop as anticipated (a real question), the discovery layer will become *the* view of the library collection for library patrons. In fact, for many users it may actually become the library. This has several consequences:

   - What is not represented in the discovery layer will be much less visible.
   - There will be pressure to incorporate more services into the discovery layer—better fulfillment, for example, through resource sharing, Google Book Search, purchase, or other options.
   - The integrated discovery experience will more clearly expose lack of integration with services behind, and will drive greater integration. One can see, for example, potentially more interest in the direct-to-content approach of something like PubGet.
   - And as somebody suggested to me afterward, there will need to be strategies for managing those who resist the loss of a specific database interface.

2. **A driver for other operations.** If the discovery layer becomes the central focus for access to collections, then one can imagine discovery patterns begin to affect supporting operations like selection and acquisition. The patron-driven acquisition model is being explored in the e-book market—will it be extended to other licensed materials?

3. **Data wells and the provider landscape.** A discovery layer depends on an aggregation of data—a "data well"—which involves considerable coordination costs. These include the processing involved in normalizing the data and the business interactions involved in assembling the data. The level of normalization may vary—how much work, for example, do you do in clustering author names across A&I databases, catalogs, and so on? It does not make sense to do this work too many times, so one might expect a small number of providers to emerge

who syndicate "data wells"[3] to others as well as use them in their own services. It will also be interesting to see how strong the tendency is to use other products from your discovery layer provider—a knowledge base in which to record licensed holdings, a resolver, and so on.

4. **Indirect discovery.** It is important to remember that a discovery layer "destination" is a part only of the library user's discovery experience. Increasingly, the library needs to think about how its services are visible to users who discover their information resources in Google, in the course management system, and so on. I discussed some issues in a recent post[4].

NOTES

1. http://litablog.org/2010/06/video-top-tech-trends-washington-dc-annual-2010/
2. http://litablog.org/2010/06/top-tech-trends-liveblog-2/
3. http://orweblog.oclc.org/archives/002068.html
4. http://orweblog.oclc.org/archives/002105.html

Sorting out demand . . . Top Tech Trends 3

http://orweblog.oclc.org/archives/002124.html

My third trend was somewhat diffuse and was inspired by a remark I read a couple of years ago by Gavin Potter, a contestant in the competition Netflix ran to improve its algorithm.

> "The 20th century was about sorting out supply," Potter says. "The 21st is going to be about sorting out demand." The Internet makes everything available, but mere availability is meaningless if the products remain unknown to potential buyers. (*This Psychologist Might Outsmart the Math Brains Competing for the Netflix Prize*[1])

Libraries spend a lot of time sorting out supply. The fragmentation of supply (across suppliers, databases, formats, business models, etc.) has meant that we have created quite a complex staff, systems, and service environment to cope. Furthermore, this has evolved piecemeal to manage evolving patterns of provision. There are separate workflows and supply industries for bought materials (think the integrated library system and catalog), for licensed materials (think knowledge base, *A*-to-*Z* lists, metasearch, ERM), and for digital materials (think repository infrastructure). What is more, this infrastructure is institution-scale—it is repeated in each library. There is significant workflow and systems redundancy across libraries. At the same time, large buildings have also been required to support this supply, as the model has perforce been to assemble materials close to the user.

This focus on supply has been because the transaction costs—in time, effort, or money—for a university, or a student or faculty member, or a member of the public of interacting with the range of information sources is quite high, and a major role of the library is to reduce those costs by integrating the sources of supply and bringing them close to the user.

However, the transaction costs for the user have come down. Google has been a major part of this. But so has the general consolidation in a network environment: Amazon, Google Books, the discovery layers I mentioned as my second trend,[2] WorldCat, and so on.

As supply consolidates, attention shifts to sorting out demand. Of course, libraries have always worked here, but not as much as they might have. What might this mean in our increasingly digital environment? Here are some overlapping examples:

- **Ranking, relating, recommending.** We are used to systems which provide hints and hooks for us, which guide us through large collections, which make suggestions. We get alerts, reminders, recommendations. Often, sites will mobilize four sources of metadata (professional, contributed, automatic, and usage) to build such functions into their services. (A related blog entry: "Recommendation and Ranganathan—retread."[3])
- **Community is the new content.** We expect services not only to know about resources on the web, but also to know about us. We are seeing services contextualized by their knowledge of people using those services and their relationships. Sites create value by facilitating the creation of community around "social objects" (think of reading sites, Mendeley, BlipFoto . . .). (A related blog entry: "The context web."[4])

- **Connective services.** People encounter bibliographic resources in various research and learning contexts: reading lists, citation managers, personal collections, reading clubs, bibliographies, and so on. The connective tissue between these tools and library resources could be better. (A related blog entry: "Reading lists, citation management, and bibliographic tissue."[5])
- **Indirect discovery.** Users find materials in Amazon, in Google, in Google Scholar, in Google Book Search, and so on. How do we make connections between those services and the library? (A related blog entry: "Indirect discovery."[6])
- **Embedding in other environments.** It may be appropriate to tailor materials for the course management system, for the course resource pages, for reading lists, and so on. I was in Trinity College Dublin recently, where colleagues were talking about their work to adapt the Microsoft Research Information Centre framework for use by groups of humanities scholars (see the poster presented at LIBER[7]). A part of the project is to build connectors to the bibliographic resources of the library. Colleagues reported that researchers preferred interacting with selective resources in this custom environment than going to the general-purpose library pages.
- **Institutional assets.** Finally, one might note a major emerging area of engagement: consultation, curation, and other services around the institutional research and learning outputs that are becoming central to a wider range of activity. This is, of course, a big topic in itself.

I concluded my remarks by remembering one of my favorite accounts of the mission of the librarian, which seems increasingly apt as time passes. It is from Dan Chudnov, and it is "help people build their own libraries."[8]

NOTES

1. www.wired.com/techbiz/media/magazine/16-03/mf_netflix?currentPage=1
2. http://orweblog.oclc.org/archives/002116.html
3. http://orweblog.oclc.org/archives/002123.html
4. http://orweblog.oclc.org/archives/002063.html
5. http://orweblog.oclc.org/archives/002092.html
6. http://orweblog.oclc.org/archives/002105.html

7. www.statsbiblioteket.dk/liber2010/presentations/posters/Arlene_Healy.pdf
8. http://onebiglibrary.net/story/because-this-is-the-business-weve-chosen

There is more to discovery than you think . . .

http://orweblog.oclc.org/archives/002153.html

Colleagues at the University of Minnesota have produced another[1] must-read report on the discoverability of library resources[2]. Importantly, it provides a framework within which to think about evolving issues and in this way makes a real contribution to our understanding of the environment and ability to plan for change.

Much of the "discovery discussion" has settled on a new library service category, the *discovery layer.* Think of WorldCat Local, Primo Central, Summon, and the EBSCO Discovery Service. These have been usefully described by Jason Vaughan in a recent report[3].

However, these are a part only of the broader discovery environment. The crucial word here is *environment,* because, as noted by the authors of this report, a single system or service will not address all requirements.

One environmental development in recent years has been the emergence of what I have called an "inside-out" requirement alongside an "outside-in" requirement. Libraries have managed an outside-in range of resources: they have acquired books, journals, databases, and other materials and provided discovery systems for their local constituency over what they own or license. This has resulted in our familiar array of catalog, resolver, metasearch, and now the integration apparatus of the discovery layer.

Of course, the institution also produces a range of information resources: digitized images or special collections, learning and research materials, research data, administrative records (website, prospectuses, etc.), and so on. And how effectively to disclose this material is of growing interest across the institutions of which the library is a part.

> Think, for example, of a distinction between "outside-in" resources, where the library is buying or licensing materials from external providers and making them accessible to a local audience (e.g., books and

journals), and "inside-out" resources, which may be unique to an institution (e.g., digitized images, research materials), where the audience
is both local and external. Thinking about an external noninstitutional
audience, and how to reach it, poses some new questions for the library.
(*Outside-in and inside-out*[4])

The discovery dynamic varies across these types of resources. The contribution of the University of Minnesota report is to try to explain that
dynamic and develop response strategies.

So, among the issues they address are:

- An inventory of institutionally managed or created resources. What
  is the audience of each? Which need to be disclosed to the external
  world? How?
- An inventory and categorization of external aggregator services
  (e.g., WorldCat, RePEc, Arxiv, Flickr, Merlot, Google, etc.). To which
  should internal resources be disclosed, and how? Which services
  aggregate metadata, and which aggregate content itself? Which are
  of interest to local audiences? Which should be integrated into local
  discovery systems (maybe the HathiTrust, for example)?
- A categorization of user personas, stylized descriptions of particular usage patterns. I was particularly interested to see the chart on
  page 13 which looks at some differences between undergraduate,
  graduate, and faculty search behaviors. They recognize that discovery systems may need to be scoped to particular user categories.
  Although it is not explored in detail, they also note the need to support manipulation and personal curation of digital resources.
- A review of practices at other libraries.
- A review of metadata associated with internal resources.

An important feature is that the general discussion is tied back to the particular requirements of the University of Minnesota, which means that the
relevance to other institutions should be clearer.

On a small note, I was interested in the pattern they established
throughout the report to describe resources:

The vision of a new discovery environment, that surfaced from the work of the phase 2 Discoverability group, suggests that a synthesis of tools and services need to be coordinated in such a way to enable users to discover, access, and interact with relevant data from internal, external, owned, licensed, and freely-available data sources.

Describing resources as *owned, licensed* and *freely-available* is probably more helpful than the print/electronic/digital schematic that is sometimes used, as it recognizes a crucial element of workflow/supply chain difference that plays into how systems are built and used. (I discussed some of these issues in a *Portal* article a while ago, "Reconfiguring the Library Systems Environment."[5])

This is a report everybody should read . . .

Full disclosure: I spoke about "Discovery and Delivery" at the University of Minnesota Libraries Planning Speaker Series[6]. This series was one input into the libraries' interesting strategic priorities document: "Supporting the Lifecycle of Knowledge."[7]

NOTES

1. http://orweblog.oclc.org/archives/002012.html
2. http://conservancy.umn.edu/handle/99734
3. www.alatechsource.org/taxonomy/term/106/web-scale-discovery-services
4. http://orweblog.oclc.org/archives/002047.html
5. www.oclc.org/research/publications/library/2008/dempsey-portal.pdf
6. https://wiki.lib.umn.edu/Staff/UniversityLibrariesSpeakerSeries
7. www.lib.umn.edu/pdf/ULibraries_strategic_planning.pdf

JUNE 10, 2012

Making things of interest discoverable, referenceable, relatable . . .

http://orweblog.oclc.org/archives/002199.html

I came across the Ernest Hemingway phrase "gradually, then suddenly" in an online discussion recently. Here is the context on the useful Goodreads quotable quote page.[1]

It seemed a statement appropriate to our times, and especially apt to a recent phenomenon: the growing importance of large-scale knowledge bases which collect data about entities and make relationships between them. Wikipedia is already an "addressable knowledge base,"[2] which creates huge value. DBpedia aims to add structure to this. Perhaps more important, Wikidata is an initiative to create a machine- and human-readable knowledge base of all the entities in Wikipedia and allow them to be augmented with further data and links.

This is one of several examples which, although different in purpose, scope, and sustainability model, collect and organize data about "things." These are important because they collect and organize data in ways that support answering questions, and are machine-processable. They make "facts" or "things" discoverable, referenceable, relatable. They become reference points on the web, or support services that become reference points on the web.

- Freebase[3]: "An entity graph of people, places and things." Freebase is now owned by Google and is a contributor to their newly publicized Knowledge Graph (more below). Alongside this, it is worth noting the strong interest in Schema.org,[4] a way of adding descriptive markup to web pages. It is sponsored by Google, Microsoft, Yahoo!, and Yandex. An important role is that it allows search engines to harvest structured data.

- DBpedia[5]/Wikipedia/Wikidata: "The DBpedia knowledge base currently describes more than 3.64 million things, out of which 1.83 million are classified in a consistent Ontology, including 416,000 persons, 526,000 places, 106,000 music albums, 60,000 films, 17,500 video games, 169,000 organizations, 183,000 species and 5,400 diseases." As mentioned above, Wikidata is an initiative of the Wikimedia Foundation, which will create an editable knowledge base of entities in Wikipedia. This will allow structured data about those entities to be shared across Wikipedia and across different language versions of Wikipedia, and with others. It will show up in the "info boxes" on Wikipedia.

- Factual[6]: Aims to "1. Extract both unstructured and structured data from millions of sources. 2. Clean, standardize, and canonicalize the data. 3. Merge, de-dupe, and map entities across multiple sources."

- Wolfram Alpha[7]: "A computational knowledge engine: it generates output by doing computations from its own internal knowledge base, instead of searching the web and returning links."

Think of two important recent developments: Apple's use of Siri in its iPhone and Google's inclusion of Knowledge Graph data in its results. Siri created a splash when it appeared. Among the sources it uses to provide answers are Yelp and Wolfram Alpha. Here is a results page from Google (see figure 4.1). The panel on the right shows the Knowledge Graph data . . .

And here is how Google describes the rationale of the Knowledge Graph:

> But we all know that [Taj Mahal] has a much richer meaning. You might think of one of the world's most beautiful monuments, or a Grammy Award-winning musician, or possibly even a casino in Atlantic City, NJ. Or, depending on when you last ate, the nearest Indian restaurant. It's why we've been working on an intelligent model—in geek-speak, a "graph"—that understands real-world entities and their relationships to one another: things, not strings.
>
> The Knowledge Graph enables you to search for things, people or places that Google knows about—landmarks, celebrities, cities, sports

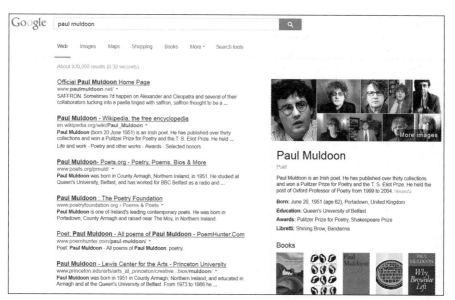

FIGURE 4.1 Screen shot of Google search results

teams, buildings, geographical features, movies, celestial objects, works
of art and more—and instantly get information that's relevant to your
query. This is a critical first step towards building the next generation
of search, which taps into the collective intelligence of the web and
understands the world a bit more like people do.

Google's Knowledge Graph isn't just rooted in public sources such
as Freebase, Wikipedia and the CIA World Factbook. It's also augmented at a much larger scale—because we're focused on comprehensive breadth and depth. It currently contains more than 500 million
objects, as well as more than 3.5 billion facts about and relationships
between these different objects. And it's tuned based on what people
search for, and what we find out on the web. (*Introducing the Knowledge
Graph: Things, not strings*[8])

The phrase "things, not strings" is telling.

One of the added values of library descriptive practice has been that it
provides structured data about the "things" of interest in a body of literature: authors, works, illustrators, places, subjects, and so on. A major motivation for library linked data is to more widely release that value and to
make those "things" more discoverable, referenceable, and relatable on the
web—in ways in which other services can build on. An important aspect
of this is to link the "things" established in library resources to "things"
established in these emerging web-scale knowledge bases. If this does not
happen, library resources will be less valuable and the library contribution
may be overlooked.

VIAF[9] is an example here. It synthesizes data about people—their names
and bibliographic contexts—from multiple national libraries and makes it
available in a way that makes an identity readily referenceable: Paul Mul-
doon[10].

We provide a lot of contextual data, including links to different names,
creations, and so on. And we relate it in various ways to other resources,
including WorldCat, Wikipedia, some national library authority files, and
so on. And links to VIAF are appearing in other places, including Freebase.

We hope that this "relatedness" will become richer, but also that applications will begin to exploit the referenceability and relatability we and the
participating national libraries are providing.

NOTES

1. www.goodreads.com/quotes/show/102579
2. http://orweblog.oclc.org/archives/001264.html
3. www.freebase.com
4. http://schema.org
5. http://dbpedia.org/About
6. www.factual.com/about
7. www.wolframalpha.com
8. http://googleblog.blogspot.com/2012/05/introducing-knowledge-graph-things-not.html
9. www.viaf.org/
10. http://viaf.org/viaf/64048541

JANUARY 2, 2013

Discovery versus discoverability . . .

http://orweblog.oclc.org/archives/002206.html

I have been interested in the different dynamics of the "inside-out" and "outside-in" library for a while (see here[1] for example).

One especially interesting characteristic is the quite different approach to discovery in each case, even though this distinction has not yet crystallized in clear service categories.

I was struck by the distinction during a recent discussion of "discoverability" in a publishing context, where the focus was on the active marketing of resources through a variety of channels. This is an emphasis that has not been common in a library environment, but, which, I argue here, is becoming more important. It is not enough simply to make resources available on the network; more active promotion is required if they are to be discovered.

What do I mean by *outside-in* and *inside-out*?

Throughout much of their existence, libraries have managed an *outside-in* range of resources: they have acquired books, journals, databases, and other materials from external sources and provided discovery systems for their local constituency over what they own or license. They aggregated scarce materials, services, and expertise close to their users. They provided a local gateway which was central to many of their users' information lives.

The discovery focus was very much on improving a set of well-known systems that provide access to the collection (acknowledging that the library had in fact little direct influence over how access to the journal literature was presented). And this remains the main focus. This discovery apparatus has evolved, and now comprises catalogs, A-to-Z lists, resource guides, maybe a discovery layer product, and other services. "Discoverability" might be interpreted in the context of how well those systems served their users.

However, in a digital and network world, there have been two major changes, which shift the focus toward "inside out."

First, access and discovery have now scaled to the level of the network: they are web scale. If I want to know if a particular book exists, I may look in Google Book Search or in Amazon, or in a social reading site, or in a library aggregation like WorldCat, and so on. My options have multiplied, and the breadth of interest of the local gateway is diminished: it provides access only to a part of what I am potentially interested in. As research and learning information resources have become abundant in this environment, the library collection and its discovery systems are no longer the necessary gateway for library users. While much of the discovery focus of the library is still on those destination or gateway systems which provide access to its collection, much of its users' discovery experience is in fact happening elsewhere.

Second, the institution is also a producer of a range of information resources: digitized images or special collections, learning and research materials, research data, administrative records (website, prospectuses, etc.), faculty expertise and profile data, and so on. How effectively to disclose this material is of growing interest across libraries or across the institutions of which the library is a part. This presents an *inside-out* challenge, as here the library wants the material to be discovered by its own constituency but usually also by a general web population.

These factors shift the discoverability challenge significantly. The challenge is not now only to improve local systems, it is to make library resources discoverable in *other* venues and systems, in the places where their users are having their discovery experiences. These include Google

Scholar or Google Books, for example, or Goodreads, or Mendeley, or Amazon. It is also to promote institutionally created and managed resources to others. This involves more active engagement across a range of channels.

Think of a couple of obvious examples. Libraries have worked to make their knowledge bases visible to Google Scholar because they want to link available library resources to their users' discovery experience. They want to make their resources discoverable in Scholar. Users should be able to access a copy of a resource the library has acquired wherever the discovery takes place. In fact, having an institutional resolver work with a variety of services (e.g., Mendeley, PubMed Central) is increasingly important, and it would be very interesting to see some research which shows the balance between internally and externally generated resolver traffic across a group of libraries. Anecdotal evidence suggests the growing importance of external sources.

Second, think of the recurrent discussion about the discoverability of institutional repository resources in Google and what steps should be taken to improve it (see, for example, the work by <u>Kenning Arlitsch and colleagues</u>[2]).

We have not yet seen clear integrated library strategies emerge for the inside-out case, but various approaches have emerged . . .

- Collection-specific interpretation and promotion through social media or other targeted activity—see <u>here</u>[3] for some blogs about special collections and archives, for example.
- Syndication. While this term may not be generally understood, I use it here to cover the idea of placing links, metadata, or services in the flow of potential users. Syndication is a major activity of OCLC as WorldCat enables linking, for example, between Google Books and other services and individual library collections.
  - **Links**. Adding links for relevant resources to Wikipedia, for example. Or to course pages, etc.
  - **Metadata**. Providing metadata about collections to relevant aggregations (the University of Minnesota "discoverability" <u>reports</u>[4] do an interesting analysis of aggregations relevant to their collections). Adding RSS feeds where appropriate.

- **Services.** Adding "share" buttons to resources (to facilitate tweeting, pinning, etc.). Creating widgets, mobile apps, toolbars. . . . In some cases, providing protocol-level access to resources.
- **Search engine optimization.** Working to ensure that crawling and indexing are as efficient as they can be. SEO is, effectively, promoting interoperability with search engines through use of good practices.

There is growing interest in connecting the library's collections to external discovery environments so that the value of the library investment is actually released for those for whom it was made. There is also now a parallel interest in making institutional resources (research and learning materials, digitized special materials, faculty expertise, etc.) more actively discoverable. In each case, there is a shift toward inside-out thinking, as the library thinks about promotion and visibility in external services. In our network environment, it is clear that "discoverability" involves an array of changing, tactical responses, working across a range of services and approaches. This active attention will become a stronger focus for libraries.

NOTES

1. http://orweblog.oclc.org/archives/002102.html
2. www.oclc.org/resources/research/events/20120316seo.pdf
3. http://pinterest.com/lorcand/librarians-talking-about-collections-they-love
4. http://conservancy.umn.edu/handle/48258

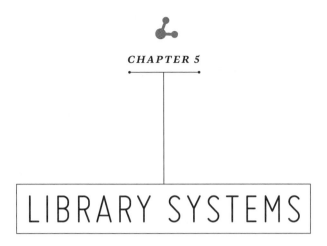

CHAPTER 5

LIBRARY SYSTEMS

ONE OF THE big challenges facing libraries is how to manage their inventories and provide access to all the information they would like to make discoverable to their users. The systems that manage these processes—tools ranging from the Integrated Library System to search indexes to OpenURL link resolvers—are complicated, customized, and rarely cohesive across a single institution, let alone across multiple institutions.

This section includes posts related to the software tools that libraries use to provide services to their users, along with discussion of the implications these systems have on broader provision of information services.

FEBRUARY 22, 2005

The integrated library system that isn't

http://orweblog.oclc.org/archives/000585.html

One can read the phrase *Integrated Library System* (ILS) in two ways: as a system for the *integrated library,* or as an *integrated system* for the library. Although the latter is what was probably meant by the term, neither is an accurate description of what the ILS has become. In fact, it is a misleading term whose continued use is bemusing. It is clear that the ILS manages a progressively smaller part of the library activity. There has been a real shift in emphasis toward e-resource management (see the metasearch/resolver/ERM/knowledge base suite of tools), and in some cases toward digital asset management. Libraries now manage a patchwork of systems which do not always play well together.

Think about the systems that support current library processes, and some possible directions. Items marked with *ILS* are typically a part of the ILS offering; those marked *NILS* are usually not.

Acquisitions (ILS). Libraries are part of larger organizations which "acquire" a variety of materials and services, and have built enterprise systems to support this. It is likely that in many settings, libraries will make more use of the generic institutional systems in the future.

Catalog (ILS). The local library catalog—let's not use the user-unfriendly and jargonish "OPAC"—is not a *central* part of most users' information behavior. Users need to be able to discover items of potential interest to them and locate them in the library. The catalog does not do a great job with the former: it does not make its data work very hard. As it covers a part only of a user's information needs, and a part only of the library collection, it may exert a progressively weaker gravitational pull on the user. More about this below.

Cataloging (ILS). Libraries have various cataloging workflows. They may acquire records from various resources, roll their own, participate in a shared cataloging environment. However, libraries are also creating metadata for other resources which may be poorly supported in their cataloging environment. They may have two workflows (their local system and a cataloging system such as Connexion from OCLC).

Circulation (ILS). This appears to be core function of the (current) ILS, and it is where such systems started. However, even here there is an interesting trajectory in some environments toward groupwide circulation systems. See OhioLINK, for example, where the line between interlibrary loan and circulation becomes blurred.

Metasearch/portal (NILS). Much could be said about this intractably difficult challenge! (See here for a short[1] and here for a long[2] discussion of metasearch/portal activity.) Some libraries are looking at wrapping a metasearch product around their various database offerings, including, in some cases, the catalog. Some libraries are putting a lot of effort into metasearch activity: it is useful, but metasearch will always be a partly broken service given the diversity of the target resource.

Resolver (NILS). The resolver is emerging as a critical part of library systems infrastructure, with the OpenURL binding resources together in various ways. The resolver moves the user from a discovered item to an instance of the item. We are likely to see OpenURLs used to tie together more systems in the future. See, for example, the current Google Scholar discussions, where a user might discover an item through Google and then be passed through to a resolver to locate local instances. This has been discussed in relation to articles; it could also happen with books, where the resolver talks to the catalog.

ERM/knowledge base (NILS). A resolver or metasearch engine requires "intelligence" about available collections. What is available? How do I connect to it? Under what terms and to whom is it available? Again, new services are emerging to help with this area, which may need to talk to acquisitions systems and catalog.

Portable bibliography (NILS). Citation managers (Endnote, RefWorks[3] . . .) and reading lists[4] are becoming more important. This lightweight bibliographic apparatus, a metadata bus if you like, provides interesting integration opportunities.

Digital asset management (NILS). Libraries are managing digitized local collections—maybe images from their special collections, historic newspapers, and so on. At the same time, many are looking at the systems infrastructure required to support institutional repository-type services, where they provide management and disclosure services for research or learning materials produced within their institution.

Important other things. Libraries may manage e-reserve systems, ILL systems, virtual reference systems, and so on. Various approaches to identity management may be in place.

So, there is a fragmented systems base, and service demands on some traditional service components are morphing as circumstances change. Here are some comments on this environment.

THINKING ABOUT COLLECTIONS

Reductively, one can think about four collecting areas which are managed in different "boxes":

1. **The bought collection.** Print books and journals, CDs, DVDs, and so on. This has been the core of the library collection, and it is around this that the ILS was built. These materials are cataloged and are "circulated" by the library.

2. **The licensed collection.** A&I services, e-journals, and so on. These are now a major focus of investment and attention, and new systems components (metasearch/resolver/ERM/knowledge base) are being put in place to manage this. This area presents new metadata challenges in the form of data-describing resources, the services through which they are made available, and the terms under which they are available.

3. **The local digitized collection.** Libraries are digitizing their rare or unique materials, releasing their research and learning potential in new contexts. This activity is in the cottage-industry stage. Metadata creation may be expensive. Digital asset management solutions are not quite routine yet.

4. **The managed institutional research and learning output.** This is the institutional repository and learning object repository space.

The balance of investment between these collection areas is different in different libraries; but, more interestingly, it is probably changing within individual libraries. It is interesting to think what the relative balance between them will be in, say, ten years time, and what implications that has for systems support.

THINKING ABOUT SERVICES

One downside of this fragmented systems and collections environment is that it becomes more difficult to build services out on top of the collections. Too much effort is going into maintaining and integrating a fragmented systems infrastructure.

This becomes more of an issue as the pressure on the library to be seen to be "making a difference" grows. Increasingly, the library needs to bring its services to the users within their work- or learnflow, and be seen to be adding value to the collection of resources.

THINKING ABOUT DIRECTIONS

Here are some thoughts:

- The systems environment needs to become simpler. We will see more hosted solutions, better integration options in a "web services" environment, and some consolidation of supply.
- For ILS vendors, there seems to be an interesting shift away from their historic core toward e-resource management, and in some cases toward digital asset management.
- We will see less focus on the integration of library resources with each other as an end in itself, and more on the integration of library resources with user environments (personal, learning management system, etc.).
- Following on from this, data and services need to be made available in ways which better facilitate their recombination in different user contexts. This touches on what I have called intrastructure,[5] the applications tissue that allows us to more easily stitch together systems and services. RSS feeds, URL-based web services, bookmarklets, data import and export: these are all boundary-crossing services which enable better stitching.
- I think that we are entering a period where opportunities to centralize services and data will be looked at more seriously again, as a way of reducing cost and complexity, and of releasing resources to focus on user experience.

NOTES

1. www.cilip.org.uk/publications/updatemagazine/archive/archive2004/october/lorcan.htm
2. www.oclc.org/research/staff/dempsey/recombinant_library/default.htm
3. http://orweblog.oclc.org/archives/000510.html
4. http://orweblog.oclc.org/archives/000467.html
5. http://orweblog.oclc.org/archives/000505.html

MAY 15, 2005

The user interface that isn't

http://orweblog.oclc.org/archives/000667.html

Increasingly, we need to think about library services in the context of the full web of user experience. This is easy to say, but it is rather more difficult to tease out what it means. One way to think about it is to think about some of the characteristics of the major web presences which have become the first—and sometimes last—resort of research for many of our users. And then to think about library services within that context. This may not provide very many answers, but it does give us some good questions!

This post is prompted by the current discussion of user interfaces on the lita-1 and web4lib discussion lists. Making our interfaces more like Google, Yahoo!, or Amazon may or may not be sensible, but it is a small part only of the rather bigger issue. Which is that however good the catalog interface is, it may be unseen by many library users because they spend most of their time elsewhere.

Here is one view of important characteristics of these services. It is followed by some consideration of library services.

1. **A comprehensive discovery experience.** For many users, Amazon, Google, or Yahoo! represent the universe of available resources. The users of Google or Yahoo! feel they have prospected the available web. The users of Amazon feel that they have prospected the available book resource. They may know that this is really not the case, but, given available tools, the transaction cost of looking further is often too high. These are one-shot discovery experiences for the users: they have sufficient scale for the users to be assured that they have been exhaustive. This scale means that they present very large information spaces, spaces in which any boundary walls are very far away, maybe even invisible.

2. **Predictable, often immediate, fulfillment.** Once the existence of an item is discovered, these services offer fulfillment services. The simplest is where discovery, location, and fulfillment are concatenated into a simple click of a URL, and the resource is returned as a web page. More complex is where a user opts to buy a resource from Amazon. Once bought, it is possible to track the status of the transaction at any stage. In more complex scenarios, the service may help you locate a provider of an instance of the discovered resource, and fulfillment services on that instance. So Google may offer several fulfillment options within Google Print: go to publisher, to Amazon, or to a used-book store, for example. Amazon may offer several sources for fulfillment. In each case, there is a focus on the complete chain—discovery, location, fulfillment—and a concern to efficiently manage the user experience up to satisfactory fulfillment. Indeed, it is interesting to see the current emphasis on access to resolver data by Google Scholar. This is important as successful fulfillment is central to the Google experience: Google wants to avoid "dead-ending" the user.

3. **Open to consumers.** This is a clumsy expression for an important concept. These services recognize that they are a part of the web experience of their end-users, and are keen to be woven into the fabric of their web experience. They are immediately accessible on the web.

They are densely interconnected internally, allowing users to traverse data within the service in much the way that they are used to traversing the web. They work the data they have hard, allowing you to use any piece of data as a springboard to other resources. They also provide mechanisms for users to move between services. Think of URLs for a moment: these are central to the fabric of the web and our experience of it. Amazon has become a de facto source of sharable book details, because you can use an Amazon URL as a "handle." If somebody wants to send somebody else a reference to a book, it is very easy to send them an Amazon URL. Google or Yahoo! let you share a results set as a URL. One of the nice features about the new Google Maps service is that you can drag the area you are interested in into your window and then capture a URL for that particular view.

4. **Open to intermediate consumers.** Amazon, Google, Yahoo!, eBay, and now the BBC[1]: they all recognize that they are not the ultimate destination for all web users. They recognize the value of other services. However, they also recognize the value of making their own data and services available in such a way that they can be surfaced and reused by intermediate consumers,[2] who mix them into new offerings to users. See, for example, the use of Amazon data in LivePlasma[3]: in this case, LivePlasma is an intermediate consumer of Amazon's data, remixing it within its own application for presentation to the user. Through toolbars, RSS feeds, and web services, these services are potentially woven into multiple destinations and user experiences. They want to make it as easy as possible to make their services available at the point of need.

5. **A co-created experience.** Many large Internet presences involve the users in the creation of the service or in their own experience of it. Each is leveraging a growing amount of data to create additional value. This may be user-contributed data, as with Amazon reviews or eBay ratings, or data that is collected by the services about resources and about user behaviors and preferences. Think of how Google and Amazon reflexively use data to modify the service, whether in personalization features, page ranking, or targeted advertizing. They may lack

highly structured data, but they sure make what data they have <u>work very hard</u>[4].

Given these characteristics, these services exercise great gravitational pull on users. They do this because they have scale, and because they give the user a sense of control. So, let's turn to library resources and think about them under the same headings.

1. **A comprehensive discovery experience.** The library discovery resource is fragmented. It may not be clear to individual users which database to look at, what part of the universe they are prospecting in any individual database, or when they have "finished" a search. The division of the library resource into the catalog, lists of electronic resources, and other databases may be confusing. These characteristics reduce the user sense of control and increase transaction costs. It is not always clear what part of the information space you are in, or it may seem like a rather limited information space: you bump into the walls. This is the area into which metasearch is stepping as a solution. However, it faces many challenges, which prompted me to wonder <u>in another post</u>[5] whether we should also be exploring much greater consolidation of library resources for discovery purposes.

2. **Predictable, often immediate, fulfillment.** Items in the catalog may be immediately available, or it may be possible to put in a reserve. Libraries are currently putting in place a variety of systems to manage the discovery (metasearch, lists of e-journals and databases . . .), location (resolution) and fulfillment services. In fact, much of the activity in this space is really about streamlining the supply chain between the user and the resource so that it disappears from view, thereby reducing the user's transaction costs in using this material. Where an item is not available, then various resource-sharing options may be available. The quality of service offered to the users may be variable depending on how much of the intermediate processes are hidden from them, and how much information is available to them about the status of any particular request. So, what we have here is a discovery-location-fulfillment chain which is variably automated, which

may still be fragmented by type of resource (book, licensed . . .), and which varies quite a bit in quality of service across institutions.

3. **Open to consumers.** Most of our information systems are rather closed. They do not all offer the ability to link with persistent URLs. Many may offer few internal navigation options. The user experience in moving between them is one of moving from one environment to a very different one, where one may have to adjust to very different interaction behaviors, redo searches, separately save results, and so on. They are often designed as if they were the sole focus of a user's attention, with special functions, help screens, and other features which are rarely used. A major focus of interesting work[6] reported by Dan Chudnov and colleagues in several places is to improve the ability of users to move across library resources in ways in which they are used to from their experiences with more open web environments.

4. **Open to the intermediate consumer.** Library systems tend to be also closed from a technical point of view. RSS feeds, web service interfaces, flexible data export: it may not be straightforward exposing their services to intermediate consumers like course management systems or campus portals. This becomes a major issue as it is vital for libraries to place their services at the point of need within the user workflow: their services must be provided so that they can be recombined with other service environments much more effectively. So, we may want a search box for the library catalog to be visible within several nonlibrary environments.

5. **A co-created experience.** Our systems are not very engaging in this way: we do not make great use of contributed data, nor do we adapt reflexively in light of user behavior or usage data. Our systems are rather inert.

So, unlike the major online presences, our systems have low gravitational pull, they do not put the user in control, they do not adapt reflexively based on user behavior, they do not participate fully in the network experience of their users.

The more I think about these issues, the more I think that a major question for us moving forward is organizational. What are the organizational frameworks through which we can mobilize collective resources to meet the challenges of the current environment? How do we overcome fragmentation, streamline supply, reduce the cost of the system and service development which is incurred redundantly across many institutions?

NOTES

1. http://orweblog.oclc.org/archives/000664.html
2. http://orweblog.oclc.org/archives/000629.html
3. www.liveplasma.com
4. http://orweblog.oclc.org/archives/000535.html
5. http://orweblog.oclc.org/archives/000615.html
6. http://orweblog.oclc.org/cgi-bin/mt-search.cgi?IncludeBlogs=1&search =chudnov+openurl+clicks

JULY 6, 2007

The network reconfigures the library systems environment

http://orweblog.oclc.org/archives/001379.html

One of the main issues facing libraries as they work to create richer user services is the complexity of their systems environment. Consider these pictures, which I have been using in presentations for a while now. (See figure 5.1.)

Reductively, we can think of three classes of systems—(1) the classic ILS focused on "bought" materials, (2) the emerging systems framework around licensed collections, and (3) potentially several repository systems for "digital" resources. Of course, there are other pieces, but I will focus on these.

In each case, what we see is a back-end apparatus for managing collections, each with its own workflow, systems, and organizational support. And each with its own—different—front-end presentation and discovery mechanisms. What this means is that the front-end presentation mirrors the organizational development over time of the library back-end systems, rather than the expectations or behaviors of the users.

You have the catalog here, maybe several options for licensed resources (*A*-to-*Z*, metasearch, web pages of databases, and so on) over there, and

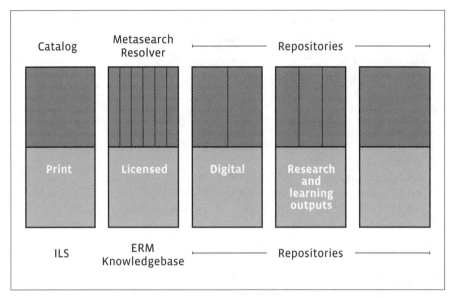

FIGURE 5.1 Library systems

potentially several repository interfaces (local digitized materials, institutional repository) somewhere else.

This is one reason that people have difficulties with the library website. Effectively, it is a layer stretched over a set of systems and services which were not designed as a unit. Indeed, in some cases, they were not originally designed to work on the web at all. So what do we have?

ILS: a management system for inventory control of the "bought" collection (books, DVDs, etc.). The catalog is bolted onto this and gives a view onto this part of the collection. In effect, in virtue of its integration with inventory management, the catalog provides discovery (what is in the collection), location (where those things are), and request (get me those things) in a tightly integrated way. The ILS and catalog may be part of a wider apparatus of provision, and may have mechanisms for interfacing to resource sharing systems of one sort or another. The management side may have interfaces to a variety of other systems for sharing and communicating data: procurement, finance, student records. And there will be a flow of data into the system, from jobbers, as part of a shared cataloging environment, and so on.

Licensed: This has been an area of rapid recent development as the journal literature moved to electronic form. On the back end, we now see a variety of approaches, and the front end can be very confusing with lists of databases and journals presented in various ways, often in uncertain relation to the catalog (where do I look for something?). We are now seeing the emergence here of an agreed set of systems around knowledge base, ERM, resolution, and metasearch, and there is rapidly developing vendor support. This is the range of approaches for which Serials Solutions has proposed the ERAMS name. These systems require the management of new kinds of data, and mechanisms are being put in place, certainly not yet optimal, for the creation, propagation, and sharing of this data. With journals data, discovery, location, and request are not so tightly coupled as they were with the catalog. Discovery has happened in one set of tools (A&I databases), but then the appropriate title may have to be located in another tool (the catalog, for example) and, if not available locally, requested through yet another system. The importance of the resolver, and the enabling OpenURL, has been to tie some of these things together and remove some of the human labor of making connections between these systems. And metasearch has been seen as a way of reducing human labor by providing a unified discovery experience over disparate databases. However, this whole apparatus is still not as well seamed as it needs to be, and users and managers still do more work than they should to make it all work.

Repository: Libraries are increasingly managing digital materials locally and supporting repository frameworks for those. This includes digitized special collections, research and learning materials in institutional repositories, web archives, and so on. There are a variety of repository solutions available, some open source. Typically, the contents of the repository back end may be available to repository front ends on a per-repository basis. Here, discovery (what is there), location (where is it), and request and delivery are typically tightly integrated. Repositories may also have interfaces for harvesting or remote query. On the management side, metadata creation and material preparation may still be labor-intensive.

OK, so here are some general observations about this environment:

There is still a major focus—in terms of attention, organizational structures, and resource allocation—on the systems and processes around the

ILS and the bought collection. In academic libraries, we will surely see some of this move toward the systems and processes around the licensed collections, given the rising relative importance of this part of the collection. The repository strand of activity, associated with emerging digital library activities, may, in some cases, be supported from grant or other special resources. It will need to become more routine.

The fragmentation of this systems activity, the multiple vendor sources, the different workflows and data management processes, and the absence of agreed simple links between things mean that the overall cost of management is high.

There is also another cost: diminished impact and lost opportunity. The awkward disjointedness described above also means that it is difficult to mobilize the consolidated library resource into other environments, course management or social networking systems, for example. It is difficult to flexibly put what is wanted where it is wanted.

There has been much discussion of library interoperability, but it has tended to be about how to tie together these individual pieces, or about tying pieces to other environments (how do I get my repository harvested, for example). There has been less focus on how you might abstract the full library experience for consumption by other applications—a campus portal for example.

This in turn means several things.

- We will see more hosted and shared solutions emerge, which offer to reduce local cost of ownership. And, of course, we are seeing vendors consider more integration between products. In particular, it is interesting seeing the concentration on support for the licensed e-resources emerge strongly, as well as discussion about integrated discovery environments.
- Over time, we can expect to see some more reconfiguration in a network environment. Shared cataloging and externalizing the journal literature have been two significant reconfigurations in the past. The pace of current developments suggests that we may be ready for other ways of collaboratively sourcing shared operations. For example, does it make sense for there to be library-by-library

solutions for preservation, social networking, disclosure to search and social networking engines, and so on?

The next picture tries to capture an important direction that has emerged in the last year or so. (See figure 5.2.)

For many of the reasons identified above, we are seeing a growing interest in separating the discovery and presentation front end from the management back end across this range of systems. Why? Well, because it is becoming clearer as I suggested in my opening that legacy system boundaries do not effectively map user preferences. And because fragmentation adds to effort and accordingly diminishes impact.

What about the discovery side? So, we saw metasearch, a partial response to fragmentation of A&I databases. We are now seeing a new generation of products from the "ILS vendors" which look at unifying access to the library collection: Encore, Primo, Enterprise Portal Solution. However, discovery has also moved to the network level. So, folks discover resources in Amazon, Google, Google Scholar. And OCLC is working to create discov-

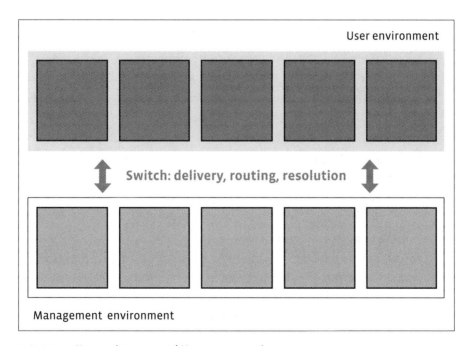

FIGURE 5.2 User environment and Management environment

ery experiences which connect local and network through WorldCat Local, WorldCat.org, and Open WorldCat.

And on the management side? Here the variety of workflows and systems adds cost, as resources are managed on a per-format basis. We can expect to see simplification and rationalization in coming years as libraries cannot sustain expensive diversity of management systems. The National Library of Australia's discussion[1] of a "single business" systems environment and Ex Libris's discussion of Uniform Resource Management are relevant here. It is likely that there will be a growing investment in collaboratively sourced solutions, as libraries seek to share the costs of development and deployment.

As discovery peels off, then the issue of connecting discovery environments back to resources themselves becomes very important. It is interesting to look at Google Scholar in this regard, as different approaches are required for the three categories identified above. It has worked with OCLC and other union catalogs to connect users through to catalogs and the ILS; it has worked with resolver data to connect users through to licensed materials; and it has crawled repositories and links directly to digital content.

Given this great divide, several issues become very important:

- Routing, resolution, and registries become critical, as one wants to enable users to move easily from a variety of discovery environments to resources they are authorized to use. We need a richer apparatus to support this. (I have discussed[2] the role of registries elsewhere.)
- Libraries have thought about discovery. There is now a switch of emphasis to disclosure: libraries need to think about how their resources are best represented in discovery environments which they don't manage. (I have also discussed[3] disclosure in more detail elsewhere in these pages.)
- And, again, how we present library services for consumption by other environments becomes an issue. For example, we are lacking an ILS Service Layer,[4] an agreed way of presenting the functionality of the ILS so that it can be placed, say, in another discovery environment (shelf status, place a hold, etc.).

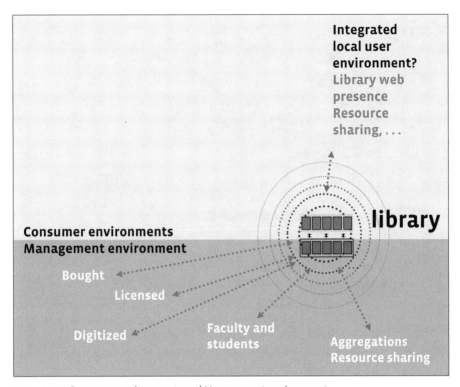

FIGURE 5.3 Consumer environments and Management environment

- Better discovery puts more pressure on delivery, whether from a local collection, throughout a consortium, or in broader resource sharing or purchase options. Streamlining the logistics of delivery and providing transparency on status at any stage for the users (as they can do with UPS or Amazon) become more important. (See figure 5.3.)

And finally . . .

We are used to thinking about better integration of library services. But that is a means, not an end. The end is the enhancement of research, learning, and personal development. I discussed above how we want resources to be represented in various discovery environments. Increasingly, we want to represent resources in a variety of other workflows. These might be the personal digital environments that we are creating around RSS aggregators, toolbars, and so on. Or the prefabricated institutional environments such as the course management system or the campus portal. Or emerging

READER COMMENT

Oren Beit-Arie
Chief Strategy Officer, Ex Libris Group

I've been following Lorcan's blog for a few years now. Not only did it help me stay informed and updated, but it helped me validate my own thinking about so many topics we share interest in.

Lorcan's weblog was invaluable—

> For the breadth of issues, the wide range of topics, the thoughtful analysis, and his shameless predictions.
>
> For the anecdotes, the examples, and the proposed language and definitions that helped formalize our thinking around complex and emerging topics.
>
> For getting me to stop and think. Triggering new ideas in my mind, and helping me realize how foolish were other ideas that I had previously thought were good . . .
>
> And, of course—not the least: for the dry, crisp humor. Yes, working in library land can also be funny . . .

service composition environments like Facebook or iGoogle. As well as in network-level discovery environments, like Google or Amazon, which are so much a part of people's behaviors.

Libraries need to focus more attention on reconfiguring library services for network environments. This is the main reason for streamlining the back-end management systems environment. It does not make sense to spend so much time on non-value-creating effort.

NOTES

1. http://orweblog.oclc.org/archives/001307.html
2. http://orweblog.oclc.org/archives/001105.html
3. http://orweblog.oclc.org/archives/001084.html
4. http://orweblog.oclc.org/archives/000927.html

Untangling the library systems environment

http://orweblog.oclc.org/archives/002015.html

NISO organized a meeting[1] on library resource management a couple of weeks ago: I notice that the presentations[2] are now available on the web. They make an interesting collection, and I return to them in a moment.

I have written about the library systems environment in these pages from time to time. A blog entry[3] from summer 2007 formed the basis of a *Portal* article of the same name ("Reconfiguring the Library Systems Environment"[4]). See figure 5.1, above, at "The network configures the library systems environment."

Libraries manage a variety of materials workflows, each supported by a different systems apparatus. In each case, there is a vertical arrangement, as materials are disclosed through discovery and delivery services which in turn relate to back-end management services in closely coupled ways. Bought (often print) materials go through an ILS workflow and are disclosed through the catalog, which is usually a part of the ILS itself. Systems to manage these materials in resource-sharing arrangements may also be present. Licensed materials have an emerging apparatus of management systems support (ERM, knowledge base, A-to-Z lists, and so on) and are disclosed in a variety of ways, including metasearch and resolvers. A routine approach has not emerged for digital materials, and they are managed in a variety of repository and other frameworks, and delivered to per-repository user interfaces. Different approaches may be taken with different categories—digitized special materials, web archives, institutional research materials, and so on—and metadata may be exposed for harvesting. Although not pictured here, one might add that there may also be additional workflows associated with archival materials or special collections. (Slide 4 of Mackenzie Smith's presentation[5] is an interesting depiction of the internal library systems environment showing the range of actual systems supported. See figure 5.2, above, at "The network configures the library systems environment.")

The complex array of systems—at different stages of maturity and created in quite different technical environments—has encouraged a move toward some rationalization and integration. In particular, we can see a drive to integrate the management workflows across material types. Examples here are OCLC's Cooperative Webscale Management Systems initiative, Ex Libris's URM, and the open source OLE project. At the same time, we see two trends on the discovery side. The first is a drive toward deeper integration across types, both through greater use of metasearch and through actual consolidation of files. Although it will not be comprehensive of all available materials, we will see much more of the latter approach for efficiency reasons. The second is a realization that library resources need to be disclosed more effectively to a variety of other environments, whether they are other institutional systems (e.g., course management) or external. See figure 5.3, above, at "The network configures the library systems environment.".

So, finally I note two major challenges. One is that on the management side libraries have to pull together a variety of systems and services whose legacy business and technical boundaries may no longer map very well onto user requirements. A second is that they have to project their resources into a variety of user environments and workflows over and above whatever integrated local library website environment they create. These include personal (people have a growing variety of ways of finding, saving, and collecting information resources); institutional (think, of course, management systems, student portals . . .); and network-level services (search and discovery services; social networking, bookmarking and bibliography sites . . .). Related to this is the challenge of integrating community in library services: there is a gap between libraries as inevitably social organizations and the social component of the library experience on the web. A redrawing of this image today would have to include a better sense of user participation.

In this context, here are some incomplete notes on some of the presentations at the NISO meeting:

- **General overviews** were given by Oren Beit-Arie[6] and Marshall Breeding[7] in a wide-ranging opening keynote and conclusion, respectively. Oren presents a picture not unlike the one suggested above, discussing the need to move from content-based verticals to service-based horizontals. The context for much of what he says is provided by a summary of responses from interviews with librarians. Here are the headline requirements (adapted slightly): a single interface for discovery and delivery of all library/institutional assets; consolidated workflows, uniting traditional library functions with those of the "digital library"; collaboration to increase productivity, leveraging "network effect"; re-use of metadata; SOA-based interoperability; software-as-a-service deployment option; user-provided data. He characterizes evolving services within a traditional/transitional/transformational framework, where traditional involves doing the same thing differently, transitional involves doing new things in support of the transitional, and transformational involves doing new things. Moving services to the cloud is given as an example of the traditional, as is evolution of the cataloging environment; exploiting network effects (e.g., collaborative collection development, tagging of library images in Flickr . . .) is given as an example of transitional; and the mobilization of usage data to transform services (new metrics of scholarly evaluation, recommender systems, analytics and ranking of results) is given as an example of transformational services.

- **System sourcing** decisions and their implications figure large in the agenda given the recent focus on open source approaches. Marshall Breeding[8] cryptically notes "many unannounced open source projects" which may change the current low defection rates from established ILS vendors. How will open source initiatives work with emerging software as a service trend?
- **Recommendation** and other ways of mobilizing usage (or intentional) data figure in several places, in line with general trends. I suggested[9] recently that we will see services which don't use direct user input in the form of tagging or review, and indirect in the form of usage data to support ranking, relating, and recommending, as bleached, rather like black-and-white TV in a color world. See Kevin Kidd's presentation,[10] as well as Oren's, on this issue.
- **Scalar emphasis** has become an important question for libraries. At what scale should things be done, as institution-scale is increasingly the wrong level for many activities? Oren discusses the transitional effect of the network in broader collaborative settings, where the power of the network can be leveraged to improve services. Shared

cataloging and resource sharing may be earlier instances of this. Consider now the potential for recommendations where circulation or other usage data is aggregated at a higher level. Consider incentives also in this context. Where are library users most likely to want to invest their effort? Kat Hagedorn[11] discusses a collaborative project of the HathiTrust, New York University, and the partners in the ReCAP shared print facility with the involvement of OCLC Research and CLIR. What policy and service apparatus needs to be in place to provide confidence of supply from Hathi-Trust and ReCAP sufficient to allow NYU to relegate materials from its own collection? Such "cloud library" provision will become more common as libraries seek to transfer resources away from "infrastructure" and toward user engagement. Kyle Bannerjee describes[12] Orbis Cascade's work with OCLC on the integration of local, consortial, and global discovery and delivery of resources. He suggests that operations should move to the highest appropriate level in the network, and speculates about what other services should move to the network level. Rachel Bruce[13] looks at library systems from the point of view of national-scale "shared services." What these and other presentations show is how decisions about level of operation—personal, local, consortial, national, global—are as important as particular discussions of functionality or sourcing. Libraries face interesting choices about sourcing—local, commercial, collaborative, public—as they look at how to achieve goals, and as shared approaches become more crucial as resources are stretched.

- Academic library systems are part of an **enterprise infrastructure**, which is discussed here by Mackenzie Smith[14] of MIT and Diane Mirvis[15] of the University of Bridgeport. For me, these were the most interesting presentations here as they point to a set of influences that are not discussed very often. As more activity takes place on the network, as students, faculty, and administrators create and use data from many sources, and as there is more pressure for new types of integration on both user and management side, it will be interesting to see how organizational and system boundaries change within institutions.

NOTES

1. www.niso.org/news/events/2009/lrms09
2. www.niso.org/news/events/2009/lrms09/agenda
3. http://orweblog.oclc.org/archives/001379.html
4. www.oclc.org/research/publications/library/2008/dempsey-portal.pdf
5. www.niso.org/apps/group_public/download.php/2895/smith_lrms09niso.ppt
6. www.niso.org/apps/group_public/download.php/2885/beitarie_lrms09niso.ppt
7. www.niso.org/apps/group_public/download.php/2887/breeding_lrms09niso .pptx
8. www.niso.org/apps/group_public/download.php/2887/breeding_lrms09niso .pptx
9. http://orweblog.oclc.org/archives/002013.html
10. www.niso.org/apps/group_public/download.php/2892/kidd_lrms09niso.ppt
11. www.niso.org/apps/group_public/download.php/2891/hagedorn_lrms09niso .ppt
12. www.niso.org/apps/group_public/download.php/2884/banerjee_lrms09niso.ppt
13. www.niso.org/apps/group_public/download.php/2888/bruce_siteversion_lrms 09niso.ppt
14. www.niso.org/apps/group_public/download.php/2895/smith_lrms09niso.ppt
15. www.niso.org/apps/group_public/download.php/2894/mirvis_lrms09niso.pptx

AUGUST 17, 2011

The ILS, the digital library, and the research library

http://orweblog.oclc.org/archives/002188.html

Job adverts are interesting for a variety of reasons. They give a sense of skills and attributes in demand. They say something about how the hiring institution wants to present itself. And they can indicate trends.

I have been interested to see three research libraries look for senior digital library posts in recent months.

- Associate Director for Digital Library Programmes and Information Technologies,[1] Bodleian Libraries, University of Oxford.
- Associate Vice President for Digital Programs and Technology Services,[2] Columbia University Libraries/Information Services.
- Head of Digital Library,[3] Information Services, the University of Edinburgh.

Now, these are different posts in different institutions, but there is the common ground that you might expect as research libraries look at creating digital infrastructure, engage with research data needs, explore new modes of scholarly communication, and so on. Each is challenging and interesting and offers a wonderful opportunity to be centrally involved in advancing how libraries support changing research and learning practices.

However, I was struck by something else they have in common. Responsibility for the integrated library system (or library management system) appears to be a part of each post, yet it is not foregrounded in the position description. For these libraries, maybe, the ILS is a necessary part of doing business, but is not the site of major development. Designing and developing digital infrastructure now includes the ILS but is no longer led by it. Or maybe there is some other reason . . .?

Now, considerable time and effort goes into these systems, and they will be reconfigured in coming years. Picking up on my opening remarks though, it is interesting to see where the adverts place the emphasis.

NOTES

1. www.lisjobnet.com/job-ads/762-a110606-associate-director-for-digital
   -library-programmes-and-information-technologies/
2. https://academicjobs.columbia.edu/applicants/jsp/shared/frameset/Frameset
   .jsp?time=1313628502453
3. www.jobs.ed.ac.uk/vacancies/index.cfm?fuseaction=vacancies.furtherdetails
   &vacancy_ref=3014396

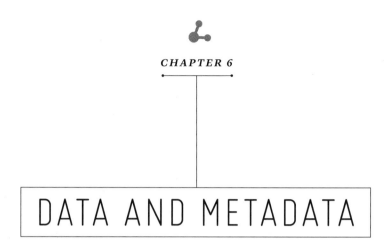

CHAPTER 6

DATA AND METADATA

LIBRARIES IN THE Internet age are decreasingly focused on traditional items and increasingly focused on their digital counterparts, or on delivering digital copies of items to users who need them. The discovery and delivery process requires extensive and shareable metadata as well as the digital objects themselves.

From his perspective atop perhaps the largest collection of bibliographic data germane to libraries, Dempsey describes the tapped and untapped potentials of data. This section comprises selected posts focusing on data and metadata themselves, as opposed to the systems designed to store or manage them. What are libraries doing with data, and what untapped sources are there?

JANUARY 8, 2005

Making data work harder

http://orweblog.oclc.org/archives/000535.html

As more activities move into a network space, so more areas of our life are shedding data. This data is increasingly being mined for intelligence which drives services. And with data, quantity, as they say, has a quality all of its own.

A major attribute of both Google and Amazon is how they squeeze as much value as they can from the data they have, and the value of that activity increases with the volume of data. Data about uses and users, as well as data about the used. The more people use Amazon, the better its recommendations. The more of the web that Google harvests, the better the associations[1] it can make between words. Which in turn will improve its collocation of stories in Google News, or its matching of ads to results. The more digital copies of books Amazon has, the better its forward and backward citation[2] linking. The more articles Google Scholar indexes, the better it can do ranking by citation[3].

IBM has just acquired the identity resolution company SRD, the better to relate names and identities across multiple data streams:

> With this newly acquired technology, as users add more and more data sources, accuracy goes up, Wozniak said. "Once you have a database of resolved identities, it can find people across multiple layers of separation," he said.[4]

The more bibliographic data OCLC has, the better it can associate the multiple manifestations[5] of works, as it mines the relationships created by many catalogers. The better, also, it can provide useful intelligence about the "flavor" of a collection, and how it compares with others. We have been doing more research work[6] in this area recently, and also preparing for new collection analysis services to appear later this year. We are also trying to make this data work better in the open web environment in Open World-Cat[7]: subjects and authors are now clickable, pulling in related results.

Historically, ISI has been notable in the way in which it has generated intelligence from data. And the work[8] at the University of Southampton on e-prints data is pioneering (see in particular CiteBase and OpCit).

However, for a community which invests so much intellectual, staff, and financial resources in data creation and management, we do not get as much value from data as we should.

See, for example, Dorothea Salo's recent argument[9] that although we have good data, we don't use the structure in the data in our user interfaces. See also Roy Tennant's recent use[10] of my phrase "murky bucket" in his *LJ* column, where Roy asks how well our current bibliographic apparatus supports ongoing needs. My view, which Roy kindly notes, is that we need increasingly to think about how we want to use data programmatically—to "FRBRize," to do collection analysis, to generate interesting displays.

We do have rich data. It could be better. But more important, we need to make our data work harder to create value for our users.

NOTES

1. http://orweblog.oclc.org/archives/000532.html
2. http://orweblog.oclc.org/archives/000503.html
3. http://orweblog.oclc.org/archives/000528.html
4. Lisa Vaas, "IBM Buys Identity Company to Nail Down Who's Who," January 7, 2005, *eWeek*, at www.eweek.com/c/a/Database/IBM-Buys-Identity-Company -to-Nail-Down-Whos-Who/
5. www.oclc.org/research/projects/frbr/default.htm
6. www.oclc.org/research/projects/mi/default.htm
7. www.cni.org/tfms/2004b.fall/abstracts/presentations/CNI_nilges_going.ppt
8. www.eprints.org
9. http://cavlec.yarinareth.net/archives/2005/01/04/the-power-of-presentation
10. www.libraryjournal.com/article/CA485777?display=Digital+LibrariesNews &industry=Digital+Libraries&industryid=3760&verticalid=151

MARC up?

MARCH 20, 2005

http://orweblog.oclc.org/archives/000616.html   Tag: Noteworthy

Terry Willan, of Talis, has a thoughtful post[1] on the current discussion about the relationship between MARC and XML on the xml4lib[2] mailing list.

He reminds people of the three layers in the classical library metadata stack: encoding (ISO 2709 or Z39.2[3]), content designation (as expressed in the various MARC formats), and content values (which is the focus of cataloging rules and controlled terminologies). I was interested to see this, as I have been emphasizing the importance of these distinctions in recent presentations (see, for example, "Metadata: Practice and practice"[4] and "Metadata practice and direction: A community perspective"[5] for two related presentations).

Dublin Core took a different approach. It initially focused on the "designation" part of the stack (what are the elements of importance), and latterly produced several encoding recommendations. However, there are no generally deployed content standards associated with the Dublin Core: it did not set out to develop any, leaving this to community agreement. And, indeed, several such agreements have arisen. Similarly, other metadata initiatives—IEEE LOM, for example—have not focused to the same extent on content standards.

This then plays into one of the major experiences of the initial harvesting projects: they soon discovered that the absence of content standards creates interoperability issues.

I mention content standards, because I was surprised that consideration of AACR3 was not brought more into the xml4lib discussion. Based on recent conversations with colleagues within and without OCLC, I think that two issues are vital as AACR3 is worked through:

1. The majority of data is going to be consumed by programs: it needs to be designed in such a way that it helps rather than hinders this process.

2. The value of existing approaches is being questioned, especially in the full glare of the Amazoogle world. This suggests that a clear focus on cost and benefit is important in revising the code: valuable cataloger time should be spent where it creates most value.

NOTES

1. http://panlibus.blogspot.com/2005/03/when-will-xml-replace-marc.html
2. http://sunsite.berkeley.edu/XML4Lib/
3. www.niso.org/standards/standard_detail.cfm?std_id=470

4. www.oclc.org/research/presentations/dempsey/clirmetadata.ppt
5. www.oclc.org/research/presentations/dempsey/nisometadata.ppt

MAY 31, 2005

All that is solid melts into flows . . .

http://orweblog.oclc.org/archives/000663.html

Like most people ;-), I tend to think about metadata as "schematized statements about resources": *schematized* because machine understandable; *statements* because they involve a claim about the resource by a particular agent; *resource* because any identifiable object may have metadata associated with it.

Metadata is useful because it relieves a potential user (person or program) of having to have full advance knowledge of the characteristics or existence of a resource. In other words, metadata provides "intelligence" which supports more efficient operations on resources. Examples of operations are discovery, preservation, purchase, reformatting, embedding, analysis, extraction of components, and so on.

Now, I say this by way of introduction because much of our metadata discussion still focuses on refining descriptive metadata for information objects. However, it is clear that as we move into more complex digital environments that this is one part only of the metadata picture. Libraries have developed practices which focus on the inventory needs of relatively "solid" information resources (books, journals . . .). But all that is solid is melting into flows. . . . We need more types of metadata than just descriptive; and we need to represent more entities in our world than "solid" information objects.

In the network world, at least four things have changed.

1. Information objects have become fluid. They can flow between different environments of use more readily, and they can be mixed <u>recombinantly</u>[1] in new forms. To take a conservative example, think about the potential impact of the Google Print/Libraries initiative on our current bibliographic apparatus. We will have print originals, Google digital copies, library digital copies. Technical and rights metadata

will come into play with the digital copies. But the germane issue here is how will we relate these various instances within our current bibliographic apparatus? How will this articulate with emerging FRBR[2] practices? And looking beyond this, how do we manage the decomposition of these objects and their recombination[3] in multiple content packages (e-portfolio, exhibition, courseware, and so on)?

2. As more business processes are moved into applications, we need to manage data about many more business entities. Think about emerging e-resource management systems, for example, where we need to manage information objects but also licenses, policies, and a range of other data. See the ERMI initiative,[4] for example, as one place where these issues are being addressed.

3. We need to manage interactions between these entities. This raises issues of rights and tracking, among others. So, for example, the COUNTER[5] initiative is looking at how we manage and share usage data.

4. We need to be able to programmatically derive more metadata, whether this is resource metadata promoted from digital resources themselves, or usage and tracking data collected from interactions within a digital environment, or data captured from users. Think of how Amazon reflexively adapts to your use of it, based on the data about use and usage it collects.

In turn, here are some issues that these directions suggest, presented in no particular order:

Multiple business entities. Here are some of the entities that we need to model within our systems: users, rights, licenses, policies, services, "complex" information objects, "simple" information objects, organizations. Where it makes sense, we need to take from the broader community. With limited effort, we should only develop approaches where none else suitable exist.

Abstraction and models. The liquidity of resources and the multiple entities involved in our activities suggest the benefits of some abstraction and modeling if we are to be able to build viable digital information environments. See, for example, the entity-relationship model advanced as part of the ERMI work above, whose purpose is to help clarify what needs to be modeled within e-resource management systems. See the entity-relationship model presented by Michael Heaney in his discussion of collection-level description, whose purpose is to help clarify what needs to be modeled in a collection description schema. See the model[6] in PREMIS. See FRBR. See INDECS. See, no doubt, multiple other initiatives. What is the appropriate level of engagement between these activities and where does it happen?

Rights, policies, licenses. These all become more important in a liquid world. We tend to think of rights as a way of locking commercial resources down. But, increasingly, we want to be able to say something (make "statements") about appropriate uses of any resource. This is especially so as resources flow recombinantly[7] between many parties and packages. As more interactions are automated, then we also need to encapsulate "intelligence" which guides decisions in machine-readable form. Policy and license data potentially become more important. This data is becoming available in digital form, but for human inspection only. It needs to be "schematized" for machines to make use of it without human intervention.

All of this raises the importance of modeling and representing events, which I speak about elsewhere[8].

We have made some progress with automatic promotion of metadata from resources. We need to do more, especially as our existing manual processes do not scale very well. Much existing metadata creation for digital resources does not look sustainable unless more cost is taken out of the process.

This note is prompted by discussion about the protocols entry I did below[9] where I suggest that we would benefit from focusing in on a small number of simple protocols and building services from those. However, metadata presents us with more challenges moving forward, which make it less easy to suggest where the "simple enough" balance is.

We should not be adding cost and complexity, which is what tends to happen when development is through multiple consensus-making chan-

READER COMMENT

Carl Grant
Associate Dean, Knowledge Services and Chief Technology Officer, University of Oklahoma Libraries

There are few writers who have greater impact on my thinking than Lorcan Dempsey. His blog consistently brings together diverse threads of knowledge, thought, and experience and turns them into coherent and rational insights for librarians. His blog is simply an invaluable resource for the profession.

nels which respond to the imperatives of a part only of the service environment. This is especially so as libraries work hard to demonstrate value in changing times.[10] The Blue Ribbon Panel,[11] set up to review NISO strategy, suggested that it needs to develop a framework within which to establish gaps and direction. Perhaps this issue is something which might form part of their deliberations.

NOTES

1. http://orweblog.oclc.org/archives/000657.html
2. www.oclc.org/research/events/frbr-workshop/program.htm
3. http://orweblog.oclc.org/archives/000657.html
4. www.library.cornell.edu/cts/elicensestudy/dlfdeliverables/home.htm
5. www.projectcounter.org
6. http://orweblog.oclc.org/archives/000672.html
7. http://orweblog.oclc.org/archives/000657.html
8. http://orweblog.oclc.org/archives/000672.html
9. http://orweblog.oclc.org/archives/000654.html
10. http://orweblog.oclc.org/archives/000667.html
11. http://orweblog.oclc.org/archives/000673.html

NOVEMBER 7, 2006

Metadata . . .

http://orweblog.oclc.org/archives/001191.html

Günter Waibel has a nice entry[1] on metadata and explores correspondences across the GLAM sectors—libraries, archives, and museums. He notes a specific content type in each domain, bibliographic, archival, and material culture, respectively. Then he compares the metadata stack for each type of material, using a useful typology: data structure (e.g., MARC), data content (e.g., AACR2), data format (e.g., ISO 2709), and data exchange (OAI). Check it out for fuller enumeration of acronyms. Of course, one can add other acronyms along various dimensions . . .

Reading the entry prompted several thoughts, largely from a library perspective:

Conceptual models. The library community has FRBR; the museum community has the CIDOC Conceptual Reference Model[2]. INDECS,[3] and the work built on it, is in a similar space in the rights world.

Each attempts to identify and define concepts important to a domain and, importantly, the relationships between them: they aim to provide a model of the world of interest, which in turn provides a basis for design of metadata approaches. Of course, although I say "world" there are things in the world which are not included. FRBR, for example, identifies some of the concepts and relationships of interest, and not others. Other models have been developed in more specific areas. A couple which are influenced by FRBR are Michael Heaney's work on collections,[4] and, more recently, Andy Powell and Julie Allinson's work on the model[5] underlying the e-prints application profile[6].

> This work uses a combination of FRBR and the DCMI Abstract Model to create a *description set* for an eprint that is much richer than the traditional flat descriptions normally associated with Dublin Core. The intention is to capture some of the relationships between works, expressions, manifestations, copies and agents.[7]

Abstract model. The Dublin Core Abstract Model[8] is a data model whose purpose "is to provide a reference model against which particular DC encoding guidelines can be compared, in order to facilitate better mappings and translations between different syntaxes." More broadly, its supporters see it as having application beyond DC, potentially providing a consistent framework for how one groups properties about resources. In a way, it shifts emphasis from particular fixed "data structures" in the typology above toward constructs like application profiles.

The data structures mentioned by Günter, and other data structures, will typically designate some elements whose values are taken from controlled lists or vocabularies. We are used to thinking about controlled vocabularies for people (e.g., authority files), places (e.g., gazetteers), and things (e.g., subject schemes like LCSH, MESH, and so on). This is clearly an area of strong shared interest for libraries, archives, and museums, even if approaches have diverged. There are other controlled lists. For example, Thom Hickey talks about[9] MARC relator terms and codes, where the redundancy he discusses would seem to limit the usefulness of the controlled approach. This is a pity, as relationships between entities are probably among the most useful things that we can record about them, especially as we try to improve navigation, clustering, and retrieval in large bibliographic systems. We have lists for languages or countries and so on. ONIX has codelists[10]; indeed its approach is to "control" a large part of the data. An advantage of control is predictability, simplifying design and processing. A more permissive or discretionary approach may appear attractive to some, but ultimately may make data less useful and applications harder to build.

In the library community, the ISO 2709/MARC/AACR stack is in widespread use but is not universal.

Although they are intricately connected, the data structure (MARC), the data content structure (AACR/RDA), and the conceptual model (FRBR) are managed through different structures and on different schedules. One might argue that while they are conceptually distinct, in practice they are closely linked and mutually interdependent.

At the data structure level, a library may have some interest in MARC, various flavors of Dublin Core, MODS, EAD, and potentially IEEE LOM and ONIX. Given the variety of levels at which this data can diverge, issues of transformation are complex.

One could go on. Does this all seem a little too complex in our fast-moving world?

I hope that the Working Group on the Future of Bibliographic Control, established[11] by the Library of Congress, considers some of these issues. (Disclosure: I am an at-large representative on the committee.)

Note: I have benefited from some discussion with colleagues on these matters and am certainly interested in more general views about the "future of bibliographic control."

NOTES

1. http://hangingtogether.org/?p=152
2. http://cidoc.ics.forth.gr
3. www.indecs.org
4. www.ukoln.ac.uk/metadata/rslp/model
5. www.ukoln.ac.uk/repositories/digirep/index/Model
6. www.ukoln.ac.uk/repositories/digirep/index/Eprints_Application_Profile
7. Andy Powell, DC-2006 Special Session—ePrints Application Profile, 2006, at http://efoundations.typepad.com/efoundations/2006/09/dc2006_special_.html
8. http://dublincore.org/documents/abstract-model
9. http://outgoing.typepad.com/outgoing/2006/10/relator_codes_a.html
10. www.editeur.org/codelists.html
11. www.loc.gov/loc/lcib/0609/cataloging.html

DECEMBER 31, 2006

Emergent knowledge and intentional data

http://orweblog.oclc.org/archives/001236.html

I have written about "intentional" data on and off, data recording user preferences or choices. Such data has a variety of uses in our domain: we are all familiar with Amazon's "people who bought this also bought this" feature. One of the major lessons of Google is to show how important such data is to improving the retrieval experience. The page-rank algorithm uses "intentional" data (the choices made by people in linking to other sites) to inform the order in which results are returned. One of the reasons I like FictionFinder[1] is that it uses holdings data to rank results to similar effect. In this case, purchasing choices made by libraries influences the ranking, and it works well. And we are familiar with the use of citation data in broader scholarly discussion and assessment.

In general, consumer sites on the web make major use of such data, and it is especially valuable when they can connect it to individual identities. They use it to build up user profiles, to do rating and comparisons across sites, to recommend, and so on. Of course, this is increasingly important in an environment of abundant choice and scarce attention: they are investing more effort in "consumption management."[2] We are all familiar with the benefits, and the irritations, of organizations that want to build a deeper understanding of what we do and make us offers based on that.

Libraries have a lot of data about users and usage. And there are now some initiatives which are looking at sharing it. However, in general, libraries do not have a data-driven understanding of individual users' behaviors, or of systemwide performance of particular information resources. This is likely to change in coming years, given the value of such data. So, we are seeing the growth in interest in sharing database usage data. And technical agreements and business incentives for third-party providers will support this development. And, of course, libraries want to preserve the privacy of learning and research choices.

We are also seeing more research into the usefulness of usage data, and I am thinking in particular here of the MESUR (MEtrics from Scholarly Usage of Resources) project:

> The project's major objective is enriching the toolkit used for the assessment of the impact of scholarly communication items, and hence of scholars, with metrics that derive from usage data. The project will start with the creation of a semantic model of scholarly communication, and an associated large-scale semantic store that relates a range

of scholarly bibliographic, citation and usage data obtained from a variety of sources. Next, an investigation into the definition and validation of usage-based metrics will be conducted on the basis of this comprehensive collection. Finally, the defined metrics will be cross-validated, resulting in the formulation of guidelines and recommendations for future applications of metrics derived from scholarly usage data.[3]

In the context of this discussion, I was interested recently to come across a paper on "Emergent Knowledge" by Chunka Mui (available for fee on Amazon[4]). As more of what we do moves into a network environment, so does the amount of data that we shed grow. Data about behaviors and choices, and other data. Mui talks about how this data can be gathered and mined to create "emergent knowledge." He presents this taxonomy of emergent knowledge:

1. **Identity**. People and objects increasingly reveal their identity to systems and services, enabling better tracking and profiling. We are familiar with the use of transaction data where we can connect identities and track behaviors.
2. **Location**. Connecting identities to locations is generating value in many service areas. Geo positioning and geo locator services are growing.
3. **Health and diagnostics**. Remote monitoring and diagnostics.
4. **Preferences**. The ability to connect identities (of people and objects) through transactions, and potentially at particular locations, provides many opportunities to mine data as discussed above.
5. **Quality of service**. Mui gives the example of how the Hartford Insurance Company actually analyses the recordings it has of telephone transactions, connecting that with outcome and process information to create a cycle of learning and improvement. (Think virtual reference . . .).

Much of what I am talking about above relates to Identities and Preferences in this taxonomy. And, incidentally, this type of application is one more reason why it would be good to be able better to unambiguously identify the range of resources of interest to libraries.

I am prompted to caricature those portentous lines of T. S. Eliot from *The Rock* often raised in library conversation (where is the knowledge we have lost in information, etc.). We might well ask ourselves where is the data we have lost in information management, and the knowledge we have forsaken thereby.

NOTES

1. http://FictionFinder.oclc.org
2. http://orweblog.oclc.org/archives/001120.html
3. www.mesur.org/MESUR.html
4. www.amazon.com/gp/product/B000F7CC90/qid=1143828293/sr=1-4/ ref=sr_1_4?s=books&v=glance&n=551440&tag2=killerplatforms

MAY 20, 2007

Four sources of metadata about things

http://orweblog.oclc.org/archives/001351.html   Tag: Coinage

I think it is useful to think of four sources of descriptive metadata in libraries. These are not mutually exclusive, and one of the interesting questions we have to address is how they will be mobilized effectively together.

I don't have good names for these. How about: professional, contributed, programmatically promoted, and intentional?

PROFESSIONAL

The curatorial professions have made major investments in knowledge organization, through the development and application of cataloging rules, controlled vocabularies, authorities, gazetteers, and so on. One of our major challenges is releasing the value that has been created through those approaches in web environments. There is much to think about here, and many folks are thinking about it. Currently, these approaches do not tend to work well across silos, they are not made available as web resources themselves so that they can be part of the connected fabric of the web, they only work with the other approaches I mention in particular projects or services, their "relating" power is underused, and higher-level services based on data mining or statistical analysis are limited. Now, these types of issues are being addressed, but are some way from routine systemwide application. I believe that these approaches will continue, within a reconfigured system, and we need to make that data work harder. My personal view is that the curatorial professions need to invest more in the shared production of resources which identify and describe authors, subjects, places, time periods, and works.

CONTRIBUTED

A major phenomenon of recent years has been the emergence of many sites which invite, aggregate, and mine data contributed by users, and mobilize that data to rank, recommend, and relate resources. These include, for example, Flickr, LibraryThing, and Connotea. These services have a different focus, and create real value in the way that they organize resources. They also have value in that they reveal relations between people. Libraries have begun to experiment with these approaches, but individual libraries may not have the scale to iron out local or personal idiosyncrasy or emphasis. This is another area which lends itself to shared attention. There are real advantages to be gained. So, for example, as we digitize photographic and other community collections, we will want to mobilize knowledge about those collections that does not exist within the library. Or, if you think about a service like WorldCat Identities, at some stage we will want to allow those "identities" themselves to comment, augment, amend. What this means is that we will have to get rather more sophisticated about managing assertions about resources from different sources.

PROGRAMMATICALLY PROMOTED

We are handling more digital materials, where it is possible to programmatically identify and promote metadata from resources themselves or groups of resources. We will also do more to mine collections, including collections of metadata, to discern pattern and relations. We are increasingly familiar with clustering, entity identification, automatic classification, and other approaches. Look at the home page for books that Google is creating to see a resource created from mining Scholar, Google Book Search, and big Google to deliver a range of related materials.

INTENTIONAL

I have used this term to refer to the data that we are collecting about use and usage. PageRank is based on aggregate linking choices. Amazon recommendations are based on aggregate purchase choices. We use holdings data in ranking algorithms, which aggregate selection choices of libraries. This type of data has emerged as a central factor in the major web presences as they seek to provide useful paths through massive amounts of data.

To repeat, these approaches are not mutually exclusive and will increasingly be deployed alongside each other. For example, authority lists may support programmatic identification of personal or place-names in large text resources. The shared interests revealed in social networking applications may be abstracted into a form of intentional data to drive recommendations or "related work" services. Patterns of association and interaction will develop between tags and subject headings. And so on.

Much of our discussion pits these approaches against each other. This seems like the wrong approach. Clearly, there will always be choices about where one invests effort, especially as the network continues to reconfigure what we do, but the starting point should be how we create better services and what approaches support that, and not a "techeological" position around one or other approach which confuses ideology and technology.

POSTSCRIPT[1]

It occurred to me that what I call here crowdsourced, programmatically promoted, and intentional data are all ways of managing abundance. Our model to date has been a "professional" one, where metadata is manually created by trained staff. This model may not scale very well with large volumes of digital material. Nor does it necessarily anticipate the variety of ways in which resources might be related. The other sources will become increasingly important . . .

NOTE

1. This paragraph originally appeared in "Metadata sources," published September 20, 2009, but was moved to this item for purposes of the book.

Metadata and Heraclitus

http://orweblog.oclc.org/archives/001754.html

I was very struck a couple of years ago by a comment made by my colleague Eric Hellman. He talked about metadata in terms of rivers and lakes. In the library cataloging model, we have had lakes—accumulating stores of data that do not change frequently over time and are fed by a few principal sources. In the ERM/knowledge base model, we have rivers—stores of data that change frequently as products and services change and which are fed by many streams.

And as Heraclitus[1] is reported to have said: you cannot step into the same river twice. The data river for licensed materials is always in flux.

Now, I think that we will need to get used to cataloging data becoming more river-like also, more in flux, as that environment too becomes more dynamic. Here are some examples. . .

Work-based approaches. We are getting used to thinking about clustering records as works. Works are dynamic: new manifestations or expressions may continue to appear and be linked in various ways to the work or expression to which they belong. If we move to represent the other FRBR entities in appropriate ways, we may link bibliographic data to data about subjects, names, and so on.

We have a similar relationship issue as materials are digitized and may live in different places. How do we represent the relationships between items and digitized versions of them?

Rights data has become more important as we want to do more with books than buy them and make them available physically to a local audience. In particular, digitization has caused us to ask questions about what can be done with the book content. This has caused us to look at data in new ways and to think about what data is needed.

We are becoming used to collecting data from users—tags, ratings, reviews, additional details . . .—about materials in an ongoing way.

Update: I changed the order of the Heraclitus sentence this morning and then noticed that Roy had quoted the earlier version in a nice amplification[2] of the river theme. I do sometimes wonder about the etiquette of changing stuff, but usually only note big changes.

NOTES

1. http://worldcat.org/identities/lccn-n78-95675
2. www.libraryjournal.com/blog/1090000309/post/1110032511.html?nid=3565

Name authorities, crowdsourcing, and Máire Mhac an tSaoi

http://orweblog.oclc.org/archives/001848.html

I was sad to read of the death of Conor Cruise O'Brien (Wikipedia,[1] World-Cat Identity[2]) before Christmas. See the obituary[3] in the *Times* and John Naughton's note[4] for context.

O'Brien was the husband of Máire Mhac an tSaoi, noted scholar, writer, and poet in the Irish language. Mhac an tSaoi is known under various permutations of English/Irish and married/original versions of her name(s). Here is how she describes herself in a chronology attached to her autobiography, *The Same Age as the State*[5] (where she writes as Máire Cruise O'Brien):

"Máire Cruise O'Brien (née Máire MacEntee, in Irish [Gaelic] Máire Mhac an tSaoi, under which name she publishes in that language)."

Here is the LC data as given in the VIAF entry[6]. Interestingly, the preferred form is Máire O'Brien, and a search in the Library of Congress catalog[7] will lead you to "O'Brien, Máire, 1922-."

Now, in reading the obituaries of Conor Cruise O'Brien, I was interested to see the form "Máire Mac an tSaoi" used, which is not a version given in the LC authority file. (It differs in that it has "Mac" rather than "Mhac.") Checking elsewhere, I notice that this is also the form used in the review of recent Irish history by Roy Foster, *Luck & the Irish: A Brief History of Change, 1970-2000.*[8] (Incidentally, John Naughton speculates above that Foster may be the author of the *Times* obituary mentioned above.)

I also notice that WorldCat shows this form of the name for one item,[9] *An Galar Dubhach*, but this may be a mistake as it is shown as Máire Mhac an tSaoi in the National Library of Ireland (in which catalog, incidentally, Máire Mhac an tSaoi is the preferred form) and in the British Library[10] (where Máire O'Brien is the preferred form).

Now, I have forgotten, or more likely may never have known, what one might expect here ("Mhac" or "Mac") or why the masculine "Mac" is being used (see the Wikipedia article[11] on Irish names for an explanation of this point), and I don't know what choices Máire Mhac an tSaoi may have made about her name. I have made some limited inquiries but have not researched the issue in any depth.

Anyway, all of this is prelude to the point I want to make. LC and national libraries around the world create authorities data. There may be collaborative structures like NACO[12] to support this.

These types of service seem remarkably well suited to social approaches. Once I came across several examples of "Mac an tSaoi" and discovered that it was not recorded in any authority file, I thought that it would be nice to make that known to LC or the National Library of Ireland or the BL or . . . However, I have no way of easily doing that, which seems a shame. Authorities work—and think NACO here—is a professional activity, hedged around by rules and procedures; it is, after all, "authorities" work. However, it would seem sensible to open it up to suggestion and information (see figure 6.1).

Incidentally, WorldCat Identities,[13] which is programmatically built on top of authorities and bibliographic data, does not handle Máire Mhac an

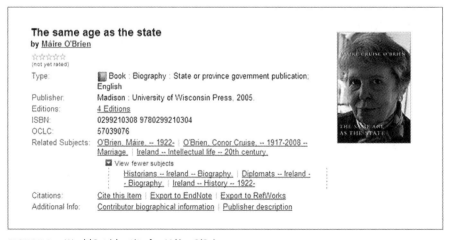

FIGURE 6.1 WorldCat identity for Máire O'Brien

tSaoi very well with entries split across several versions of her name and combining her work with some others. This is a good example of why we are working on approaches to allow readers to suggest splitting or merging of Identities.

NOTES

1. http://en.wikipedia.org/wiki/Conor_Cruise_O'Brien
2. http://worldcat.org/identities/lccn-n50-43483
3. www.timesonline.co.uk/tol/comment/obituaries/article5372017.ece
4. http://memex.naughtons.org/archives/2008/12/23/5902
5. www.worldcat.org/oclc/57039076/editions?editions
6. http://orlabs.oclc.org/viaf/LC|n86102319
7. http://catalog.loc.gov/webvoy.htm
8. www.worldcat.org/oclc/173749429
9. www.worldcat.org/oclc/16550767
10. http://catalogue.bl.uk/F/GSLH1JYYU2PDFFFV3674GFQ6DIIHHDLS4U32
    EHK5K9PASNMEL9-16346?func=full-set-set&set_number=151051&set
    _entry=000001&format=001
11. http://en.wikipedia.org/wiki/Irish_name
12. www.loc.gov/catdir/pcc/naco/nacopara.html
13. www.worldcat.org/identities

JUNE 14, 2009

Data flows in the book world

http://orweblog.oclc.org/archives/001974.html

One of the recommendations of the Library of Congress Working Group on the Future of Bibliographic Control[1] was that ways should be found of harnessing publisher data upstream of the cataloging process. The rationale was that this would make data about materials available earlier and reduce overall creation effort.

OCLC recently organized an invitational symposium[2] which had this issue as a central topic. The report is an interesting set of notes from the different perspectives of the multiple players involved. It discusses current practices and incentives to do things differently.

In a follow-up activity to the LC report, R2 Consulting is mapping the flow of MARC records in North American. The symposium notes say: "This list of distributors is much larger than originally anticipated and consists of a very diverse group of entities."

And, as I discussed the other day, the Research Information Network has published a report about UK practices, "Creating Catalogues: Bibliographic Records in a Networked World (Splash page)",[3] which also recommends greater re-use of records across the publishing and library worlds.

So, there certainly seems to be a convergence of interest here. Indeed, the potential benefits of such sharing have been a topic of discussion for many years. For example, at the OCLC Symposium, Brian Green, Executive Director of the International ISBN Agency, and I reminisced about UK initiatives to which we had been party almost, gulp, twenty years ago to try to create the conditions for an "all-through" system of bibliographic record exchange between the various players in the book world.

Now, clearly, quite a lot has happened, and as R2 reported above, data flows through many parties. And publisher data does flow into CIP, and into various organizations which support libraries. Amazon has done much to underline the importance to publishers of having book metadata to support a variety of operations. That said, the renewed emphasis on publisher-library data flow, certainly from the library side, suggests that much more might be done.

Why has more not happened to promote the flow of metadata through the system, from publishers to libraries? Three things occur . . .

First, there is the mechanical issue of data exchange. ONIX has now emerged as a shared approach to disseminating publisher data. However, it is interesting reading the remarks about ONIX in the report of the OCLC Symposium. NetLibrary reports that 10% of publishers supply data in ONIX, representing 50% of the supplied content. NLM also reported that 10% of publishers supply ONIX, but that these account for 80% of materials cataloged at NLM. There were also lots of comments about the consistency of ONIX data. However, one would expect improved technical apparatus to support data flow, not create the need for it.

This prompts the second question: what incentives exist and are they aligned across the system? Historically, metadata may have been created for different purposes. Publishers had an interest in the supply chain, and libraries an interest in inventory control. There may be a shared interest in discovery, but it has been approached differently in each area. In fact, one library interest is a recognition that more descriptive material (table of contents, summary, etc.) is in fact very useful for users of their catalogs and other systems, even though they have not historically made it a part of their catalog data. There may also be an interest in getting basic descriptive data earlier, to allow more time to be spent on other parts of record creation. What incentives exist for publishers to make data available to libraries? Amazon and other agents in the supply chain provide an incentive to make appropriate metadata available to support discovery and sales. Data is supplied for CIP purposes. Are there additional incentives? One may be to have enriched metadata flow back to publishers. Are there incentives here which are strong enough for a framework to emerge within which there is greater flow?

And third, related to this, and probably most important, is that the incentives on either side have not been strong enough to encourage organizations to develop services in this area which would make the flow a reality.

POSTSCRIPT

The conversation with Brian Green prompted me to look up various pieces I wrote at the time which reflected some of the discussion we remembered. (I note that while I have difficulty opening Word files from that time, the RTF file is still readable.)

"Publishers and Libraries: An All-Through System for Bibliographic Data?" *International Cataloguing and Bibliographic Control.* 20 (3), July/ September, 1991, 37–41.[4]

"Users' Requirements of Bibliographic Records: Publishers, Booksellers, Librarians." *ASLIB Proceedings,* 42 (2), February 1990, 61–69.[5]

Bibliographic Records: Use of Data Elements in the Book World. Bath: Bath University Library, 1989.[6]

NOTES

1. www.loc.gov/bibliographic-future
2. www.oclc.org/publisher-symposium/summary/default.htm
3. www.rin.ac.uk/creating-catalogues
4. www.ukoln.ac.uk/services/papers/ukoln/dempsey-1991-01/ubcim.rtf
5. www.worldcat.org/oclc/56916306
6. www.worldcat.org/oclc/19267913

DECEMBER 6, 2009

Beyond bibliographic records

http://orweblog.oclc.org/archives/002030.html

Our cataloging model revolves around the "manifestation," the particular edition or version of a work that is to be added to the collection. This is also the unit of bibliographic exchange: we ship around MARC records which have data about "manifestations."

These are the "inputs" into our catalogs and bibliographic systems. There is no necessary reason that they should also be the only outputs, although this is in fact what is usually the case. Searches tend to result in lists of entries for manifestations, each of which displays some subset of the data in the bibliographic record.

Recent catalogs have only changed this model slightly. Faceted browse, for example, typically allows manifestations to be brought together by some "facet": subject, place of publication, or date, for example. The facets themselves, potentially interesting ways of organizing data for presentation to a reader, don't tend to be used in this way.

What is an example of an alternative? WorldCat Identities provides an example of how a person or organization might be used as an organizing principle for displaying data. Here, we pull data from many records, recombine it, and present it in an integrated way. So an Identities page has, for example, a list of books by a person and about a person; it has alternative forms of the name of that person; it has related persons (or organizations); it has a concept-based tag-cloud representing the publications by and about that person; and so on.

We have done some work on similar sorts of pages for works. It would be nice to think of this type of organization for places.

In fact, our bibliographic records contain data about lots of entities about which people have an interest, or about which they ask questions. These include works, people, places, subjects, time periods. . . . However, our manifestation-record-oriented view means that we do not always exploit these data in ways in which they can be mobilized to answer those questions.

Of course, we do also manage other data as "records": name and subject authorities, for example. But these are not used extensively as structured data, and are often collapsed to strings in the bibliographic records. Other futures for this type of data are interesting to consider, but not here.

Now, I was prompted to write this by an interesting post by John Mark Ockerbloom, who talks about "concept-oriented" catalogs. (*Note:* by "concept" John means "thing" or "entity" or "object." In some ways, "concept" is confusing here because it might be thought that he is meaning a "subject" in library terms, something about which we have a lot of coded data. That said, we don't have agreed words for all that we want to talk about.)

> As more and more knowledge resources become available to users, via the expansion of the Internet, the streamlining of interlibrary loan services, and the mass digitization of print library materials, well-defined, well-documented, and well-connected concepts will become increasingly important for readers that want to find what is most useful to them in a sea of information. While we will never have well-defined concepts for everything readers might be interested in, the concepts that have been defined by someone, somewhere, can serve as valuable guideposts for subsequent information seekers, if we're smart about managing and using them.[1]

John notes as examples WorldCat Identities and FictionFinder[2] (an earlier prototype designed to show how data could be mobilized around works. I always liked the way this allowed you to search for "settings": for example, you can search for detective novels set in Edinburgh, etc.). He also notes the Subject Maps[3] work he is involved in at the University of Pennsylvania.

Libraries have managed bibliographic records, containers of data. The directions above point to a growing interest in seeing how they might more actively manage the data itself, making it work harder to provide information about entities of interest to their readers.

NOTES

1. John Mark Ockerbloom, "Understanding concept-oriented catalogs," December 4, 2009, at http://everybodyslibraries.com/2009/12/04/understanding-concept -oriented-catalogs
2. http://fictionfinder.oclc.org
3. https://labs.library.upenn.edu/subjectmaps

CHAPTER 7

PUBLISHING AND COMMUNICATION

AS THE INTERNET has become more pervasive in life, the way we communicate has shifted dramatically. This is true whether we are commenting on our profession or society informally through blogs or social media, or publishing the results of our research to the scholarly record. (The post "Communication," below, summarizes the venues used for these purposes.)

The items selected for this chapter focus on scholarly communication, social networking, and forms of writing and publishing, and they trace the rapid evolution of the digital age over the past decade.

DECEMBER 14, 2004

Aura, Google Print, and digitized library books

http://orweblog.oclc.org/archives/000509.html

Walter Benjamin famously asserted[1] that "that which withers in the age of mechanical reproduction is the aura of the work of art." In his terms, the aura is that which is original or authentic about a work. Aura depends on the position of a work within a tradition and its uniqueness. Reproduction diminishes each, the argument goes.

I was looking at *Books and Culture* (<u>scanned copy</u>,[2] <u>find in a library</u>[3]) in Google with a colleague earlier. It was nice to see the "auratic traces" (see figure 7.1) left by the staff at the University of Michigan on the scanned copy—the cataloger's marks, the UM perforated stamp.[4] Maybe we will see books emerging with annotations, autographs, coffee stains: that would be good.

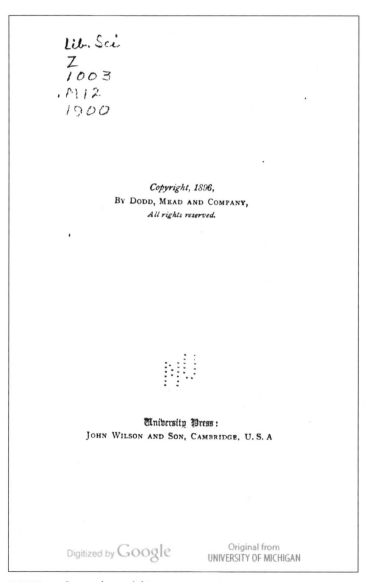

FIGURE 7.1 Scanned copyright page

NOTES

1. http://scholar.google.com/scholar?q=walter+benjamin
2. http://print.google.com/print?id=yGZZXIrbUKQC&pg=1
3. www.worldcatlibraries.org/wcpa/ow/77e88fd6e2135226.html
4. Source: http://hdl.handle.net/2027/mdp.39015034569833?urlappend=%3Bseq=6

OCTOBER 20, 2005

The discretion of bloggers

http://orweblog.oclc.org/archives/000832.html

It is quite difficult to be private: we leave traces everywhere. What we spend, who we speak to on the phone, where we live, our credit history: it all goes into the *record*.

I have just spoken at the very congenial Access 2005[1] conference, in Edmonton. The conference had active blogger participation (aggregated at Planet Access[2]), and the presentations will be podcast. I think this is marvelous; I find it enormously useful seeing a commentary or record of presentations.

READER COMMENT

Rick Anderson
Associate Dean for Scholarly Resources and Collections,
J. Willard Marriott Library

Lorcan Dempsey's ability to locate, pull together, and make sense of the disparate and sometimes contradictory conversations taking place in the scholarly communication environment is nothing short of astounding, and his blog has long been essential reading for anyone who wants to have any idea what's going on. It's not just that he locates the good stuff and brings it to a handy location, either—it's that he understands not only what people are saying, but also sees the issues that are implied but unstated, and he finds implications for libraries and scholars in commentary and developments that are not, at first blush, obviously relevant to that community. And, of course, he generates unique insights of his own. Having read what Lorcan says, one finds oneself constantly muttering, "Of course; why didn't I think of that?"

It did set up a particular dynamic as I was speaking though. Usually, during a conference presentation, I have a sense of being *"off record"*: so one might make the odd aside that would not be included in a written article, for example, or have that not-quite-validated detail in a presentation, knowing that it was not going to go beyond the room.

Now, however, everything is going into the *record:* one is always *on record.* One might rely on the discretion of bloggers, but it is all there in the podcast. . . . The private, public conference space is becoming a public, public space ;-).

Mmm . . . Update: a colleague points out that videos of presentations at last year's VALA are available[3]. I never knew!

NOTES

1. http://access2005.library.ualberta.ca
2. http://access2005.library.ualberta.ca/planetaccess
3. www.vala.org.au/vala2004/2004pprs/vide2004.htm

JANUARY 3, 2006

Keeping the public in publishing?

http://orweblog.oclc.org/archives/000911.html

We are used to buying books. To sharing them. To giving and receiving them as gifts. To quietly marking them. Even sometimes to proclaiming ownership in a bookplate. We are used to copying parts of them for study, to quoting from them.

Books circulate—through libraries, private collections, bookstores, and used bookstores. They are sold and resold. They exist redundantly: multiple copies are issued, and they can be tracked down in various places.

A by-product of this redundancy is the persistence of the scholarly record: lots of copies keeps stuff somewhere.

My *Concise Oxford Dictionary* offers "prepare and issue . . . for public sale" as a definition of "publishing." "Publishing" is a making "public," and the materials published are available to the public in various ways. They are also available for use and disposal at the buyer's discretion.

However, this line of thinking may sometimes mislead. For example, John Sutherland, distinguished critic and historian of literature, writes about the Google digitization initiatives and the announcement of Microsoft's support for digitization at the British Library:

> What is coming is something akin to the Oklahoma land rush of 1899. A half-dozen massively wealthy digital pioneers all going hell for leather to "propertise" the hitherto democratically owned "public domain"— that deposit of printed material that currently (but not for much longer, alas) you, I, and nobody own. It will be the biggest privatisation in history, and the most profitable. Once the public domain is propertised, it will remain proprietary material forever. (*EducationGuardian. co.uk | E-learning | Ivory towers will fall to digital land grab*[1])

He goes on to talk about the knowledge base of the university, and how it "is added to and refreshed, in the form of new books for the library and so on" and says "but it is essentially a university-owned asset."

But it is not a university-owned asset, or it is only partly a university-owned asset, if by "own" we imply unrestricted use and re-use. "Publication" does not put materials into the "public domain"; they are only in the public domain when copyrights expire or are not in place. The ongoing proprietary interest of the copyright holder has always been something that libraries have managed, and its interpretation, as we know, has sometimes been a cause of tension between publishers and libraries. Like books, journals were published and distributed, and often have institutional and personal subscription rates which recognize institutional and library patterns of use. In the print world, however, even when copyrights were still in force, the sharing, distribution, and occasional resale of the materials could make institutional "ownership" more visible than the ongoing proprietary interest of rights holders.

Of course, moving into the digital arena changed this. And we have seen with journals a very different model emerge where institutional "ownership" has given ground before the proprietary interest of the copyright holder. "Licensing" has replaced "buying" as the visible model. And there is an ongoing library discussion about appropriate models for sharing and preserving journal materials which are not now "owned" redundantly by libraries.

Two recent initiatives have made this type of discussion of much more general interest. The first is the mass-digitization initiatives of Google and others where the interests of the copyright holders has been asserted, questioning whether the universities can in fact do as they will with the "knowledge base" that they have acquired.

The second is more recent still and is more interesting given its potential impact. As people realize what restrictions they face when they "buy" music on iTunes, the changing nature of "publishing" will become apparent. In many cases "rent" may be a more apt description than "buy." And from music back to books, here is Adam Green:

> While waiting in my dentist's office this morning I started reading
> *BusinessWeek* and came across a story about <u>Sony's new ebook reader.</u>[2]
> The hardware sounds nice, but there is no way copy-protected ebooks
> are going to succeed. As I keep telling my kids when it comes to music,
> if there is DRM you are renting not buying. A day will surely come
> when you switch hardware or the company switches DRM schemes
> and your music will go away. Personally, I don't care that much about
> music, but when DRM is applied to books I get a little crazy. For book
> buyers *owning* the book is at least as important as reading it. I'm not
> even going to talk about the way books smell or the way they feel in
> your hands. I accept that digital books may replace physical ones, but
> interfering with my ability to own a book, and even pass it on to my
> kids or future grandkids, is not something I will tolerate. When people
> predicted the effects of computer technology on society 20 years ago,
> nobody imagined that software licenses would eventually spread to
> books and music. I'll predict now that ebooks will never become pop-
> ular while DRM is in place. (*Darwinian Web: Adam Green's thoughts on
> the evolution of the Internet*[3])

So, moving forward we are looking at an environment where individual consumers will become more aware of the issues of the shift in models, and some pressure to change may come as a result.

For libraries, in addition to current access issues, it highlights the longer-term question of what their responsibility to the cultural and scholarly record is, and how it will be discharged. In the print world, the "publication" and distribution of multiple copies of materials, and the individual behavior of libraries and related institutions, have resulted in a collective record lodged in many individually curated collections. Some few institutions have significant parts of this "knowledge base," readily accessible to their users. With persistence, a large part of the collective "knowledge base" is accessible through catalogs, bibliographies, finding aids, and so on.

The changed pattern of distribution of digital "publications" will need a different model, one which requires more concerted systemwide strategizing and action.

NOTES

1. http://education.guardian.co.uk/elearning/comment/0,10577,1614951,00.html
2. www.businessweek.com/technology/content/dec2005/tc20051229_155542.htm
3. http://darwinianweb.com/

APRIL 10, 2006

Sharable and licensable

http://orweblog.oclc.org/archives/000995.html

We have several mass-digitization initiatives under way. And there seems to be an expectation that these will continue, that more of our current collective book and journal collection will be digitized. There are a variety of drivers for this, both for libraries and for the other organizations which have stepped up to serve and to resource such initiatives.

We are used to thinking that the library "owns" its print collections, that subject to certain restrictions, it can do what it will with them. Among these restrictions are copyright ones.

Our Google 5 analysis[1] suggested that more than 80% of books in the Google 5 library collections were published post-1923. This means that about 20% of books in those collections are out of copyright.

We do not currently have very easy ways of knowing which post-1923 works have gone through the copyright-renewal process.

And one of the interesting service requirements to emerge around the mass-digitization initiatives is rights tracking and notification. Libraries want to know the copyright status of materials at various points in potential workflows, including at the point of selection for digitization.

What this means is that a large part of library collections is still in copyright. The library "owns" the cost of storing it, shelving it, keeping it at the right temperature, and so on. It can be shared and borrowed in its current form. However, the library does not "own" it to the extent that the library can freely reformat it and allow it to be used by many parties.

In this sense, the gap between the materials that libraries "own" and the materials that libraries license is smaller than we are used to thinking about.

NOTE

1. www.dlib.org/dlib/september05/lavoie/09lavoie.html

APRIL 16, 2007

Books are technology, too

http://orweblog.oclc.org/archives/001324.html

The Google digitization of books appears to have caught the public imagination. Recent weeks have seen high-profile articles in the *Economist* (subscription required[1]) and the *New Yorker*[2] as well as several newspaper pieces (see the links and response on this OUP blog entry[3] for example).

Google Book Search is a major endeavor, and Google has brought an impressive service online with impressive speed. The media stories tend to have different hooks. Inevitably, some pivot on a description of confrontation between publishers and Google; others discuss it in the context of a general digital turn, or the future of the book.

In some of the more reflective discussion, I am interested to see a particular strand emerge. And that is the acknowledgement that the book, in its material form, is itself a designed and evolved technology, rather than a permanent or unchanging feature of our experience. Simply, this may involve talking about the "technology" of the book. Or it may take more elaborate form.

Of course, the material book—its technology, circulation, reception, institutions—is a strong if diffuse field of enquiry. However, now, it is as if the change in perspective brought about by the digital turn has made the technology of the book more popularly visible and discussed just as that, as a particular technology which can be compared to others. And, having become used to talking about the impact on practice and potential of new technologies, we may now use that language to also describe earlier forms and their impact.

Seeing it in this way reinforces an awareness that the book itself, the codex, represents particular technological choices which in turn have influenced how we create and engage with the intellectual and cultural record, and in turn with broader experience and intellectual development.

This, for example, comes from a recent discussion of copyright and book digitization by the writer John Lanchester. Incidentally, it is encouraging to see a piece which is so appreciative of a library and library staff. He talks about the *technology* of the library and of the book.

> The buildings of the Bodleian are so old, and in their golden Cotswold stone so beautiful, that it is easy not to see how insistently modern an institution the library has tended to be. The very beginnings of the collection, in Duke Humfrey's Library above the divinity school, showed how Thomas Bodley's own bibliographic vision had to react to a technological shift. The new collection was built to accommodate the transition from the long-established, tried-and-tested technology of unique handwritten texts to the hot new mass-produced technology of the printed codex: in other words, the book. Duke Humfrey's Library has high stacks of shelves, which the reader can't directly access: the world's first closed stacks. These were designed to accommodate the increasing number of books too small to chain securely to open shelves, and were an important repository of copies from the Stationers' Company. Issues of copyright and of access to information were thus built into the institutional DNA from the start. The very layout of the buildings, with teaching "schools" tucked in the corners of the quadrangle, reflected new ideas about the connection between the library as a repository of information and the university as a place of instruction.

(John Lanchester: Who owns what in the digital age? | News | Guardian
Unlimited Books[4])

And after a marvelous description of the technology of delivery from the
stacks, he concludes that "it is impossible not to miss the point: a library
is a machine for storing and retrieving information." Later in the piece he
quotes Richard Ovenden, of the Bodleian:

> The codex was a technological leap. It works very well, has done so for
> 2,000 years, and still does so—people still find it very easy to use. What
> digitisation does is to highlight that.

Here is another example, following nicely from the last comment. The ori-
gins of the codex were discussed recently in the *New York Review of Books*,
by Eamon Duffy, in a review of two books on the role of the *book* in early
church history (available to subscribers or for purchase).[5] Here is his opening paragraph:

> These two books are built on a single perception. Early Christianity
> was more than a new religion: it brought with it a revolutionary shift
> in the information technology of the ancient world. That shift was to
> have implications for the cultural history of the world over the next
> two millennia at least as momentous as the invention of the Internet
> seems likely to have for the future. Like Judaism before it and Islam
> after it, Christianity is often described as "a religion of the Book." The
> phrase asserts both an abstraction—the centrality of authoritative
> sacred texts and their interpretation within the three Abrahamic reli-
> gions—and also a simple concrete fact—the importance of a material
> object, the book, in the history and practice of all three traditions.

Note how he talks about the book as a shift in *information technology* and
makes the comparison with the impact of the Internet explicit. In a fascinating piece, he goes on to discuss the practical and political reasons why
the codex was favored over the scroll in early church writing. In the context of my point here, consider his later references to technology.

> Why should the new religion have adopted this down-market and
> unfashionable book technology? . . . However that may be, until

recently surprisingly little has been made of this momentous foundational shift to a new book technology.

I think that this terminology is symptomatic of a positive trend, a recognition that the book itself, while central, influential, and marvelously adapted to various uses, is not some natural given. It is another sign that we are moving beyond the reductive opposition between the book and the digital turn.

NOTES

1. www.economist.com/books/displaystory.cfm?story_id=E1_RRRTQQG
2. www.newyorker.com/reporting/2007/02/05/070205fa_fact_toobin
3. http://blog.oup.com/2007/03/playing_nice_wi/
4. http://books.guardian.co.uk/comment/story/0,,2051729,00.html
5. www.nybooks.com/articles/article-preview?article_id=19992

AUGUST 20, 2007

Communication

http://orweblog.oclc.org/archives/001394.html

Update: my comments about the published literature below are about the library literature, a very specific set of journals and organizations. I am not trying to make any statement about the general value of the "published literature" relative to blogs or other media.

We have lots of places to "publish" positions, views, findings. . . . Consider some options . . .

One. A little while ago, I wrote a couple of hundred words or so in a post to the discussion board on a Facebook group. Not a very active or large group. It took a while to prepare, as I had to think about it, and the topic had been bubbling away under the surface for a while. A colleague read it and asked why I had not put it on my blog. I responded that it was probably a little more provocative than I would normally be here and also that it was specific to the experiences of various folks within that particular Facebook group. However, it does have a limited readership, and it does underline one of the widely discussed issues with Facebook: that it is a one-sided platform: what happens in Facebook stays in Facebook. However, I felt about it like I felt about posts to mailing lists or about blog posts in early days of the blog: it is for the moment.

Two. I write quite a bit on this blog. It has been an interesting experience. From a writing point of view, I find it quite liberating. Over the years, I have written quite a lot for the professional literature. However, I write slowly. For me, the main procedural difference here is twofold. The first is that entries never get long enough to worry about structure. And the second is a continuing sense that that this is still a fugitive medium. This means that an entry can be dispatched relatively quickly. I did it for a year internally at OCLC before we decided to externalize it. So it has a strong focus on work topics, although latterly I notice that I have to resist using it to talk about a wider set of topics. It is good to have a place to "publish" short pieces, to comment on what is going on, and to have stuff commented on. And I also find it a useful place to work through things, which makes me better prepared in (some ;-)) discussions. The downside is that I have become something of a blog bore: increasingly, I want to refer people to blog entries in conversation as it is somewhere to which a range of thoughts have been "externalized."

It is also nice to see posts or concepts discussed here get into wider circulation. It is interesting to see blog entries being cited[1] in the "literature." Although it is very difficult to get a real sense of readership. That said, I do sometimes wonder about the opportunity cost of writing here in the context of a broader set of writing opportunities (or reading time, or whatever . . .).

In this context, I was interested to read Andy Powell's comments about Jakob Nielsen's "Write Articles, Not Blog Postings"[2] piece. Nielsen is talking about the effort-impact ratio. If you are going to spend effort, make sure it has impact. Andy's response is that the blog works just fine. He goes on to compare the blog with the professional/scholarly literature.

> Now, impact means different things to different people, but for me, as a non-researcher (i.e., as someone that doesn't have to worry about impact factors and the RAE), writing something for a peer-reviewed journal that won't see the light of day for another year or so doesn't make a lot of sense. I'm happy with the impact of this blog thank you very much. There are times when it does seem to make sense, to me,

to write for something with a quicker turnaround—*Ariadne*³ for example—but I must admit that it isn't 100% clear to me exactly when that makes sense and when it is sufficient to simply put something in the blog. [*eFoundations: Write blog postings, not articles :-)*⁴]

And thinking about impact, or influence, Dan Cohen urged⁵ his fellow professors to take up blogging some time ago: "A large blog audience is as good as a book or a seminal article. A good blog provides a platform to frame discussions on a topic and point to resources of value."

I sometimes wonder about *curation* and about *record,* especially given the volume of material now "published" here. It has gone beyond "just for the moment." Much of what is in blogs is not worth holding onto; some is, as is shown by citation patterns. We don't have good models here. There is a tension between the now (where the library literature and associated apparatus are difficult to access, to the extent, I suggest, that it is the new "gray" literature, while the network literature is readily available) and the record (where we don't have professional practices and services to ensure continued access for the "blog" literature, while we do for the classical literature). And yes—we are seeing some closing of this gap. But slowly.

Three. However, I think we have a very dreary "published" literature. We have a set of niche publications, many of little sustained interest. The literature is a citation farm for those involved in formal research activity, and in the US, a necessary career convenience for those librarians who work within the tenure system. I remember once sending an e-mail to a university colleague asking had she a copy of an article. This was on the basis of a related article which I thought was very good. She responded bemusedly that I shouldn't be reading this article, that it was just something churned out toward an application for tenure. There are certainly many interesting articles published, but I wonder about the system as a whole.

The state of the library literature is a big topic, one which I don't propose to address here. A major issue is that much of it is cut off from the web, which reduces its impact inside and outside the library community. My own incentives to publish in the existing print literature are much reduced in recent years: why hide away something that has taken a lot of effort to produce in a journal with limited readership? And no traction outside the library community.

Since being at OCLC, I have encouraged my colleagues to publish more in the professional and scholarly literature. However, I have recently been involved in several discussions about where to offer something for publication without any really satisfactory outcome. *D-Lib* and *Ariadne* suffice for some types of material but not for all.

Now, something like *College & Research Libraries* does land on a lot of desks; it would be nice if I could pass around URLs for articles published there. It seems to me that I see more references to EDUCAUSE publications or to *First Monday* than I do to *C&RL*. How often do you see mentions of *LRTS* articles in discussions of metadata or knowledge organization outside the library community?

So, I am left with two thoughts:

1. There is a growing gap between the positions that the library profession takes with respect to the literature more generally and the state of its own literature.

2. What responsibility should libraries take, if any, to the curation of the "blog literature"? This is another area where the balance between institutional and network-level response is interesting to think about.

References: See Walt Crawford's recent "On the Literature"[6] and Stu Weibel's remarks on blog curation economics[7].

NOTES

1. http://scholar.google.com/scholar?hl=en&lr=&q=orweblog&btnG=Search
2. www.useit.com/alertbox/articles-not-blogs.html

READER COMMENT

Tony Hey
Vice President of Microsoft Research Connections, Microsoft Research

As a Dean of Engineering at the University of Southampton, I necessarily became very engaged with the ongoing revolution in scholarly communication and university research libraries. In thinking about the future of research journals and libraries, I have always found Lorcan Dempsey to be a profound and observant commentator. His blog posts contain much insightful and stimulating discussion on these issues. I am delighted that these are now being published for a wider audience.

3. www.ariadne.ac.uk

4. http://efoundations.typepad.com/efoundations/2007/07/write-blog-post.html

5. www.dancohen.org/blog/posts/professors_start_your_blogs

6. http://citesandinsights.info/v7i9a.htm

7. http://weibel-lines.typepad.com/weibelines/2007/08/blog-curation-e.html

JANUARY 6, 2008

The less common reader

http://orweblog.oclc.org/archives/001525.html

The much-discussed, and somewhat contested, NEA report on reading[1] came out at around the same time as *The Uncommon Reader*,[2] a fictional account by Alan Bennett[3] of the late discovery of reading by the queen[4] (of England). The conjunction was discussed in the *New York Times:*

> Perhaps the most fantastical story of the year was not "Harry Potter and the Deathly Hallows," but "The Uncommon Reader," a novella by Alan Bennett that imagines the queen of England suddenly becoming a voracious reader late in life. (*A Good Mystery: Why We Read—New York Times*[5])

"Fantastical," the author, Motoko Rich, suggests because: "At a time when books appear to be waging a Sisyphean battle against the forces of MySpace, YouTube and 'American Idol,' the notion that someone could move so quickly from literary indifference to devouring passion seems, sadly, far-fetched."

> *The Uncommon Reader* posits the theory that the right book at the right time can ignite a lifelong habit. (For the fictional queen, it's Nancy Mitford's *Pursuit of Love*.) This is a romantic ideal that persists among many a bibliophile.

This same tone is evident in the *Financial Times* review:

> His storytelling, though, is rather less magical. By taking us into the workings of minds other than our own, Bennett argues, reading makes better people of us. This is a quaintly old-fashioned view of literature

that one might find comforting had history not so comprehensively rubbished it. (*FT.com / Books / Fiction—The Uncommon Reader*[6])

I read the book when it came out and was a little puzzled by some of the emphasis of these and other reviewers. While the book does indeed celebrate the power of reading to transform the queen's life, its main message for me was somewhat different. It is a discussion of how little of this "literary" reading there actually is. So, I reread it over the holiday. It is a quick read . . .

The queen discovers a City of Westminster mobile library outside the kitchen doors of the palace and borrows a book. This triggers a sustained late-life reading wave. She reads quickly, passionately, and in ever-increasing circles (her initial choices are guided by Hutchings, who worked in the kitchen and was in the mobile library when she came across it; he suggests books by gay authors). She soon comes to regret the many wasted years where she did not read; she is mortified when she thinks of all the authors she has met without any insight into what they wrote. And, yes, the author connects her progressively more discriminating reading tastes with a general refinement of sensibilities. She becomes concerned, for example, with the bad impression she makes on a maid, something that before she would not have noticed. She wonders why, and the narrative voice suggests that she is yet to connect this "access of consideration" with her reading. She talks of books opening up "other lives" and "igniting the imagination." She rebukes her private secretary, who wondered had she not been briefed about the authors she met: "Briefing closes down a subject, reading opens it up."

But what comes across more strongly than this personal refinement is that her new interest does not extend the range of her personal connections with others. She does not find the world hospitable to readers. Indeed, her reading becomes a barrier to engagement, not a bridge built on new shared reading interests. Sir Kevin is concerned that while not quite "elitist," reading tends to "exclude" and sends out a bad message. Not many people actually read, he suggests. He further suggests that reading is selfish, a "withdrawal," that it makes "oneself less available," and is "solipsistic." She makes people she meets uncomfortable as she asks about what they are reading; if they cannot come up with any current reading materials, she offers then whatever she has in her bag. Her staff worry about this, as "most people, poor dears, aren't reading anything." Those that receive her books in this way, they reckon, sell them on eBay. Her equerries come up with some suggestions of titles for those that otherwise might be at a loss when the queen asks about their reading. "Though this meant that the Queen came away with a disproportionate notion of the popularity of Andy McNab[7] and the near universal affection for Joanna Trollope,[8] no matter; at least embarrassment had been avoided." Her family approves of books, so long as they don't have to read them; they wish she did not quiz them about their reading habits or check that they had read books she had given them. As her behavior continues to change and she devotes more time to reading, she becomes somewhat perfunctory in the performance of her duties. Her staff fear the worst: "The dawn of sensibility was mistaken for the onset of senility."

This is all conveyed in a gently satirical tone. Although there are some broad swipes at the business language of Sir Kevin, and at East Anglia, New Zealand, and Canada! The treatment gets sharper when other figures of authority are involved. In the opening pages, she discombobulates the president of France by wanting to talk about *Genet*.[9] He is unbriefed and so unprepared. She rings the archbishop of Canterbury wanting to talk about reading in church services; after their conversation, he returns to watching *Strictly Come Dancing* on the TV. There are some very barbed swipes at the prime minister (not named, but presumably Tony Blair[10]). He did not "wholly believe in the past or in any lessons that might be learned from it." When the queen begins giving the prime minister books, an unequivocal message comes back through "channels": "Yes. Lending him books to read. That's out of order." Toward the end of the book, the queen begins to think about writing a book herself, something more "radical" and "challenging" she tells the prime minister. He is not worried, as *radical* and *challenging* are both words that trip off his tongue: they have been bleached of any meaning for him.

So, she experiences an awakening through reading, and wants to share her discoveries and pleasures with those around her. However, she runs into incomprehension, opposition, and distaste.

The book's title plays on *The Common Reader,* and on the fact that the queen is not a "commoner" like her subjects. However, as I read the book, I increasingly heard something else. The queen is also "uncommon" because she *is* a reader, unlike all the others she comes in contact with. Reading turns out not to be common, in the sense in which reading is being used here; there are no common readers. Rather than being a celebration of the redemptive power of literature, this is an elegy for its demise, or at least for the demise of a particular type of reading as a common pursuit. It may be more appropriate to point to what *The Uncommon Reader* shares with the NEA report than to offer it as a contrast.

Note: updated for style.

NOTES

1. www.nea.gov/news/news07/TRNR.html
2. www.worldcat.org/oclc/163582083
3. http://worldcat.org/identities/lccn-n82-70229
4. http://worldcat.org/identities/lccn-n80-126296
5. www.nytimes.com/2007/11/25/weekinreview/25rich.html
6. www.ft.com/cms/s/0/33dffd1c-665c-11dc-9fbb-0000779fd2ac.html
7. http://worldcat.org/identities/lccn-n094-33040
8. http://worldcat.org/identities/lccn-n78-87580
9. http://worldcat.org/identities/lccn-n79-60478
10. http://worldcat.org/identities/lccn-n095-58170

SEPTEMBER 18, 2008

Naming opportunities

http://orweblog.oclc.org/archives/001772.html

[Warning: retrospection ahead.]

In a longish and intermittently productive professional writing career, I have had lots of opportunities to come up with titles for publications. With variable results.

Some I like. "Full disclosure"[1] captured, I thought, the gist of the report to which it is attached. This was a study into the extent of the retrospective catalog conversion challenge in UK libraries and archives. The rationale was similar to the "hidden collections" discussion. If the existence of particular collections is not disclosed, they may not be discovered, and their value to research and learning is diminished.

Some were awful. "A Utopian place of criticism?"[2] was a rather opaque title for a rather dense article. It is an example of the strained literary allusion that is more of an indulgence for the authors than a helpful hook for the reader.

Some were mistimed. "Libraries, networks, and OSI"[3] was a well-received[4] contribution. Despite the advice of colleagues, I was reluctant to drop OSI from the title because a lot of work had gone into the OSI bits. As it turns out, I should have heeded the advice. Interest in OSI had peaked and gone into decline by the time the second edition came out. Its impact would have been greater if it had been called "Libraries and networks," or some such: OSI got in the way.

> Note 1: An early lesson in the importance of brand
>
> Note 2: How many current readers know what OSI was ;-)

Anyway, this nostalgic note was prompted by the appearance on my desk of "No brief candle: Reconceiving research libraries for the 21st Century" (PDF,[5] WorldCat[6]), from CLIR, which despite the strained literary allusion in its title has some interesting contributions to which I will no doubt return in these pages.

NOTES

1. www.ukoln.ac.uk/services/lic/fulldisclosure/report.pdf
2. www.ukoln.ac.uk/dlis/models/publications/utopia
3. www.worldcat.org/oclc/185576057
4. http://epress.lib.uh.edu/pr/v2/n1/lynch.2n1
5. www.clir.org/pubs/reports/pub142/pub142.pdf
6. www.worldcat.org/oclc/236082910

MAY 3, 2009

Blogging

http://orweblog.oclc.org/archives/001948.html

I seem to spend less time looking at blogs, library or otherwise. I don't know if this is just me or if it is a general experience. The demands of work, life, and Twitter perhaps. No doubt Walt Crawford will inform[1] us in due course whether the volume of library blogging, at least, is up or down, whatever about the quality or interest.

However, as soon as I say that I realize that it is probably not true. I do look at quite a lot of things that are sort of quasi-blogs/quasi-news (e.g., on CNET) which I do not tend to think of as blogs because they do not have a strong personal voice. I occasionally look at some other things which are clearly "blogs," if in some managed space. The blogs at HarvardBusiness .org[2] are an example, and they seem a bit flat, as if produced to order.

In this context, I was quite interested to read the job advert for the editor of the BBC internet blog.

> The BBC internet blog is the key audience facing accountability blog for senior staff in the BBC's online and technology teams (e.g., BBC Online, BBC iPlayer, Future Media & Technology, Online Media Group, A&Mi, Vision Multi-platform). It aims to showcase the work of these teams and to respond to live issues in the blogosphere and elsewhere on what the BBC does in technology and online. The blog is a fast moving editorial proposition which aims to publish a blog post every day. (*BBC—Jobs—Job Details*[3])

This prompts me to think that perhaps the word *blog* has become overburdened and as a result somewhat fuzzy in use. Sometimes we use it for the mechanics, for a mode of delivery which has become a useful and general web publishing medium: a stream of messages which are individually commentable, addressable, and signed, which can be subscribed to as a stream and which can be aggregated and mixed in various ways. Other times we may mean this, but we are principally thinking of the personal voice that comes through . . .

So, I probably spend as much or more time looking at blogs in that mechanical sense. But I probably spend less time listening to individual, idiosyncratic voices . . .

NOTES

1. www.lulu.com/content/paperback-book/the-liblog-landscape-2007–2008/ 4898086
2. http://blogs.harvardbusiness.org
3. http://jobs.bbc.co.uk/fe/tpl_bbc01.asp?newms=jj&id=27386&aid=15716

E-books and/or digital books

http://orweblog.oclc.org/archives/001999.html

I was in a meeting with a group of folks from research libraries the other week. I was interested in a particular terminological issue: "e-books" and "digital books" were each being used in conversation. I asked was there a pattern of consistent use here. "Not complete consistency" was the answer, but there was certainly a tendency to use "e-books" for materials available for license from external providers, and a tendency to use "digital books" for materials digitized from library collections.

So, in this context, it is easy to see how each expression has a different— if overlapping—set of associations. E-books may evoke an environment currently fragmented by provider platforms, with restrictions on use, and managed in a licensed e-resource workflow. They are for reference, information, reading. Digital books may evoke a digital library environment, an aspiration to provide higher-level research services based on text mining, entity identification, and so on, and various funding and cooperative initiatives which aim to increase the corpus. The Monk Project[1] or the international Digging into Data Challenge[2] are examples of a direction here.

Over the next few years, it will be interesting to see how these environments evolve as e-books/digital books grow in number and usage. E-books and digital books—to continue to use these ambiguous terms—will become more important in the practice of research and learning. There are at least three big drivers in the environment the group above was discussing. The first is around moving physical collections to the cloud as libraries balance service between local collections, shared off-site collections, and digital collections. There are early discussions about policy and service frameworks within which libraries can reduce their print inventory and the opportunity costs associated with it (see here[3] for example). The second is around the demand environment, as books in digital form offer a better fit with research and learning workflows which are increasingly network based. The increasing availability of books in digital form supports patterns of discovery, analysis, and use now common with other resources. Think, for example, of the practice of "strategic reading" (or "reading avoidance"), where researchers are found to prospect the literature broadly in a digital environment, searching, consulting abstracts, scanning for terminology and diagrams, and so on (interestingly described by Allen Renear and Carol Palmer here[4]). For many purposes, people will prefer the digital versions and will shift use. This is not to say that people will not continue to read physical books, but it is interesting to consider the pattern of adoption (and continued development) of the journal literature. The third is around the environment of supply, where there is major current activity. The post-settlement Google Books institutional product offering, Amazon's attempt to "iPodify" books, the rise of the iPhone, and a range of other developments point to rapidly changing opportunities.

So the relationship with the book literature is going to change in significant ways, which may make the e-book/digital book distinction advanced above less relevant. In fact, Google Book Search already moves beyond it in important ways. And libraries are exploring various syndication models (with Amazon, for example, or Kirtas) or in collaboration with publishers such as the Cambridge Library Collection,[5] for example. Fragmentation, of technical platform, of format, of business model, and so on, will complicate service provision.

This poses major questions for libraries at all levels. From a (current) workflow point of view, we will see a shift of more activity out of the "bought" materials workflow into the "licensed" materials workflow. From a collections point of view, we will see a rebalancing between local, shared, and third-party print and digital provision in ways now being worked through. There are bigger issues, already with us with the journal literature, about the curation of the scholarly record, about sharing of materials, and about assuring the type of access that is compatible with use and re-use in research and learning.

I was very interested to read the following remarks by David Nicholas in Update[6] recently . . .

> "E-books are going to be the real paradigm-buster," he told the audience at UCL.
>
> The availability of e-journals had already led to users leaving the library space. "If books leave the physical space too what do librarians do then? It's possible that the publishers will become the new librarians—encouraging users into their virtual space, their walled gardens."
>
> Though many are now thinking that "data" is the area to get into, Professor Nicholas disagreed: "I think books are the big one. It is only because books are not available electronically, that we see such high levels of e-journals use."
>
> Once e-books are everywhere "all kinds of knowledge discovery and learning will be possible. Instead we're chasing Facebook, YouTube, etc."

I think that libraries may be underestimating the impact and pace of change in the book world . . .

NOTES

1. www.monkproject.org/
2. www.diggingintodata.org/
3. www.oclc.org/us/en/nextspace/012/research.htm
4. www.sciencedaily.com/releases/2009/08/090818182058.htm
5. www.cambridge.org/features/cambridgeLibraryCollection/default.html
6. www.cilip.org.uk/publications/updatemagazine

MAY 30, 2010

"Reading at library-scale" and/or "distant reading"

http://orweblog.oclc.org/archives/002099.html

Franco Moretti has an interesting short book called *Graphs, Maps, Trees: Abstract Models for Literary History*.[1] He proposes a way of reading literary history which involves abstracting patterns across large stretches of a literary field rather than examining "concrete, individual works." In particular, he works with three organizing models: graphs, maps, and trees. He calls this type of reading "distant reading," a method which can be applied to large bodies of literature and which yields a different form of insight than close textual analysis of a selective canon.

Via a <u>conference report</u>[2] by Eric Lease Morgan, I recently came across John Unsworth's use of the phrase "reading at library-scale."

> My own research career as a faculty member, for the last 20 years, has been devoted first to understanding the impact of technology on the humanities and, more recently, to designing tools that would allow humanists to work at library-scale, using the computer as a kind of attention prosthetic that allows us to perceive patterns made up of very small pieces of information across very large expanses of text. Having perceived those patterns, of course, it is still up to us, as human beings with expertise in a relevant domain, to make sense of them and to persuade others to share that sense. (*Abstract—reading at library scale*[3])

Unsworth and Moretti both feature in an article published in the *Chronicle* a couple of days ago: "The Humanities Go Google."

This considers "distant reading" or "reading at library-scale" in the context of Google Book Search.

> Data-diggers are gunning to debunk old claims based on "anecdotal" evidence and answer once-impossible questions about the evolution of ideas, language, and culture. Critics, meanwhile, worry that these stat-happy quants take the human out of the humanities. Novels aren't commodities like bags of flour, they warn. Cranking words from deeply specific texts like grist through a mill is a recipe for lousy research, they say—and a potential disaster for the profession. (*The humanities go Google*[4])

Now, the article sets up an opposition which may be a convenient hook for a story, but is probably less important than some of the ways in which humanities scholarship will develop when large amounts of material are available for computational analysis in this way.

READER COMMENT

 Rick Lugg
President, Sustainable Collection Services (SCS), LLC

Lorcan is a one-man environmental scan. He sees patterns, coins terms, parses distinctions, turns glimmers into useful concepts. Sometimes I have no idea what he's on about. That's when his work is most interesting.

In this context, I was interested to read how "distant reading" involves a cross-disciplinary team: "To sort, interrogate, and interpret roughly 1,000 digital texts, scholars have brought together a data-mining gang drawn from the departments of English, history, and computer science." Unsworth also discusses collaborative multidisciplinary work of the type which produced MONK,[5] for example.

From a library point of view, it is interesting to see humanities scholarship acquiring some of the features—and support requirements—more characteristic of the sciences.

NOTES

1. www.worldcat.org/title/graphs-maps-trees-abstract-models-for-a-literary
-history/oclc/60671819/editions?referer=di&editionsView=true
2. http://infomotions.com/blog/2010/05/cyberinfrastructure-days-at-the
-university-of-notre-dame
3. http://ci.nd.edu/presenters/pre_Unsworth.htm
4. http://chronicle.com/article/The-Humanities-Go-Google/65713
5. www.monkproject.org

SEPTEMBER 26, 2010

Library literature again . . .

http://orweblog.oclc.org/archives/002139.html

First a mention of two recent articles . . .

Rick Anderson has a very nice piece in *EDUCAUSE Review* about budgets, libraries, and scholarly publishers. It is an interesting reflection on systemic change, always difficult to manage as it involves reconsidering why things are done as well as how they are done.

> Scholarly publishers are looking at libraries right now and seeing what has always been the best and most reliable market for their products suddenly changing into a highly unreliable one. There is very little likelihood that library budgets will grow significantly (if at all) anytime soon; in fact, there is a strong likelihood that they will shrink again next year—in many cases, for the second year in a row. Furthermore, even if budgets begin growing again, it is highly unlikely that they will ever rise to their pre-2008 levels or that libraries will resume buying books the way they did in the past. Traditional library collection development has meant buying large amounts of materials in the hope that those materials will turn out to be what patrons need, but financial constraints are now forcing libraries to move in a more patron-driven and less speculative direction. Having figured out how to do so, most libraries will probably continue to develop their collections this way for some time to come, if not permanently. (*If I were a scholarly publisher*[1])

This article is what might be called an "intervention." It contributes to an important debate and deserves to be widely read by library managers. To achieve its goals, it needs to be published somewhere that aggregates the attention of a senior audience. It is interesting that it is published in *EDUCAUSE Review,* which aggregates the attention of a senior IT and information management audience in higher education. In that sense, *EDUCAUSE Review* is a platform publication, in the way that, say, variously, *Harvard Business Review, IEEE Spectrum, Communications of the ACM,* or *Nature* are. These publications aggregate attention in their communities, and beyond. They provide a platform for their authors.

The second is an article by Ted Striphas: "Acknowledged Goods: Cultural Studies and the Politics of Academic Journal Publishing." This is academic writing in the idiom of cultural studies. He argues that although the institutions of communication are central objects of study among his colleagues, those colleagues are unreflective about the institutions of scholarly communication upon which their discipline depends.

> This type of thinking is symptomatic of the sense of alienation I suspect many people in cultural studies feel from the instruments of production, distribution, and propagation of both our work and our

field. We access these instruments all the time. We depend on them significantly for our livelihoods. What would cultural studies be without its publications, and without the formidable network of social, economic, legal, and infrastructural linkages to the publishing industry that sustains them? Nevertheless, many of us are reluctant to pause long enough to take stock of the choices we make—or that are made for us—when publishing our work, much less to consider how those choices may reverberate well beyond the immediate confines of cultural studies. (*Acknowledged goods. Worksite*[2])

Reading this, I was struck by the parallel with the library literature. Libraries acquire and manage literature for others, and are very familiar with individual publisher practices, and the business of distribution which underlies scholarly communication. However, librarians can sometimes seem strangely unreflective about the structure of their own disciplinary literature.

Here are some issues that prompt this statement . . .

I am not thinking of open access in particular here, although Doug Way recently published an interesting article exploring rates of deposit among authors of the library literature.

To examine the open access availability of Library and Information Science (LIS) research, a study was conducted using Google Scholar to search for articles from 20 top LIS journals. The study examined whether Google Scholar was able to find any links to full text, if open access versions of the articles were available and where these articles were being hosted. The results showed the archiving of articles is not a regular practice in the field, articles are not being deposited in institutional or subject repositories at a high rate and the overall percentage of available open access articles in LIS was similar to the findings in previous studies. (*The Open Access Availability of Library and Information Science Literature*[3])

I have not checked to see how the number of publications in our field compares to other disciplines, or if the work to find out has been done. However, we appear to have a proliferation of journals, many of little sustained interest. These are supported by editors, editorial boards, authors, purchasers.

> The literature is a citation farm for those involved in formal research activity, and in the US, a necessary career convenience for those librarians who work within the tenure system. I remember once sending an e-mail to a university colleague asking had she a copy of an article. This was on the basis of a related article which I thought was very good. She responded bemusedly that I shouldn't be reading this article, that it was just something written toward an application for tenure. There are certainly many interesting articles published, but I wonder about the system as a whole.[4]

The literature is very fragmented; few journals rise to the "must-read" category.

This last point relates to the absence of a "platform publication" in the sense described above in the library community. There is no natural venue within the library literature for an intervention of the type I began with, which will aggregate the attention of a large part of library management. I wonder why this is so. Does it matter?

A personal coda: My colleague John MacColl and I founded the *Ariadne* magazine many years ago, based on an idea and proposal by John. The original purpose was probably twofold: to provide a platform publication for discussion of the future of libraries in a network environment and to provide a venue for discussion of the JISC and other digital library projects which were becoming such a feature of the higher education scene. While

---

READER COMMENT

Candy Schwartz
Professor, Graduate School of Library and Information Science, Simmons College

I have always found Lorcan's blog to be a treasure trove for teaching librarians-to-be. He provides well-crafted think pieces which can provoke discussion forums, and he also points to innovative library practices which I can use as illustrations in class.

it does a very nice job still on the second of these, the platform aspect has probably receded.

NOTES

1. www.educause.edu/EDUCAUSE+Review/EDUCAUSEReviewMagazine Volume45/IfIWereaScholarlyPublisher/209335
2. http://striphas.wikidot.com/acknowledged-goods-worksite
3. http://works.bepress.com/doug_way/2
4. http://orweblog.oclc.org/archives/001394.html

Presenting . . .

http://orweblog.oclc.org/archives/002142.html

Although I give quite a few presentations, I don't really present enough for them to become ends in themselves. I am thinking of this contentwise and stylewise.

Contentwise, I tend to talk about things that are currently on my mind unless I have been asked to describe a particular set of activities or address a particular topic. This means that I have a running set of themes which evolves through presentations. It also means that I find it difficult to go back to earlier themes, even if they remain relevant. And it means that presentations may not have a definitive or conclusive feel. As I say, this is because they tend to flow from current concerns rather than be crafted as statements about a particular topic.

Stylewise, for internal OCLC events, or when I am speaking with colleagues, I will tend to use an OCLC template. Otherwise, I tend to use an evolving one of my own. Partly, I must admit, because fiddling with the template seems a reasonable displacement activity when trying to prepare a presentation ;-). If I did more, I would probably aim for something more definitive.

But that is enough about me . . .

For the above reasons, I am quite interested in the style of presentations I see. In fact, I am probably more impressed by some nice PowerPoint (it is usually PowerPoint), or how it is used, than I should be. In recent years, we have seen several trends which depart from the heading and bullet-point style . . .

White on black. Lawrence Lessig changed presentations. Here is how Presentation Zen characterized[1] his style: "His rapid pace and quick slide transitions include a mix of short bursts of text, images, and video clips." Dick Hardt did this[2] famously. Rather than being a reflection of the words, the presentation is a foil. Now, a Lessig presentation is a unique event. Often we see influences rather than the whole package, as in the now common use of large white phrases on a black background. When done well, this can work nicely.

The Flickr turn. It is now common to see presentations that almost entirely comprise text superimposed on "found" Flickr images, where the image is an amusing or amplifying commentary on the text. Again, this can work well when done well. It is less good at leaving a record of the presentation for others to read. And it can also be tedious or distracting, as the relevance or otherwise of the image becomes the main message of the slide.

Prezi. And junking PowerPoint altogether, Prezi has recently emerged as an alternative approach, developed, according to the founders,[3] because "they felt slides limited their ability to develop and explain ideas." Perhaps this is why I have yet to see a Prezi presentation I have enjoyed. It seems that the rationale is to be not-PowerPoint, rather than actually to be something else. And in unsophisticated hands the "swoosh" effect can be off-putting. Again, there is a danger of distraction as the medium intrudes on attention too much. And what would it be like seeing a series of Prezi presentations in a row?

Of course, a good presenter is usually enjoyable whatever aid he or she uses. And those for whom presenting is central enough may take more care. That said, it is always nice to see some nice slides . . . ;-).

(I only recently realized the size of the market for blog themes that the WordPress platform has created. It is really quite interesting browsing some of the design sites of those who appear to make a living designing themes. It is also nice coming across a pleasingly designed blog. I am not sure, but I think that I am less swayed, though, by blog design than I am by presentation design ;-).

NOTES

1. www.presentationzen.com/presentationzen/2010/08/lawrence-lessig-on
   -remix-redux.html
2. http://identity20.com/media/OSCON2005
3. http://prezi.com/about

A fragmented reading experience:
Locally and anecdotally speaking . . .

http://orweblog.oclc.org/archives/002203.html

In February 2011 I noted . . .

> A while ago I was interested to observe that I had begun to resist buying
> paperback novels. . . . In thinking about it, I realized that I only wanted
> to buy the experience not the physical item. My bag and our house is
> already cluttered enough. I wanted the few hours' entertainment the
> book provided, not the small burden of owning a bundle of paper to be
> shelved. (*Buying books and/or experiences: A consumer view*[1])

In other cases, I still wanted to buy a physical item.

In the interim, the reconfiguration of publishing by the network continues. We are even more aware of the staggering impact of Amazon on
the book industry; questions about the future of print 'n' mortar stores are
more stark; there is consolidation among publishers; publishing and reading options proliferate.

While I am professionally aware day-to-day of that background, I have
been interested in how my reading behaviors continue to shift. The pull
of digital is stronger. The benefits of portability, availability, and search
weigh heavier. However, my reading has become fragmented in ways that
complicate my life as a consumer.

It is fragmented in terms of actual reading experience (Kindle versus
print versus other). It is fragmented in terms of collection, where what is
on my shelves is joined by what is on my Kindle (in its various manifestations), or elsewhere. It is fragmented in terms of discoverability (store

versus website). I often have to choose between grades of experience, and the choices involve trade-offs (portability versus aesthetics, for example).

Of course, it is also fragmented in terms of ownership, where my ability to resell, share, or move an e-book is limited in various ways. This is a major issue, although it is not my main focus here.

Here are some rather ordinary anecdotal examples . . .

ANECDOTE 1: HIGHLIGHTING

I was in the <u>Acorn Bookshop</u>,[2] a used bookstore in Grandview, Ohio, a while ago (which incidentally, is the bookstore which features in the movie *Liberal Arts*[3]). I was pleased to find a <u>Nicholas Blake</u>[4] novel, *End of Chapter*[5]. Blake is the name under which <u>Cecil Day-Lewis</u>,[6] poet and father of Daniel, wrote mystery novels. I have wanted to read one of his novels for years, without having been quite motivated enough to go out and get one (he does not figure in the catalog of the Columbus Metropolitan Library). Coincidentally, I was able to buy another couple of Blake novels in Caveat Emptor Books on a trip to Bloomington, Indiana, around the same time.

End of Chapter is set in a publishing house, and, as one might expect, is quite a nice read in a somewhat old-fashioned way. This meant that as I read I kept wanting to highlight sentences for saving to my Kindle space. Not being able to do so created a nagging friction as I read, which is a typical reaction now when I read an interesting book in print. I would always have been an inveterate maker of marginal pencil marks. Even if I rarely went back to them, they were there for future reference . . . just in case. I now want to save highlights as I read.

This requirement has also made cross-platform differences in the Kindle app a frustration. For a while, highlighting was not possible in Cloud Reader, though it now is. The major issue I have with my Windows Phone—with which otherwise I am very happy—is that the Kindle app does not allow me to highlight text. This means that I don't read books during those <u>interstitial reading moments</u>[7] on the phone. I can't bring myself to read an e-book which does not have the highlighting option.

And highlighting is important—see Steven Johnson's interesting post from which this line jumped out . . .

This ability to capture important clips in real-time as I'm reading a book has probably been the single most important advance in my reading life since the Web came along. (*Your outboard memory*[8])

ANECDOTE 2: CHOOSING BETWEEN BENEFITS

I was going to buy *Ambiguous Republic: Ireland in the 1970s*,[9] by Diarmaid Ferriter, when it came out last year. Although it is a bit dispiriting to realize that you are now old enough that the period in which you grew up is the topic of a major historical work. However, do I go with hardback or Kindle?

I want the benefits of the digital, but there are also some pleasures of ownership associated with a physical book like this. These don't really have an analog in the current e-book environment. This pleasure is also in contrast to the poverty of the Kindle collection experience. It is unclear to me why they do not do a better job of allowing you to manage collections in a congenial way—this seems like a big miss, but presumably their data shows that this is not a big enough requirement to push aside other development needs? I am sure this will get better in the future.

I would certainly lightly annotate a paper version of a book like this, but as I say above, I would prefer to keep those passages online now.

A couple of times I have expressed frustration on Twitter or Facebook about having to chose in this way, and in each case, somebody responded with the example of music, where, if you buy vinyl, you can also download MP3s. I would be willing to pay extra to get digital and print for some types of books, ones like this one. This point was also made by Nicholas Carr . . .

> There's a lesson here, I think, for book publishers. Readers today are forced to choose between buying a physical book or an ebook, but a lot of them would really like to have both on hand—so they'd be able, for instance, to curl up with the print edition while at home (and keep it on their shelves) but also be able to load the ebook onto their e-reader when they go on a trip. In fact, bundling a free electronic copy with a physical product would have a much bigger impact in the book business than in the music business. After all, in order to play vinyl you have to buy a turntable, and most people aren't going to do that. So

vinyl may be a bright spot for record companies, but it's not likely to become an enormous bright spot. The only technology you need to read a print book is the eyes you were born with, and print continues, for the moment, to be the leading format for books. If you start giving away downloads with print copies, you shake things up in a pretty big way. (*Rough Type*[10])

It seems unlikely that an e-version would be available with the hardback without some price increase. But I probably would not pay the premium that you pay for vinyl. I do not know what price point would persuade me, but I would certainly pay more. I now have several books where I have bought both print and e-versions.

My indecision meant I did not buy the Ferriter book when I first saw it—I did not know which way to go. As I write this, however, I went back and bought the hardback. Although, when I get around to reading it, I know that I will be thinking of how I miss the digital highlighting feature. :-). And I definitely won't be reading it on a plane, as I won't want to carry a book of this size around with me.

ANECDOTE 3: BORROWING

I bought *Information Wants to Be Shared*,[11] by Joshua Gans,[12] last year. I bought it on the basis of a blog entry[13] by John Naughton, who bought it on the basis of the Amazon abstract. On Amazon.com, it appears to be only available as an e-book. Now, normally for this type of item—which I would like to read, but not necessarily buy—I would suggest to the very fine folks at the OCLC Library that they acquire it. However, acquiring an e-book for lending from Amazon is not an option. So, as it was just $4.99, I went ahead and bought it. This touches on major policy and business issues, but for consumers, it is a way in which previous behaviors don't map onto current options.

Of course, these may be the "morbid symptoms" that accompany transition between orders. And we will always have choices. I just hope we have some better ones soon . . . as the reconfiguration continues.

NOTES

1. http://orweblog.oclc.org/archives/002158.html
2. www.acornbookshop.com
3. http://acornbookshop.com/Acorn_LibartsMovie.html
4. www.worldcat.org/wcidentities/lccn-n90-609288
5. www.worldcat.org/oclc/1233501
6. www.worldcat.org/wcidentities/lccn-n80-67088
7. http://orweblog.oclc.org/archives/002081.html
8. https://medium.com/the-writers-room/bcf82e3cc73
9. www.worldcat.org/816562848
10. www.roughtype.com/?p=1573
11. www.worldcat.org/oclc/829130871
12. www.worldcat.org/wcidentities/lccn-n99-280635
13. http://memex.naughtons.org/archives/2012/10/03/17200

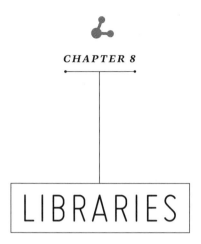

CHAPTER 8

LIBRARIES

THE POSTS IN this section relate to "memory institutions"—that is, libraries, archives, museums, and galleries. These are the organizations that preserve and make available the cultural output of society. While we often think of Dempsey as being a voice in the narrower library community, he considers this larger space in the items found below.

Here, the focus is broadly on the administration and organization of these institutions and much less on the technologies that they use to carry out their work. (Posts on these technologies are in chapter 5, "Library Systems.")

APRIL 6, 2005

Aura and digitization

http://orweblog.oclc.org/archives/000623.html

Writing here about the digitization initiatives in the "Google 5" libraries a while ago I referred to *aura:*

> Walter Benjamin famously asserted[1] that "that which withers in the age of mechanical reproduction is the aura of the work of art." In his terms, the aura is that which is original or authentic about a work. Aura depends on the position of a work within a tradition and its uniqueness.[2]

I was reminded of this while listening to Ken Hamma's <u>interesting presentation</u>[3] at the CNI Spring Task Force meeting earlier this week.

> Instead of asserting intellectual property rights in images of public domain works as nearly every art museum does now, it is argued here that publicly and proactively placing these images in the public domain and clearly removing all questions about their availability for use and reuse would likely cause no harm to the financial position or trustworthy reputation of any collecting institution and would demonstrably contribute to the public good. As those images have become digital assets and as the preferred delivery venue has become increasingly an electronic network, the ante has been raised to do so. The manner in which this might be done may require consultation with legal counsel. The fact of doing it, however, is not a legal decision but a business decision that can be evaluated by non-profits in measuring success against the mission.[4]

Ken referred to Benjamin's essay in his talk. During discussion it was argued that the distribution of images of works of art—on posters, etc.—translates into increased traffic to see the real artifacts, the works of art in situ in galleries or museums.

I wondered if one could think of this as the allure of aura. Exposure to the "mechanically reproduced" copies, drained of aura, creates a demand to experience the work of art itself.

I also wondered whether this points to an important difference between museum and library collections, and hence in our experience of their digitization. Much of what is in libraries is already a "mechanical reproduction"; it is one of many copies in a publishing process. In digitizing it, we are translating it into another medium. We experience it differently: but we are not losing that aura of uniqueness. Of course, the exception is where an individual volume has some particular characteristics which make it special, because it is rare, or is annotated, or for some other reason.

Much of what is in a museum or gallery is unique. We do indeed diminish the aura in reproduction.

NOTES

1. http://scholar.google.com/scholar?q=walter+benjamin
2. http://orweblog.oclc.org/archives/000509.html
3. www.cni.org/tfms/2005a.spring/abstracts/PB-hamma-public.html
4. www.cni.org/tfms/2005a.spring/abstracts/PB-hamma-public.html

DECEMBER 9, 2006

Two buildings

http://orweblog.oclc.org/archives/001219.html

I spoke last Friday at Numérique et bibliothèques: le deuxième choc,[1] a conference at the Bibliothèque nationale de France,[2] at Le site François-Mitterrand. Earlier in the week, I attended a meeting about the proposed UK Research Reserve at the British Library, at St. Pancras. The UKRR is a collaborative higher-education storage project looking to create a national resource which reduces redundant costs at individual libraries while assuring long-term access.

It was interesting visiting these two buildings in quick succession. Each generated major national, and international, discussion as they were being built and in their early lives as working libraries. A discussion about architecture and civic space, about the role of public institutions, and about the place of a national library in public life. And, of course, each generated discussion about how a library building should support the modern needs of its users.

I travelled between London and Paris on the Eurostar, through the Channel Tunnel. Next year, the UK terminus of this service will reach St.

Pancras, beside the British Library building. This is from a piece I wrote a few years back as a contribution to a *volume*[3] on digital library initiatives at the British Library:

> At the same time, the British Library has been involved in the construction of one of the most significant library "places" the world will have seen, a building in which the main objective is to "create an easy commerce between the lone scholar and the huge building mass required to house the collections, all the fellow (rival?) researchers and the general public." It is an enterprise emphatically set against the "withering of experience": the architect, Colin St. John Wilson, discusses scale, how to accommodate the demands for personal space with flow, of daylight as a source of ambient light, and closes by describing the "difficult to define 'body language' that responds to the invitation to touch (the travertine barrier, the leather handrail, the oak-ribbed carapace of the column)." He hopes that the arrival in nearby St. Pancras of the Channel Tunnel Rail Link will make the court yard a social assembly place, the clock tower a rendezvous point. St. John Wilson acknowledges the influence of Alvar Aalto—himself a creator of libraries—and endorses Aalto's view that a building should be judged not on the day of its opening but after thirty years of use. (*Library Places and Digital Information Spaces: Reflections on Emerging Network Services*[4])

The event at the Bibliothèque nationale de France marked ten years since the opening of the building there.

NOTES

1. www.bnf.fr/pages/zNavigat/frame/infopro.htm?ancre=journeespro/jp_entretiens06.htm
2. www.bnf.fr
3. http://worldcat.org/oclc/43459217
4. http://homes.ukoln.ac.uk/~lisld/publications/alex.html

JUNE 15, 2008

Academic library and organization

http://orweblog.oclc.org/archives/001656.html

Being in the UK for a few days has reminded me of how common the "merged service" is in UK universities. This is where IT services, library, possibly management information services, and various other services may be combined in one unit. Of course, organizational boundaries and labels vary from institution to institution.

In general I think that these merged services are an artifact of an earlier time. The library was early into automation and networking and accordingly was associated with IT. But IT is now pervasive of everything, so the rationale seems weaker. Aligning the library organizationally with enterprise systems, networking, security, and so on seems to make less and less sense.

Indeed, personality and institutional positioning may have been a driving factor in developing this model in the UK. It seems much stronger in the UK than it is in other countries.

It seems to me that it now makes more sense to associate the library with emerging support for e-learning and e-research, creating a set of capacities aligned around academic systems and services, and the management of research and learning data.

JUNE 6, 2010

Outside-in and inside-out redux

http://orweblog.oclc.org/archives/002102.html

I have been using this phrase, "outside-in and inside-out," to discuss a contrast in information management practices that is becoming more important. Here is how I spoke about it a little while ago in these pages:

> Think, for example, of a distinction between "outside-in" resources, where the library is buying or licensing materials from external providers and making them accessible to a local audience (e.g., books and

journals), and "inside-out" resources which may be unique to an institution (e.g., digitized images, research materials) where the audience is
both local and external. Thinking about an external non-institutional
audience, and how to reach it, poses some new questions for the library.[1]

And here is how I have been talking about it in presentations in the context
of the "collections grid."[2] (See figure 8.1.)

"Below the line" are digitized materials (special collections, slides, etc.)
and the digital outputs of research and learning practices. Here a set of
common interests emerge, in terms of digital library infrastructure, management of unique materials (something, of course, archives and museums
have always done), disclosure to the outside world, and so on. This requires a
new set of skills and orientations and a new way of interacting with clients.

I was reminded of this when reading an interesting post by Mark Dahl
earlier where he talks about this shift in concrete terms. He notes the slow
diminishment of "above the line" activities:

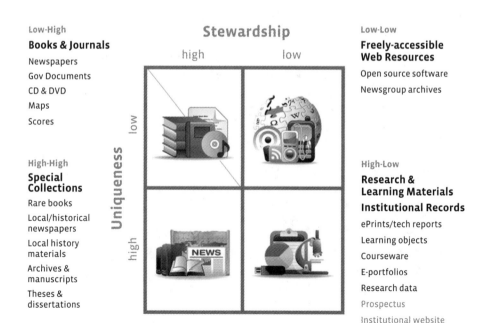

FIGURE 8.1 Collections grid

> As content shifts to the network and as discovery is disintermediated from the library, the work needed to support the library's traditional roles as buyer, archiver, and gateway to information is slowly diminishing.[3]

He then discusses several "thematic digital projects" where faculty are working with digital resources to enhance teaching, learning, and research. One example is "accessCeramics: a contemporary ceramics image resource"[4] a collaboration between the library and the art department at Lewis and Clark College, where the author works.

He sees a role over and above the creation and management of document- or image-based repositories we have seen emerge in recent years, and which I mention above.

> But I think there are more interesting opportunities when we actually wade out into the messy world of teaching and research and offer up our expertise at organizing information. A way of doing this is to establish some kind of a digital initiatives program that faculty can engage with directly. We see this at large institutions such as University of Virginia[5] and Columbia,[6] but also now increasingly at liberal arts colleges like Hamilton,[7] the University of Richmond,[8] and Kenyon.[9] The programs at these institutions in one way or another offer support to faculty for teaching or research related digital projects.[10]

(Incidentally, given the University of Virginia is mentioned, it might be appropriate to point to the Scholars' Lab.[11])

NOTES

1. http://orweblog.oclc.org/archives/002047.html
2. http://orweblog.oclc.org/archives/001897.html
3. http://synthesize-specialize-mobilize.blogspot.com/2010/06/code4lib-nw
   -digital-initiatives.html
4. http://accessceramics.org
5. www.iath.virginia.edu
6. www.columbia.edu/ccnmtl
7. http://academics.hamilton.edu/dhi
8. http://digitalscholarship.richmond.edu
9. https://lbis.kenyon.edu/NGLgrants
10. http://synthesize-specialize-mobilize.blogspot.com/2010/06/code4lib-nw
    -digital-initiatives.html
11. http://www2.lib.virginia.edu/scholarslab/about

JANUARY 28, 2011

The service turn . . .

http://orweblog.oclc.org/archives/002152.html

A while ago, I spent some time looking through the institution profiles[1] collected by ARL. One of the themes I noticed was the "service turn," where
libraries were looking at the quality of their services in support of research
and learning as important markers of distinction, more important, maybe,
than the collections which have loomed so large in historic ARL assessment of libraries.

Consider this, from the University of Illinois at Urbana-Champaign, for
example . . .

> As part of a broader re-alignment of library services ongoing since 2007
> to address transformational changes in the composition of library col-
> lections, the information-use patterns of library users, and the broader
> environments of scholarly communication and American higher edu-
> cation, the Library has committed to supporting a greater variety of
> service models—including central services, departmental library ser-
> vices, embedded librarian service programs, and virtual service pro-
> grams—as a key component of a vision of the future in which leading
> research libraries are distinguished as much by the scope and quality of
> their service programs as by their collections.[2]

Or this from the University of Minnesota...

> In alignment with the University's strategic positioning, the University Libraries have re-conceived goals, shifting from a collection-centric focus to one that is engagement-based.[3]

Coincidentally, at much the same time, a colleague pointed me to a brief article written by Scott Walter of UIUC, "Distinctive Signifiers of Excellence: Library Services and the Future of the Academic Library."

Here is a sample...

> There can be no question that a great library must provide access to great content, but do the seismic changes afoot in the ways in which access may be gained to content (including that found in unique artifacts) require us to ask new questions? For example, when access to content is no longer scarce, what are the services that will stand as the "primary measures of quality" and "distinctive signifiers of excellence" in the academic library? What effect might a broader understanding of distinctive services have on our appreciation for a range of libraries beyond those with the largest collections?[4]

He provides some examples of "distinctive services," including, for example, Columbia's Copyright Advisory Office[5] and the Library Assessment Program[6] at the University of Washington.

He goes on to argue that the development of distinctive services will not be the preserve of larger libraries...

> While the development of a distinctive library service does require vision, strategic planning, and professional expertise, it does not require access to a local collection numbering in the millions. Defining distinctive services with the clarity with which we have defined distinctive collections allows us to acknowledge that the 21st century will be marked by different, but equally valid, definitions of excellence in academic libraries, and that the manner in which individual libraries demonstrate excellence will be distinctive to the service needs, and to the opportunities to address those needs, found on each campus.[7]

It is to this article that I owe the phrase "service turn," which I use as the title above.

Two things occur to me here. One is that it relates to a general move toward "customer relationship" (or engagement, or research and learning support, or . . .) and away from infrastructure management as the primary locus of library activity (I use these terms as used by John Hagel III here[8]). This is not to say that infrastructure is not managed, but that it may increasingly be shared or outsourced. One interesting example of this trend is library space, which is being reshaped around library users rather than around collections. Another is that it will be interesting to see how such new services do or don't converge around models which can be provided collaboratively or by third parties. In other words, is local responsiveness a part of their distinctiveness?

NOTES

1. http://directors.arl.org/folder/files
2. http://directors.arl.org/file/show/illinoisurbanachampaign.doc (no longer available at this URL)
3. http://directors.arl.org/file/show/uminnesota.pdf (no longer available at this URL)
4. http://crl.acrl.org/content/72/1/6.full.pdf
5. http://copyright.columbia.edu/copyright
6. www.lib.washington.edu/assessment
7. http://crl.acrl.org/content/72/1/6.full.pdf
8. http://edgeperspectives.typepad.com/edge_perspectives/2008/09/unbundling-dell.html

MARCH 31, 2011

Internal boundary changes . . . the library in the institution

http://orweblog.oclc.org/archives/002167.html

It has been interesting in recent years to see how library boundaries within universities have shifted as relationships with other campus providers potentially change.

This is natural enough as the network has changed the way in which research, learning, and administration are carried out within the university in important ways, with follow-on information management and service impacts. The creation, management, manipulation, and disclosure of digital materials have become integral to a wide range of university activities. Think of GIS and survey data, data-intensive science, lab-books, learning management systems, digital repositories of various sorts, digital publishing initiatives, grants, and publication details.

As information management becomes pervasive of university activities, it also becomes natural to think about how information management support services are aligned across existing and new organizational units. This creates organizational choices for the university in how it arranges information management services internally, and what it chooses to externalize. These changes are usually driven by local personalities, politics, and cultures, although you would expect patterns to emerge over time.

In thinking about this topic, here are some examples that have arisen more or less successively in recent years.

LIBRARY AND IT SERVICES
Libraries and IT Centres (variously named and structured) have interacted since automation began. As with others, the library would look to the IT Centre for general support with security, networking, office support, and so on, but maybe also specific library technology support. Early discussions may have been around library automation systems, but continue around evolving infrastructure to manage digital resources. Boundary issues are common.

As requirements evolve, organizations may look at infrastructure in new ways. Interestingly, Yale has established an Office for Digital Assets and Infrastructure[1] organizationally distinct from both technology and library operations, but on a peer level with them. It is charged with creating the infrastructure required to manage digital institutional assets.

An early and telling example involves the development of so-called merged or converged services, a trend particularly noticeable in the UK. Approximately 50% of UK academic libraries are part of larger organizational units which may include some combination of academic computing, administrative computing, e-learning management, and other emerging digital infrastructure services.[2]

LIBRARY AND E-LEARNING

Most institutions now maintain a course management system, and within that, or associated with it, a range of information, communication, and group-work resources. From an informational point of view, think of reading lists, resource guides, and course reserves. Or of the desire to make library resources visible within course management workflows (learn-flows). Or of the management of course materials. Although they are now a major investment, there does not appear to be a consistent organizational pattern. So, in some cases, e-learning infrastructure may be managed by the library; in others, by the CIO's office; or in others, in some other way. Levels of coordination between library and learning management may vary.

LIBRARY AND PUBLISHING

As publishing processes evolve, as institutional research and learning resources are managed and disclosed to the world, and as self-publishing models are explored, so do boundaries between publishing, library, and resource management come down. The university press, or new publishing initiatives, may or may not be associated with the library. The University of Michigan has an interesting collection of activities under the MPublishing[3] label: "By bringing together the talents and resources of the University of Michigan Press, the Scholarly Publishing Office, Deep Blue (the University's institutional repository service), the Copyright Office, and the Text Creation Partnership, MPublishing builds upon the traditional publishing strengths of the University of Michigan while creating and shaping sustainable publishing models for the future." MPublishing is organizationally situated as part of the library service.

LIBRARY AND RESEARCH INFRASTRUCTURE

As information generation, management, manipulation, and disclosure become integral to a larger part of research, universities are considering organizational management support for these. Data curation provides one example. In some cases, these interests may have crystallized around a "cyberinfrastructure" or "digital humanities" organizational hub, or some capacity in a department or school; in other cases, it is not formalized. Libraries are also developing services here and, in some cases, may host such units. It is interesting to look at the "history"[4] of the Center for Digital Scholarship at Brown University Library.

The library has a persistent institutional role; however, we have seen other areas emerge with overlapping, similar, or converging functions. These have included IT, e-learning, publishing, e-research and digital humanities support, writing centers, research, and publication administration. As the information management function becomes integral to more activities, and these activities are unified by the network, then the university may realign information management support.

This has led to various well-documented boundary issues—between libraries and IT for example, or libraries and e-learning. It has also led to really interesting new service configurations which bring together previously disparate service areas as common interests become clear. It is surely likely that these new configurations will become more common in the next few years.

NOTES

1. http://odai.research.yale.edu
2. T. Hanson, *Managing Academic Support Services in Universities: The Convergence Experience* (London: Facet, 2005).
3. www.lib.umich.edu/mpublishing
4. http://library.brown.edu/cds/about/history

APRIL 13, 2011

LAM-inating libraries . . . redux

http://orweblog.oclc.org/archives/002168.html

The shared interests between libraries, archives, and museums (LAMs) have been an important line of work[1] for OCLC Research. It is also, of course, a recurring service, organizational, and policy issue in many contexts.

A related issue is also of considerable interest for libraries. As we move into a digital environment, library work can increasingly understand and benefit from archival and museum perspectives and professional practice.

As libraries digitize primary materials, or as they begin to curate research data or learning materials, an archival perspective becomes more important. Provenance and context are of interest, and changes to resources over time need to be tracked and managed. Appraisal practices may have lessons. The value of resources as *evidence* becomes central.

As libraries provide access to abundant digital materials, how to selectively present them or to construct narratives around them becomes more interesting. Thinking explicitly about structured learning support is a topic. The notion of *exhibition* comes into play, a central museum activity, alongside education.

NOTE

1. www.oclc.org/research/activities/lamsurvey/default.htm

APRIL 29, 2011

Advocacy: Public library as amenity and necessity

http://orweblog.oclc.org/archives/002169.html

Downward pressure on the cost of public services creates issues for public libraries. A growth in advocacy is a natural response, and this in turn creates pressing questions about value, and in particular about how different stakeholders potentially perceive value differently. Who one is addressing, and with what message, has become very important.

These topics were addressed in a strongly worded article about public libraries from Christopher Caldwell in the *Financial Times* last week. It appeared under the provocative—although misleading—title "It is the fate of libraries to die." The context is the public debate around library cutbacks and closures in the UK.

He opens by referring to recent arguments for public libraries by author Zadie Smith, and suggests that her advocacy is misdirected. He characterizes the issue as follows:

> Libraries are imperiled for a different reason: because local councils
> feel they have better things to do with the money. This winter, Keith
> Mitchell of Oxfordshire county council, discussing the possibility of

closing 20 of 43 local libraries, warned that if the libraries were not
cut, something else would be, "and that will most likely be elderly care,
learning difficulty care and care for people with mental health problems because those are the biggest bits of our budget."[1]

Caldwell has some harsh thing to say about public libraries. He calls them
"reactionary" for limiting borrowing rights to local residents. He asserts
that "like the military sector, the library sector confounds every attempt
to make it more efficient."

He suggests a parallel with a general government dynamic: "In olden
times, people wanted a state that built great monuments, even at the price
of being distant. Nowadays, people prefer a state that is intimate and
therapeutic, one that will solve the practical problems of day-to-day life."
Libraries are often monumental, but answer the needs of the individual.
Although he presents this as an issue, I would see it as more of an achieve-
ment. Libraries have married the civic and the intimate in successful ways.

One might argue with his perceptions about public libraries, but this is
less important than his main point about influencing funding decisions.
In asking what makes libraries so hard to defend against cuts, he turns to
an article by Eleanor Jo Rodger in *American Libraries*, "Public Libraries:
Necessities or Amenities?"[2] I have discussed the value of other work by
Rodger in these pages,[3] and Caldwell calls this a "magnificent essay."

Rodger starts in a similar place. As public funding is reduced, public
library funding will also be reduced as "there simply isn't enough money to

go around." She repeats the important point I highlighted in the earlier post, that local government decisions will reflect *their* understanding, not ours.

She briefly reviews the "justification" language of public libraries in the US, noting the founding educational impulse, the association of that with books and reading, support for an educated citizenry, and then a "right to information" agenda. However, she suggests that there is currently a "fuzzy mix of language about importance, equity and use" used in support of public library budgets.

She then introduces the distinction between "necessities" and "amenities" that appealed to Christopher Caldwell. Necessities are those things to which we have a right because they are seen to be centrally socially valuable. For example, fire and police services are justified by an appeal to the right of public safety. Amenities are those things to which we don't believe we have a right, but which we may prefer are provided by local government because there are economies of scale in such general provision. Garbage collection is an example here.

In several very interesting paragraphs, Rodger then discusses how public library services may be seen to be both important amenities and valued necessities. For example, equity of access to information in mixed- or low-income communities may be seen as a necessity. However, she suggests that most uses for most users tend to fall in the amenities category.

She then uses this distinction to talk about advocacy. Library users, she suggests, may be mobilized to advocate for the public library as amenity. On the other hand, she suggests that library supporters—who may not necessarily use the library—may believe in the transformative role of public libraries. They can be mobilized as advocates for the library as necessity, providing homework help or business information for local entrepreneurs.

Caldwell concludes his article with a recommendation for public library advocates: "As a matter of politics defending amenities may work better than defending necessities." This is in contrast to the transformative arguments advanced by Zadie Smith, Philip Pullman, and others which defend the library as necessity.

He doesn't really say why he thinks this is so, or how he thinks different arguments play in council corridors. (Indeed, the overall continuity of the article seems interrupted in several places, as if it were shortened from a longer piece.)

It was interesting to see the issue discussed in this way in the pages of the *Financial Times*. It was also interesting to be referred again to Eleanor Jo Rodger. Her article emphasizes the need to understand the motivations of those who make decisions about library funding, presents an interesting framework for characterizing library value, and notes how effective advocacy will depend on mobilizing different groups depending on the values which are important to them.

P.S. Rodger notes the work of my OCLC colleagues on creating support for public library funding in the US, "From Awareness to Funding."[4] This emphasizes the need to target messages to particular segments, and also notes that those who most strongly support the library believe in its transformative role. This report influenced the subsequent Geek the Library[5] library advocacy framework.

NOTES

1. Christopher Caldwell. "It Is the Fate of Libraries to Die," April 15, 2011, at www.ft.com/cms/s/0/784d85f8-6790-11e0-9138-00144feab49a.html
2. http://issuu.com/seanfitzpatrick/docs/0809/49?viewMode=presentation&zoomed=true&zoomPercent=100&zoomXPos=0.5&zoomYPos=0.25338491295938104
3. http://orweblog.oclc.org/archives/001424.html
4. www.oclc.org/reports/funding/default.htm
5. www.oclc.org/us/en/reports/geekthelibrary.htm

Collections are library assets

http://orweblog.oclc.org/archives/002191.html

I quite like using the word *assets* with reference to library collections. We tend to think of assets in positive terms, as things that are valuable. More of that later.

I was interested to see Rick Anderson remark on the vocabulary used by my colleague Constance Malpas a while ago. This was in the context of a generous note about Constance's "Cloud-Sourcing Research Collections: Managing Print in the Mass-Digitized Library Environment."[1]

I confess that I giggle and shudder simultaneously at the thought of referring publicly to books in our collection as "inventory that is increasingly devalued as an institutional asset." That kind of business-school-flavored language will, not to put too fine a point on it, utterly freak out significant segments of any university faculty, not to mention library staff.[2]

The "business" reference is apt, and I confess that my sense of "asset" in general conversation has indeed been subtly transformed by the narrower accounting sense. For example, in the glossary to Robert C. Higgins's *Analysis for Financial Management*, we read that an asset is "Anything with value in exchange." (It is always a pleasure to read something that is well written. This is a very nice example of fine technical writing.) And turning, as one does, to Wikipedia, I read an accounting definition[3]. "An asset is a resource controlled by the entity as a result of past events and from which future economic benefits are expected to flow to the entity."

What is relevant here is the idea that assets are things from which you release value. You expect a return. But assets are not ends in themselves. They are means toward creating value. Of course, this is important because assets have associated costs. Managing collections, for example, is not cost-free.

I remember being struck by some sentences about assets in Higgins's book when I read them first a few years ago:

Some newcomers to finance believe assets are a good thing: the more the better. The reality is just the opposite: Unless a company is about to go out of business, its value is in the income stream it generates, and its assets are simply a necessary means to this end. Indeed, the ideal company would be one that produced income without any assets; then no investment would be required, and returns would be infinite.[4]

Yes, financial metrics lend clarity here, but are not relevant to libraries for whom the question of value is different and less susceptible to measurement.

However, it has been interesting to see the growing debate about print "assets" in libraries. As the pressure to repurpose space grows and as the print collection releases progressively less value in research and learning, there is a growing interest in managing down print assets. Not unexpectedly, this is in parallel with an emerging interest in securing systemwide preservation of the collective print record.

It is clear that research libraries no longer see collections as ends in themselves, or they do not necessarily equate the size of the collection with the value of the library. More is not necessarily better. They also recognize the opportunity costs of managing large print collections.

As we rethink collections, I think we are seeing them more as assets in the sense I have discussed here, as investment is driven by a stronger sense of how they will be used to generate value in research and learning. Of course, some libraries have thought this way for longer: think of how a busy public library manages its collection. And, of course, some libraries will continue to have a mission-driven responsibility to collect significant portions of the scholarly record, although we will probably see more collective approaches here.

Anyway, to get a sense of what I mean, Rick Anderson's presentations[5] might help . . .

NOTES

1. www.oclc.org/research/publications/library/2011/2011-01.pdf
2. http://scholarlykitchen.sspnet.org/2011/02/28/the-digitized-book-corpus -and-the-cracking-dam
3. http://en.wikipedia.org/wiki/Asset
4. Robert C. Higgins, *Analysis for Financial Management* (New York: McGraw-Hill, 2011).
5. www.slideshare.net/CharlestonConference/let-them-eat-everything-by-rick -anderson-university-of-utah

JUNE 30, 2012

The enterprising librarian . . .

http://orweblog.oclc.org/archives/002201.html

I participated in an interesting event[1] at the School of Information and Library Science at UNC a while ago. It was a symposium to consider the "information professional" of 2050. Yes, that is 2050 :-). There was a mix of people. Some in LIS education; some in libraries; and some in industry.

One word that was used a lot was *entrepreneur*. It was used in two related ways. First was entrepreneur with a big *E*, where schools are preparing people with the skills and outlook to found or go into start-ups. Second was entrepreneur with a little *e*, where schools are preparing people to work flexibly in dynamic environments which value enterprise.

I was interested in this theme as it chimed with a quote from Manuel Castells I had used in my written submission to the symposium (these will be published later in the year). My focus was on libraries, not on the broader information field. Here is the Castells quote . . .

> In a dynamic, evolutionary perspective there is a fundamental difference between two types of organizations: organizations for which the reproduction of their system of means becomes their main organizational goal; and organizations in which goals, and the change of goals, shape and endlessly reshape the structure of means. I call the first type of organizations bureaucracies; the second type, enterprises.[2]

This is quite dense, and needs to be unpacked a little in relation to libraries. Historically, libraries enjoyed stability and a shared understanding of goals. This in turn favored a focus on managing and improving the means toward those goals—building the collection, providing reference service, creating efficiencies in technical processing, and so on. This was the focus of professional practice and education. Much of this work is inherently bureaucratic. However, in an environment of change, while overall mission and values may remain the same, new and shifting goals become the norm. Think of greater integration in the learning and research process through greater curriculum support, data curation, scholarly publishing, or support for grant writing or expertise profiles. Think of network-based reading services, or job-seeking and homework support. As goals shift in a changing environment, so does the need to think about how to marshal the means to meet them. This may need reorganization, new staff skills, changing priorities, reallocation of staff and resources, and so on. It requires a shift from bureaucracy to enterprise, an adaptive organization that reviews and reshapes what it does in light of changing requirements.

Now, just after I had written my submission, I came across an interesting looking book by Bethan Ruddock: *The New Professional's Toolkit.*[3] I was very taken with the table of contents, and the OCLC Library kindly acquired a copy for me. Here is the table of contents:

1. Project management
2. Teaching, training & communicating
3. Meeting your users' needs and measuring success
4. Marketing your service and engaging stakeholders
5. Using technologies
6. Getting and staying online
7. Generating funding and doing more with less
8. Managing money—budgets & negotiating
9. Information ethics and copyright
10. Up-skilling and professional development
11. Networking and promoting yourself
12. Professional involvement & career development

Each chapter includes practitioner case studies, some from her colleagues at Manchester. Readers will find some familiar names[4] there, including, for example, Amanda Hill, Bohyun Kim, Lukas Koster, Jenica Rogers. An expanded table of contents,[5] with links to some of the case studies, is on the book blog. Now, Bethan talks about information professionals broadly in the preface, but this looks like a publisher-encouraged widening of focus (I may be wrong :-)). In the introduction, she notes it is aimed at librarians and archivists.

What struck me immediately about this list was how the focus was very much on generic skills applied in a library or archival context. And those skills are very much about managing an enterprise: many are explicitly about managing in a changing environment. Importantly, much of the material is about *positioning* oneself or one's organization in relation to other players, a theme that becomes more important in dynamic environments of multiple stakeholders. So, for example, there is material about budgets; but there is also material about negotiating, about raising money from other sources, about demonstrating value. There is little material here about management as such, which surely would have featured in an equivalent volume some years ago, but there is material on managing projects, on training and communication, and on assessing needs and evaluating services. There is also a strong emphasis on personal skills and positioning, with discussions of personal branding in a networked environment, skills development, and professional involvement. It is taken for granted that communication, marketing, assessment, promotion, and brand management are central activities for the organization and the individual. For example . . .

> It is not just your organization and services that need promoting: you also need to promote yourself and for many of the same reasons. This isn't about boasting about how great you are, but about making people aware of your unique skills and expertise, so they can call on them as necessary.
>
> Just as your users won't know how your service can help them unless you specifically tell them, people won't know what you personally have to offer unless you make it obvious. In the workplace, you as a person can inspire trust and reliance in a way that your library or archive as a service can never do. Your users are much more likely to connect with your personal expertise: "The information service can do that. I read it on a leaflet" is a much less powerful message than: "Bethan can do that. She was talking to me about it last week." Your knowledge, expertise and personal skills can be a very valuable asset to your organization.[6]

This echoed a comment I have been using in presentations recently: "If the library wishes to be seen as expert, its expertise must be visible."

The book does focus on the individual rather than the organization, so the technology chapters, for example, are somewhat impressionistic, but they do hand off to interesting and informative case studies. And one can look elsewhere for the detail.

This "toolkit" covers some of what I took to be entrepreneurial skills. Or in language I prefer in this context, it covers some of the skills the library enterprise needs to include, and the enterprising librarian needs to have.

NOTES

1. http://sils.unc.edu/events/2012/ip2050
2. Manuel Castells, *The Rise of the Network Society* (Malden, MA: Wiley-Blackwell, 2010).

3. www.worldcat.org/oclc/758076068
4. http://lisnewprofs.com/contributors
5. http://lisnewprofs.com/table-of-contents
6. www.worldcat.org/oclc/758076068

Defining the library . . . reflexively

http://orweblog.oclc.org/archives/002208.html

It occurred to me recently that the library definitions I most like have a reflexive quality . . .

Dan Chudnov, for example, is admirably succinct and direct:

> My professional mission as a librarian is this:
> Help people build their own libraries.
> That's it. That's all I care about.[1]

This is from 2006. Interestingly, in the interim, we have seen big growth in the personal "library"—think of Mendeley or Goodreads for example.

Here are two from very different writers, each expressing the generative capacity of the library in a very pithy way . . .

> People should think not so much of the books that have gone into the National Library but rather of the books that have come out of it. A library, after all, feeds the people that go in there.[2]

This is Irish writer Seán O'Faoláin, and the library he talks about is the National Library of Ireland.

The second is Daniel Dennett's oft-noted . . .

> A scholar is just a library's way of making another library.[3]

Now, Dennett's remarks are in the context of Richard Dawkins's argument about how memes mirror the behavior of genes, "just different kinds of replicators evolving in different media at different rates." While he wants to argue that this is a good way of thinking about ideas, he acknowledges that it is unsettling, "even appalling": "I am not initially attracted by the idea of my brain as a sort of dung heap in which the larvae of other people's ideas renew themselves, before sending out copies of themselves in an informational Diaspora."

I like the way each of these emphasizes the role of the library in a cycle of creation and recreation. The library is not an end in itself but an institution which helps create new knowledge.

And finally, here are another two which come at a similar idea from different perspectives . . .

First, Ross Atkinson, a refreshingly cerebral librarian, has written:

> Because the purpose and result of absorbing information is always finally to produce further information, i.e., to continue the conversation, the function of the library must be understood as one that assists members of the community both in taking particular positions and in recognizing and assessing the positions taken by others. (*Contingency and contradiction: The place(s) of the library at the dawn of the new millennium*[4])

The opening here echoes the generative theme of the last two. But what drew me to this was the latter part, which emphasizes the library's role in providing the material and evidential base for debate and enquiry.

This leads directly into what is for me the most affecting of these accounts, coming from Irish writer and journalist, Fintan O'Toole. He is writing about public libraries in Dublin, libraries which I also heavily used and later worked in for a while.

> The library should not provide an argument for a particular case, but demonstrate that there is always another case to be made. The notion that the library is a place that has no agenda other than allowing people to invent their own agendas is what makes it an indispensable resource for a democracy. It is where we can learn not just to be readers, but to be the authors of our own destiny.[5]

O'Toole's essay is a marvelous tribute to public libraries. It does not appear to be available online, but I quoted from it at length here[6].

Agenda may be a more loaded word than Atkinson's *position*, but I immediately associated the two in my mind. The idea that a library is a place which "has no agenda other than allowing people to invent their own agendas" resonates strongly. Of course, to achieve this goal, libraries do indeed have to have an agenda.

JULY 5, 2013

Three challenges: Engaging, rightscaling, and innovating

http://orweblog.oclc.org/archives/002213.html

I was in Australia recently, primarily to attend the conference intriguingly entitled "The Edge of the World."[7] The presentation I gave is here[8]. This was the latest Theta conference, the Australian parallel to EDUCAUSE. I very much enjoyed the host city, Hobart, not least because of the smell of the sea as we walked out of the hotel.

More recently, I was pleased to attend parts of the CIC Center for Library Initiatives conference,[9] hosted by The Ohio State University, here in Columbus (far, unfortunately, from the sea). The topic was emerging forms of scholarly communication.

Finally, Kurt de Belder recently gave a presentation[10] at OCLC in our Distinguished Speaker Series, in which he spoke about the transformation of the academic library.

In Hobart, after some introductory material, I spoke about three challenges for libraries: a shift to engagement, rightscaling infrastructure, and innovation, notably institutional innovation. I only attended some of the sessions at the CIC meeting but I was struck by the correspondences between what I heard there and the challenges I identified. It also seemed to me that much of what Kurt spoke about aligned well with these challenges also.

This blog entry briefly talks about each challenge and illustrates them with examples from the CIC conference and Kurt's presentation.

Engagement, infrastructure, and innovation are related of course. As engagement becomes more important, libraries are reducing local infrastructure where it does not make a distinctive local impact (print collections and systems, for example). Greater engagement means that there may be a need for new services which requires innovation. Over time, innovations may become established and generate infrastructure requirements, which may be provided in different ways.

Libraries always did these three things, but I think the nature of the current challenge is different. Libraries are looking at more and different ways of engaging with their users as patterns of research, learning, and personal-information use change in a network environment, and are actively looking to re-allocate resources to support this shift. At the same time, the emergence of the network makes it possible to choose to source infrastructure in different ways and at different levels, introducing new choices and partner opportunities.

1. THE SHIFT TO ENGAGEMENT

By engagement, I mean that libraries are working to create distinctive value in the research, learning, and teaching workflows of their users in ways which go beyond the provision of collections.

In this context, Kurt de Belder speaks about the library as an active partner in knowledge. Scott Walter spoke recently about the service turn,[11] a direction in which libraries aim for distinction in the services they offer, as the distinctive value of collections is less strong, and content is less scarce.

And I was struck by this formulation by the University of Minnesota Libraries:

> In alignment with the University's strategic positioning, the University Libraries have re-conceived goals, shifting from a collection-centric focus to one that is engagement-based. (PDF[12])

Think of these trends:

- Users used to build their workflows around libraries. Now the library needs to build services around user workflows, especially as those workflows form around broader network services. So, for example, we see libraries expose their knowledge bases to Google Scholar; introduce support for Mendeley and Zotero alongside End- note or RefWorks; reach out to provide curricular or grants sup- port; and other ways in which they more directly support changing workflows. Kurt de Belder spoke about their support for research- ers through VREs (virtual research environments), systems to sup- port group working and research workflow (in their case, based on the SharePoint toolkit[13] developed by Microsoft Research).
- Libraries used to acquire and organize "published" materials. Now they are engaged with the full range of creation, management, and disclosure of learning and scholarly resources. For example, we are seeing library provide copyright, publishing, or bibliometric advice; engage with the emerging scholarly publishing practices of their faculty; explore research data management strategies; actively pro- mote institutional research and learning outputs through the insti- tutional repository. . . . This means that promoting institutional materials on the network becomes more important.
- Library spaces used to be configured around the management and use of print collections; now they are configured around engage- ment with researchers and learners, around experiences, expertise, and specialist facilities. For example, libraries provide better spaces for social interaction around learning or communication tasks; they promote access to specialist data, GIS, or other expertise; and they mount exhibitions which highlight relevant aspects of special col- lections and archives.

These are all examples of how libraries are reallocating resource and effort to engage more strongly with the learning and research lives of their users, focused on improving the learning experience, making research more pro- ductive and research outputs more visible.

One signal of this shift is the debate around the library subject or liaison role. Kurt describes a shift in Leiden University from collection specialists to outreach which is "service and expertise based." Liaison librarians will partner around "data curation, copyright, text and data-mining, e-publishing and dissemination, GIS, datasets."

Clearly, given its topic, the CIC conference focused on new forms of engagement with the faculty around curation and dissemination of research outputs, around new forms of scholarly publishing, and around publishing support and advisory services.

Four things occurred to me as I listened, specific to this particular discussion about publishing support, but which might be generalized to other emerging forms of engagement with research and learning.

1. These are areas where libraries are exploring a range of services, which means that each library's approach will be different. And each library's activity will be differently situated in relationship to other campus services. This was very clear in the final panel session, where participants spoke about how services were organized. There is no consistent organizational pattern, for example, for the relationship between copyright and other advisory services, library publishing services, university press, research data management, and institutional repository. In this context, I was also interested to recently see how Penn State had aligned special collections and scholarly publishing services in one division[14].

2. It is sometimes difficult to discern between edge cases and emerging services: are alternative forms of monograph peer review and publication going to emerge as important categories, for example, or will they remain experimental?

3. There is a balance between doing extensive custom work for one faculty member or department and the ability to scale services effectively across a campus community.

4. Emergent areas live beside established practices. This may lead to a more plural environment, or over time to disruption or absorption. Think of the various scenarios that might play out with open access publishing and alt-metrics for example. There were CIC panels in

each of these areas, with participation by representatives from Elsevier and Thompson Reuters.

For me, this discussion underlined the innovation challenge I discuss below. Exploration and experiment has to turn into something repeatable and scalable if it is to become part of the library portfolio. And much of the required innovation is around the institutions through which we organize to get work done—think of the changing relationship of university press and library, for example.

2. RIGHTSCALING

Libraries were predominantly "institution-scale"—they provided services at the level of the institution for their local users. However, their users now look to the network for information services (e.g., Google Scholar, Wikipedia . . .). And libraries now look to the network to collaborate or to source services (e.g., HathiTrust, cloud-based discovery or management systems, shared systems infrastructure . . .). At the same time, we are seeing a growing interest in shared management of the collective print collection, as regional and other consortia emerge to rebalance print management across groups of libraries.

In this environment, the need for local infrastructure declines (e.g., extensive print collections, redundantly deployed local systems which provide necessary but not distinctive services). The scale advantage of different ways of doing things manifests itself in both impact and efficiency. Think of HathiTrust. It has more impact, because it acts as a gravitational hub on the network. And it is more efficient to consolidate this activity rather than spread it redundantly across many libraries.

READER COMMENT

Cathrine Harboe-Ree
University Librarian, Monash University

In his July 5, 2013, blog, Lorcan reports on his attendance in Hobart, Australia, at a conference entitled "The Edge of the World." From an Australian perspective, Lorcan's blog plays a huge part in ensuring that we do not feel that we are isolated and unconnected from the intellectual and practical evolution of libraries.

Print collections provide an interesting example of emerging infrastructure consolidation. In seven years' time, say, a large part of the existing print collection in libraries will have moved into shared management, with a reduced local footprint. The opportunity costs of locally managing large print collections which release progressively less value into research and learning are becoming too pressing for this not to happen. There is a low engagement return on this infrastructure investment.

At the CIC meeting, scale came up in several contexts. John Wilkin spoke about how the consolidation of publishing activities in one unit and the sharing of infrastructure across them allowed the separate activities to benefit from scale, and achieve a level of activity that would have been impossible if they had remained separate, scattered across the University of Michigan. Charles Watkinson mentioned that it was usual to outsource technical infrastructure at Purdue. And in his closing remarks, Mark Sandler mentioned previous discussions about a single university press for the CIC. He suggested that it might be more reasonable to explore a model in which back-office infrastructure was shared, but where engagement with research, author relations, and press identity remained individual to each campus. In the vocabulary used here, he was speculating that infrastructure might scale to the level of a regional consortium, while engagement might remain at institution-scale.

On a national scale, Kurt de Belder spoke about the Dutch bibliographic infrastructure, currently provided in partnership with OCLC. He reported discussion about whether there continued to be a need for national-scale services in the current network environment, and whether in fact they should go to more global provision at the network level.

Of course, although rightscaling is an important infrastructure issue, it is not limited to infrastructure. Kurt also spoke about the lack of scale[15] as a broader library issue. He argued that each individual library could not specialize in the range of expertise required to deliver current services. He spoke, for example, about research data management services in the context of the full range of disciplines on a campus. In this context, he spoke for national and international collaboration around networks of provision to get local jobs done.

These examples show how rightscaling has become a central question for libraries. Do I build something myself? Do I do it collaboratively? Do I outsource it to a third party? Again, look at discovery systems or library management systems in this context, or look at the trend to managing down print collections alongside emerging shared print initiatives. Think of the models in use for preservation (LOCKSS, Portico). Think of newer services like analytics or recommendations where an institutional perspective may not scale and collaborative or third-party approaches will be necessary. Think of how important it is to make sure that your resolver is correctly configured in Scholar or PubMed. Questions increasingly arise around cloud provision, around collaboration, or around outsourcing to third parties.

As libraries want to emphasize impact and engagement, and de-emphasize activities which do not create distinctive local value, rightscaling becomes a key question.

3. INSTITUTIONAL INNOVATION

As behaviors and structures shift, innovation becomes central.

I think of two big trends here. The first is a shift—well under way—from thinking about the library as a fixed set of services (bureaucratic) to thinking about it as an organization which reconfigures to map changes in its user environment and expectations (enterprise). The second shift is around institutional innovation and the learning that flows from it.

I wrote about the first of these shifts a while ago. (See "The enterprising librarian,"[16] in chapter 8, "Libraries.")

Coping with change requires an enterprising orientation, one which recognizes that resources and effort must be continually adapted to meet the needs of the library user.

Institutional innovation is the second trend I note here, one which is inevitable as internal and external partnerships rebalance effort. Libraries have to develop new and routine ways of collaborating to achieve their goals, which involves evolution of organizational, cultural, and communication approaches. At the same time, they have to negotiate internal boundaries and forge new structures within institutions. In each case, they are developing new "relationship architectures" (to use a phrase of John Hagel III and John Seely Brown's).

Think, for example, of the institutional innovation required to move to shared systems and collections in the Orbis Cascade Alliance or 2CUL for example.

Or think of the innovative approach which makes new relationships within institutions (with learning and teaching support, with the office of research, the university press, emerging e-research infrastructure, IT, etc., for example, or with various educational or social services in a public setting). Evolving such relationships requires an enterprising approach and ensures continual learning, as staff interact with colleagues elsewhere to evolve new structures and services.

We are used to thinking of innovation in relation to start-ups. Here is a definition from Steve Blank[17]: "A start-up is an organization formed to search for a repeatable and scalable business model." This is useful as it reminds us that to be successful, innovation has to result in repeatable and scalable services which can be supported over time. And this brings us back to the type of engagement that is valuable and the infrastructure that is required to support it.

Much of the discussion around the examples I have used is an exploration of how to make identified new services repeatable and scalable, and of how to evolve the skills and organizational settings to support them.

CREDITS

The framework used here is influenced by the categories used in "Unbundling the Corporation."[18] Institutional change and learning is discussed in *Institutional Innovation*.[19]

NOTES

1. http://onebiglibrary.net/story/because-this-is-the-business-weve-chosen
2. Quoted in Noel Kissane, *Treasures from the National Library of Ireland* (Drogheda: Boyne Valley Honey Co., 1994).
3. http://ase.tufts.edu/cogstud/papers/memeimag.htm
4. Ross Atkinson, "Contingency and Contradiction: The Place(s) of the Library at the Dawn of the New Millennium," *Journal of the American Society for Information Science and Technology*, 52.1: 3–11.
5. Fintan O'Toole, "Reading, Writing and Rebelling: Growing Up with Public Libraries," in *The University of the People: Celebrating Ireland's Public Libraries,*

ed. Norma McDermott and Muriel McCarthy (Dublin: Chomhairle Leabharlanna, 2003).

6. http://orweblog.oclc.org/archives/000624.html
7. http://theta.edu.au
8. www.slideshare.net/lisld/hobart-19178013
9. www.cic.net/calendar/conferences/library/2013/home
10. www.oclc.org/research/news/2013/05-31.html
11. http://orweblog.oclc.org/archives/002152.html
12. http://crl.acrl.org/content/72/1/6.full.pdf
13. http://research.microsoft.com/en-us/projects/vre
14. www.libraries.psu.edu/psul/admin/adrsc.html
15. www.slideshare.net/kurtdebelder/transformation-of-the-academic-library-oclc/46
16. http://orweblog.oclc.org/archives/002201.html
17. http://steveblank.com/2010/01/25/whats-a-startup-first-principles
18. John Hagel and Marc Singer, "Unbundling the Corporation," *Harvard Business Review* (January 1, 1999).
19. John Hagel and John Seely Brown, *Institutional Innovation: Creating Smarter Organizations to Scale Learning* (Deloitte University Press, 1999), at www.scribd.com/doc/129958072/Institutional-Innovation-Creating-Smarter-Organizations-to-Scale-Learning

---

READER COMMENT

Cyril Oberlander
Library Director, SUNY Geneseo, Milne Library

Lorcan Dempsey has written a decade of insightful posts consistently illuminating powerful ideas, and connections among libraries.

A recent example of an influential post: "Three challenges: Engaging, rightscaling, and innovating." Lorcan identifies libraries resolving important challenging trends; one is about engagement and service redesign focusing on user workflows, one is the "rightscaling" of libraries that reimagine local roles, and the last is institutional innovation. Lorcan is highlighting the need for library structures designed as relationships balancing local and network values. At Milne Library, SUNY Geneseo, we understand this, as one of the homes of the IDS Project and Open SUNY Textbooks, a library lives many lives.

Thanks for the years of dialogue and commentary; I value his thinking about collaboration, service frameworks and systems, summaries from visits to libraries, and, also important, the open communication between libraries and OCLC.

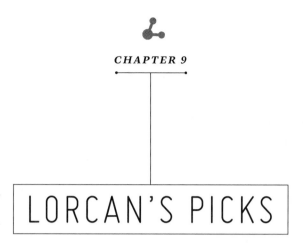

CHAPTER 9

LORCAN'S PICKS

THE POSTS IN this section were selected by Lorcan Dempsey from among the items that did not fit neatly into one of the other topical categories but which he felt would be strong additions to this collection. They range from the self-referential (the first post on the weblog, when it was on the OCLC Intranet), to discussion of Irish culture and poetry, to other observations on specific libraries and their cultural impact.

OCTOBER 20, 2003

Hello . . .

http://orweblog.oclc.org/archives/000036.html   Tag: Noteworthy

This is an experiment. One motivation is to provide a better vehicle for communicating interesting goings-on than the OR mailing list. Another is to explore what is involved in maintaining a weblog.

Mind the gap

http://orweblog.oclc.org/archives/000220.html

When I had been with OCLC for a few months, I was asked to do a keynote presentation to the biannual JISC/CNI conference. The topic was the difference between US and UK library environments. A topic I was not especially prepared for ;-).

I thought I would frame discussion with some more general remarks. I asked the library if they had anything available which would provide some starting points. They were helpful; most of what came back were books aimed at business travelers. These provided occasionally interesting comment, but frequently fell back on the stereotypical and archaic.

They did not really get at what I wanted; I did have a quick look for some more academic materials but did not turn up anything digestible in the small amount of time I had.

I recently came across *Brit-Think, Ameri-Think: A Transatlantic Survival Guide* (WorldCat[1]), by Jane Walmsley,[2] a US-born journalist who has married an Englishman and is a longtime resident of the UK. In her preface, she notes:

> The longer I stay, the more aware I become that we are very different
> peoples, grown far apart since 1776. I submit that the so-called special

READER COMMENT

 Alane Wilson
Senior Library Marketing Consultant, OCLC

I don't recall exactly what you said about enterprise blogging, but you were most skeptical that it was a productive thing for OCLC staff to be doing, that the output contributed anything to the discourse of our space, and that it was sustainable. When you did decide to begin blogging, you, of course, proved all three of those concerns to be . . . *phhht,* nothing. Very quickly, you established your blog as a "must-read" for our community.

Editor's note: At the time *Lorcan Dempsey's Weblog* was started, Alane Wilson was Senior Library Marketing Consultant at OCLC.

relationship between Britain and America is now one part history and one part wishful thinking. Sure, Yanks love London, and Brits watch *Friends,* and everybody eats at McDonald's, but that's not the point. We have developed separate attitudes and aspirations, which I classify as *Brit-think* and *Ameri-think.*[3]

The book is light in tone: it is humorous cultural generalization. It covers a range of topics and is, I think, often insightful. That said, I also often resisted what she said, or disagreed with her emphasis. Perhaps that is inevitable with any reader!

The leitmotif of the book is a schematic and necessarily reductive distinction between an individualistic *me-think* that she feels is characteristic of the US, and a more collective *we-think* that she feels characterizes the UK (although she mostly talks about England, and even then appears mostly to be influenced by London). This is not a political distinction, although it is manifest in political preferences.

Of course, the book's strengths (humorous cultural generalization) are also its faults (humorous cultural generalization). It avoids, for example, attitudes toward race and immigration, or toward social welfare, and it is in danger of trivializing or ignoring deep differences. Attitudes toward religion or patriotism come to mind.

I enjoyed reading it, although I felt she was rather unfair to what she calls the "Brits," overemphasizing their resistance to change and inaction. Again, others will have different reactions.

Nevertheless, I thought it a very valuable read. It focuses on differences in culture and values, differences not always apparent to the tourist or in intermittent business exchanges. But these differences are much more important than surface issues, like which fork to use or whether business casual is acceptable dress.

NOTES

1. http://worldcat.org/oclc/13945088
2. http://worldcat.org/identities/lccn-n84-150763
3. Jane Walmsley, *Brit-Think, Ameri-Think: A Transatlantic Survival Guide* (New York: Penguin Books, 1987).

APRIL 7, 2005

Public libraries in Dublin

http://orweblog.oclc.org/archives/000624.html

Fintan O'Toole has a wonderful essay on the public library in *The University of the People: Celebrating Irish Public Libraries*.[1] He calls it: "Reading, Writing and Rebelling: Growing Up with Public Libraries." Unfortunately, it does not appear to be on the web. The whole eight pages is almost worth quoting!

> [Public libraries] matter not because they're part of the infrastructure of public education, though of course they are that, but because they represent a different kind of education from what you can get in school. They are, in a very specific sense, an instrument of private education: an education in what it means to have a private self. They are public institutions that touch upon the most intimate parts of an emerging personality: the parts from which the ability to rebel against orthodoxy and authority may come. And they offer the prospect that that emergence can continue as long as life itself does. To say that the library offers a kind of private education is not to suggest that the reader who uses it is isolated from the community, or cut off from the surrounding society. On the contrary, what you learn at the library is something almost unique in life: a shared privacy.

The child who begins to borrow books from a library becomes aware
at more or less that same time of two things. One is the solitary pleasure of reading, as an arena in which you are free from outside inter-
ference. The other is that this pleasure has been and is being experi-
enced by many others in their own way. One of the simple things that
a library adds to a book is that white sheet gummed into the inside
cover or the title page, stamped with the dates on which other people
who borrowed it before you were supposed to return it. In this banal
bureaucratic record, there is a lesson to be learned. Books, like their
authors, have biographies, they have passed through other hands. The
private experience you are having is one that is also shared. . . .

One of the great things about borrowing a book was that you got to
bring it home, and that the book in itself transformed the house. I grew
up in a small, two-bedroomed corporation house, which was inhabited
by three adults and five children, so space was at a premium. But a
book made the space bigger by opening up private imaginative rooms.
. . . The fact that a book was borrowed rather than owned added to
the excitement, firstly because the book itself was a kind of temporary
exotic guest, and secondly because the pressure of time, the awareness
of a looming deadline for the return of the book, made you read more
intensely.

The struggle of libraries since then has been to categorize knowledge in as
comprehensive a manner as possible. A library at one level is like an orderly
chicken coop, where the books sit brooding in their neat rows of nests. But
every library user, on the other hand, is a fox among those chickens, fright-
ening the established order of knowledge into panic-stricken scatterings . . .

I found the piece particularly affecting for three reasons.

The first personal: I am the same age as O'Toole and grew up a few miles
away from where he is writing about, albeit in a larger house! He describes
library experiences that are similar to my own, down to the authors read. I
worked my way through the Richmal Crompton "William" books, and the
"Billy Bunter" series in their yellow jackets, and also "Jennings," who he
does not mention. I also promiscuously read the classics alongside myths
and legends and popular fiction. Later, I worked for several years in those

same public libraries, and indeed spent one year actually sticking white labels into the front of books. That said, I was slightly surprised to read "one of the responses of the state in the hard times of the 1980s, when mass unemployment perhaps threatened a degree of social discontent, was to virtually close down the public library service." Given this lack of opportunity, I left the Dublin Corporation public library system (now Dublin City Public Libraries[2]) in the 1980s to work in England.

The second also personal: he captures wonderfully a variety of the things I have thought about the public library, and those public libraries at that time.

The third professional: subtly, and passionately, O'Toole argues for the value of the public library, leading in his closing paragraph to a powerful statement of library purpose:

> The library should not provide an argument for a particular case, but demonstrate that there is always another case to be made. The notion that the library is a place that has no agenda other than allowing people to invent their own agendas is what makes it an indispensable resource for a democracy. It is where we can learn not just to be readers, but to be the authors of our own destiny.

NOTES
1. www.librarycouncil.ie/news/university_people.shtml
2. www.dublincity.ie/living_in_the_city/libraries

Aura again: *Habent sua fata libelli*

http://orweblog.oclc.org/archives/000627.html

This post continues the discussion of aura, digitization, and "mechanical reproduction," and relates it to remarks of Fintan O'Toole reported in another post[1].

JD is right to *suggest*[2] that aura is about more than uniqueness. It is about the "historic testimony" of the object, the traces it bears of where and what it has been.

In his essay, "Unpacking my Library," Walter Benjamin writes:

> *Habent sua fata libelli:* these words may have been intended as a general
> statement about books. So books like *The Divine Comedy,* Spinoza's *Eth-
> ics,* and *The Origin of the Species* have their fates. A collector, however,
> interprets this Latin saying differently. For him, not only books but
> also copies of books have their fates.[3]

So a copy may be testimony to an individual's life: where it was bought,
where it has been, what experiences it has been part of, who bound it. It
has a provenance and a history, which may be of broad interest. (In FRBR[4]
terms, we can say that in these cases the work and the copy equally may
have interest.)

I was recently in the Bata Shoe Museum,[5] in a party of five adults and six
children under twelve. The museum kept everybody's attention—well, for
a while anyway ;-). It is really very well done. Shaq O'Neal's large basketball
shoe in particular generated interest among the children: not only its size,
but the fact that it had been part of an unrepeatable experience fascinated.

Benjamin goes on to say:

> The phenomenon of collecting loses its meaning as it loses its per-
> sonal owner. Even though public collections may be less objectionable
> socially and more useful academically than private collections, the
> objects get their due only in the latter.

This seems strange, and is countered by our experience in the Bata Shoe
Museum, and by Fintan O'Toole's in the public library. Indeed, many curators will feel about their collections the way that Benjamin felt about his.

O'Toole talked of the fate of library books, of how they create a shared
experience:

> Books, like their authors, have biographies, they have passed through
> other hands. The private experience you are having is one that is also
> shared.

Books live in the lives of their readers. Readers also live in the lives of their
books. And, in the libraries that he is talking about, I always thought that

the mark of very good library staff was that they understood their collections based on the readers in the life of the book, but also understood their readers based on the books in the life of the reader.

So books, and copies of books, have an aura. They bear testimony to their lives and the lives of their users and owners. They may assume significance as part of a collection. They may be annotated or otherwise significantly marked.

However, to come back to my original point. For many books, the aura of the copy is low and the ability to transmit the content in new forms may be welcome. That does not mean, of course, that for some books, the user will be drawn back to the artifact, even when it itself is a mechanical reproduction.

NOTES

1. http://orweblog.oclc.org/archives/000624.html
2. http://orweblog.oclc.org/archives/000623.html#comments. "JD" commented on the original blog post.
3. http://townsendlab.berkeley.edu/sites/all/files/Benjamin%20Unpacking% 20My%20Library.pdf. Collected in *Illuminations* (ed. Hannah Arendt, trans. Harry Zohn).
4. www.oclc.org/research/projects/frbr/default.htm
5. www.batashoemuseum.ca

SEPTEMBER 17, 2005

Starbucks and other coffeehouses— an observation and a prediction

http://orweblog.oclc.org/archives/000799.html

It seems to me that the role of the coffeehouse, and, it must be said, Starbucks in particular, given its reach in the contemporary urban setting, is becoming clearer. Starbucks provides time-place alignment in busy, moving lives: in other words, it provides "on-demand place." It provides a place which is convenient at the time that it is required. This may be for downtime (a place to spend time relaxing), connect time (a place to spend time connecting to the network), rendezvous time (a place to spend time with others), work time (a place to spend time working). A colleague recently described Starbucks to me as his mobile office when he was on the road. It is not unusual to see job interviews take place there.

Starbucks has recently been in the news[1] because of its exclusive deal with Bob Dylan for sale of his latest album. The sale of music seems a natural for Starbucks and its clientele. So, the prediction? Within a small number of years, Starbucks will be selling individual tracks in a way that can be easily loaded onto customers' devices when they visit the stores.

Note: of course, as a colleague points out, one ought not overlook the primary role of providing "on-demand" coffee ;-).

NOTE

1. http://news.bbc.co.uk/2/hi/entertainment/4244934.stm

MAY 8, 2007

Glanceability

http://orweblog.oclc.org/archives/001347.html

Glanceability is about enabling "users to understand information with low cognitive effort." And further:

Glanceability refers to how quickly and easily the visual design conveys information after the user is paying attention to the display.

These quotes are from a paper, "Designing Glanceable Peripheral Displays," by Tara Lynn Matthews, Jodi Forlizzi, and Stacie Rohrbach, at Berkeley. (Abstract[1] and full text[2])

I went looking for further information about glanceability after I came across a mention of it in Tony Hirst's blog:

> However, whilst the visual component to radio is not just using limited to scrolling liveText displays, nor does it mean moving wholesale into television: the key is to support *glanceability,* a beautifully evocative word referring to the ability to look at a screen and capture the information you require *at a glance.* (*OUseful Info: Learnin' from Virgin*[3])

Broadly speaking, it seems to me that effective ranking, for example, supports glanceability, as folks will focus in on top results and may forego individually inspecting each member of a result set. And, of course, one of the issues with library websites is that they have low glanceability: they require quite a bit of cognitive effort to figure out what is available as they present a thin guiding layer wrapped around a resource fragmented by legacy categories.

I like the visual features of <u>WorldCat Identities</u>,[4] the time line and audience-level indicator. Each of these provides a hint about a resource, something that conveys quite a bit of information but which requires low cognitive effort to assimilate.

The time line gives a nice sense of shifts in reputation or reception of an author over time. Here, for example, is the time line of the very popular Victorian novelist Edward Bulwer-Lytton (<u>Wikipedia entry</u>[5]). (See figure 9.1.)

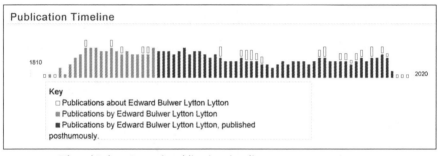

FIGURE 9.1 Edward Bulwer-Lytton's publication time line

Although there is a decline in volume, there continues to be interest in reissuing his novels and some writing about them. One thought is that this may be because of ongoing academic interest. A *glance* at the audience-level indicator supports this (see figure 9.2).

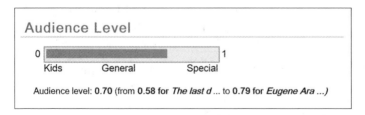

FIGURE 9.2
Edward Bulwer-Lytton's audience-level indicator

For info on audience level, see the <u>project page</u>[6].

NOTES

1. www.eecs.berkeley.edu/Pubs/TechRpts/2006/EECS-2006-113.html
2. www.eecs.berkeley.edu/Pubs/TechRpts/2006/EECS-2006-113.pdf
3. http://blogs.open.ac.uk/Maths/ajh59/010272.html
4. http://orlabs.oclc.org/Identities
5. http://en.wikipedia.org/wiki/Edward_Bulwer-Lytton%2C_1st_Baron_Lytton
6. www.oclc.org/research/projects/audience/default.htm

MAY 13, 2007

Day-Lewis stock

http://orweblog.oclc.org/archives/001350.html

Andrew Motion,[1] current UK Poet Laureate, reviews[2] the biography of one of his predecessors in that role, Cecil Day-Lewis:

> Various attempts have been made to lift the reputation of Cecil Day-Lewis since his death 35 years ago, but none of them has met with much success. The poet, who was esteemed as a member of the "MacSpaunday" group in the 1930s, who achieved wide popular success during the '40s, who was professor of poetry at Oxford in the '50s, and poet laureate for the last four years of his life, has lost his general readership and failed to stir significant interest in the academies. He is by no means the first writer to suffer such a fall from favour, and he won't be the last, but his case is a spectacular one. Has he been unfairly treated? (*The begetter of poetry* | *Review* | *Guardian Unlimited Books*[3])

Can we tell at a glance[4] if his judgment about the reception of Day-Lewis is correct? (See figure 9.3.)

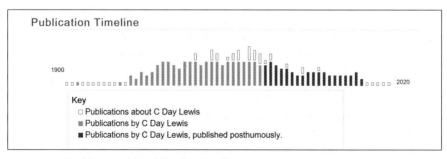

FIGURE 9.3 Cecil Day-Lewis's publication time line

Appears so. Maybe Day-Lewis is now most often invoked as the father of actor Daniel Day-Lewis[5]?

And what about his MacSpaunday colleagues? This expression (coined by Roy Campbell[6]) pulled together Louis MacNeice,[7] Stephen Spender,[8] W. H. Auden,[9] and Day-Lewis[10]. Checking their time lines shows strong ongoing interest in Auden[11] (also the subject of a *Guardian* review[12] on Saturday), but less strong interest in the others (maybe a little upward tick in MacNeice?).

Northrop Frye[13] famously complained[14] about the state of literary criticism, which operated like a stock exchange in which the stock of authors was seen to rise and fall driven by the whims of literary "chitchat." This may be the tool to track that stock!

Incidentally, Day-Lewis also wrote mystery fiction[15] under the name Nicholas Blake[16]. (See figure 9.4.)

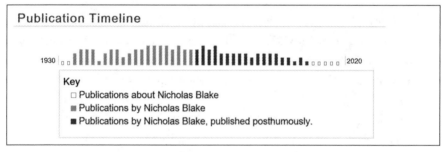

FIGURE 9.4 Nicholas Blake's publication time line

This is getting addictive ;-). Maybe I will resist further posts on World-Cat Identities[17] for a while.

NOTES

1. www.worldcat.org/identities/lccn-n78-58583
2. http://books.guardian.co.uk/review/story/0,,2077492,00.html
3. http://books.guardian.co.uk/review/story/0,,2077492,00.html
4. http://orweblog.oclc.org/archives/001347.html
5. www.worldcat.org/identities/lccn-n95-30987
6. www.worldcat.org/identities/lccn-n50-30959
7. www.worldcat.org/identities/lccn-n79-32198
8. www.worldcat.org/identities/lccn-n79-7025
9. www.worldcat.org/identities/lccn-n79-54316

10. www.worldcat.org/identities/lccn-n80-67088
11. www.worldcat.org/identities/lccn-n79-54316
12. http://books.guardian.co.uk/reviews/poetry/0,,2077778,00.html
13. www.worldcat.org/identities/lccn-n50-248
14. http://worldcat.org/oclc/230039
15. www.worldcat.org/search?q=su%3a%22mystery%20fiction%22
16. www.worldcat.org/identities/lccn-n90-609288
17. www.worldcat.org/identities

JULY 12, 2007

Narnia, memory organizations, and public diplomacy

http://orweblog.oclc.org/archives/001391.html

"Cultural Diplomacy"[1] is a report from the UK think tank Demos,[2] which I finally read on a plane ride this week. It talks about the role of cultural institutions and manifestations in international relations and, while charting international differences of approach, notes that cultural diplomacy is sometimes underappreciated as a "soft" influencer. The report talks about *cultural diplomacy, public diplomacy,* and *cultural literacy,* and emphasizes the growing importance of the latter two. Public diplomacy aims to reach broad masses of people with a favorable image of a country and, to be effective, has to enlist a broad part of the population in support of it. Hence, in part, the importance of cultural literacy. Clearly, each issue connects to the wider range of ways in which we now communicate.

> While hard power is the ability to coerce (through military or economic means), soft power is the means to attract and persuade. As one British expert has put it: "Public diplomacy is based on the premise that the image and reputation of a country are public goods which can create either an enabling or disabling environment for individual transactions."[3]

Libraries, museums, and archives are seen to have an important role in UK public diplomacy.

> Our national cultural institutions are not static depositories for cultural artefacts; they are active participants in the articulation and

communication of our own and others' sense of identity. Museums, galleries and libraries in particular "provide the means by which a nation represents its relationship to its own history and to that of 'other' cultures, functioning as monuments to the nation, and as such they have played a pivotal role in the formation of nation states." (*Reinventing the nation: British heritage and the bicultural settlement in New Zealand / Lynda Dyson in Littler and Naidoo*[4])

And, interestingly, the report recommends support for acquisitions by these organizations to maintain the "range, quality and contemporary relevance of our cultural assets." In turn, it recommends that national cultural institutions (such as the British Library) should develop explicit international strategies which take account of government goals.

Now, shortly after finishing this document, I was walking through Union Station in Washington, D.C., and was interested to see there an extensive exhibition promoting Northern Ireland and Belfast as tourist and commercial destinations. What was interesting to me was how it was constructed around the *Titanic* (which was built in Belfast and has become an important part of Belfast's promoted identity) and various cultural references. There was a reference to the poet Louis MacNeice[5] for example. And to

---

READER COMMENT

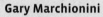 **Gary Marchionini**
Dean and Cary C. Boshamer Professor, School of Information and Library Science, University of North Carolina at Chapel Hill

Few people have blogs that reach back ten years, and even fewer long-standing blogs come from thought leaders in information science. Lorcan Dempsey's blog has long been a source of inspiration and discussion fodder for information science scholars and students. Lorcan's weblog on libraries, services, and networks provides insightful observations about technical developments in information and library science organized by broad themes of the evolving information industry. The ideas are worth a regular visit, but Lorcan's writing is fun to read as he uses springboards from classical and pop culture to make his lens on libraries old and new as much a kaleidoscope as telescope for the field.

C. S. Lewis[6]. It noted how the Mourne Mountains were an inspiration for Narnia. I imagine most people seeing this did not realize that C. S. Lewis was born in Northern Ireland, and I wondered what impact it would have on them.

Aside 1: It is interesting to see the climbing interest[7] in C. S. Lewis as reflected in continued publication of his works and works about him.

Aside 2: The seventh International JISC/CNI Conference will be held in Belfast almost exactly a year from now (July 10–11, 2008).

NOTES

1. www.demos.co.uk/publications/culturaldiplomacy
2. www.demos.co.uk
3. http://worldcat.org/oclc/54814028
4. http://worldcat.org/oclc/55645007?tab=details
5. http://worldcat.org/identities/lccn-n79-32198
6. http://worldcat.org/identities/lccn-n79-3974
7. http://worldcat.org/identities/lccn-n79-3974

JULY 25, 2007

The amplified conference

http://orweblog.oclc.org/archives/001404.html   *Tag: Noteworthy, Coinage*

It is interesting to watch how more conferences are amplifying their effect through a variety of network tools and collateral communications.

Stuart Dempster of JISC has just sent me a note about the recently held JISC e-Content Symposium (see reports of discussion on the *Strategic Content Alliance* blog[1]) and associated Digitisation Conference[2]. Check out reports of the conference on the conference blog,[3] pictures on Flickr,[4] the presentations,[5] podcasts,[6] and, hey, there is even a Facebook group[7] devoted to conference interests.

The conference content is "published" as part of a wider set of materials about the JISC Digitization Program[8] and the Strategic Content Alliance[9]. The use of the blogging environment with material organized with categories is also something we are seeing more of.

NOTES

1. http://involve.jisc.ac.uk/wpmu/sea/category/symposium2007
2. http://involve.jisc.ac.uk/wpmu/digitisation/digitisation-conference-2007
3. http://involve.jisc.ac.uk/wpmu/digitisation
4. www.flickr.com/photos/jiscdigi
5. http://involve.jisc.ac.uk/wpmu/digitisation/digitisation-conference-2007
6. http://involve.jisc.ac.uk/wpmu/digitisation/category/podcasts
7. www.facebook.com/group.php?gid=2402844750
8. http://involve.jisc.ac.uk/wpmu/digitisation/about-the-jisc-digi-programme
9. http://involve.jisc.ac.uk/wpmu/sea/about
10. http://orweblog.oclc.org/archives/002162.html

NOVEMBER 3, 2008

Flying and light posting

http://orweblog.oclc.org/archives/001805.html

I was traveling through Reagan National in Washington, D.C., a while ago. I was tired. It was early in the morning, and I was coming off a bumpy and cramped commuter flight from Columbus, Ohio (purportedly within an hour and a half's flying time of 56% of the US population, I seem to remember reading somewhere).

I passed by a display of retro Pan Am flight bags, proud with that iconic logo. They were on sale. Since then, it seems that I have been seeing retro flight bags everywhere. (See figure 9.5.)

As a young child, the logo was very familiar to me, and not a little magical. I had an uncle who worked with Pan Am, and for a while, there were always bags or other items around. It was a time when flying was exciting and even exotic. And Pan Am seemed more exciting than the rest. I notice that Wikipedia describes[1] Pan Am as a "cultural icon of the 20th century."

FIGURE 9.5 Pan Am logo

Indeed, the flight bag and that logo, in particular, seem to belong to a different era. And it is perhaps now, when the excitement has been squeezed from most flying, that the logo can come to life again as an emblem of the glamour of an experience that has mostly faded away.

Note: logo copied from the Wikipedia page[2] about the image. Note the fair use rationale.

NOTES

1. http://en.wikipedia.org/wiki/Pan_American_World_Airways
2. http://en.wikipedia.org/wiki/Image:Pan_Am_Logo.svg

SEPTEMBER 29, 2009

Reputation enhancement

http://orweblog.oclc.org/archives/002011.html

Reputation management on the web—individual and institutional—has become a more conscious activity for many, as ranking, assessment, and other reputational measures are increasingly influenced by network visibility. In particular, it raises for academic institutions an issue that has become a part of many service decisions: What is it appropriate to do locally? What should be sourced externally? And what should be left to others to do?

Think, for example, of faculty profiles: the managed disclosure of expertise and research activity. This has often been an informal personal or departmental activity. However, there is now a variety of institutional initiatives which may pull together data about expertise, experience, publications, grants, courses taught, and so on (see OSU Pro at OSU, or VIVO at Cornell, for example). Such initiatives may sit between several organizational units on campus: Research Support, PR/Communications, IT, Library. They are also at the intersection of different systems: enterprise (PeopleSoft, for example), course lists, research/grants management, bibliographic. At the same time, researchers may have presences in emerging network-level research social networks (Mendeley or Nature Network for example), in disciplinary resources (RePEc, for example), and, of course, in general use services (LinkedIn, for example). There are also commercial services which support such activity in different ways (Community of Science or Symplectic, for example).

In this context, here is a note about several unrelated initiatives which I have come across in the last week or so. I don't try and create a single narrative around them, but together I think they point to this emerging sense of reputation management (or enhancement) as an important, if not yet fully clear, service category.

We are exploring such a service category in our Research Information Management[1] theme. It looks at the intersection of library services and research administration on campus, and we are thinking about the variety of library services which might emerge (which include, in the context of this entry, bibliographic support, bibliometric advice, effective disclosure of expertise and research to the web, advice about SEO and copyright, and so on).

VIVO: Research and expertise across Cornell.[2] Some colleagues from Cornell visited last week (see details and video of Anne Kenney's presentation here[3]), and VIVO came up in discussion.

> VIVO (not an acronym) brings together in one site publicly available information on the people, departments, graduate fields, facilities, and other resources that collectively make up the research and scholarship environment in all disciplines at Cornell. (*About VIVO*[4])

Managed within the library, it draws together a lot of data from various sources. Interestingly, it is based on Vitro,[5] an "Integrated Ontology Editor and Semantic Web Application."

Bibliometrician.[6] The University of Leicester Library advertised for a "bibliometrician" whose role would be "to provide high-level expertise and advice to the University on the use of bibliometrics and related policies in the external and internal evaluation of the quality of the University's research."

Mendeley.[7] My colleague John MacColl wrote a blog entry[8] about Mendeley last week. Mendeley describes itself as being like "iTunes for research papers": "Organize, share, and discover research papers! Mendeley is a research management tool for desktop & web. You can also explore research trends and connect to other academics in your discipline." John contrasted Mendeley and institutional repository incentives and user experience for researchers. Mendeley is one of several social networking sites aimed at researchers.

Manchester escholar.[9] The University of Manchester launched its repository service. The first line of its mission reads: "sustain and enhance the research reputations of individuals and organisations affiliated with the University of Manchester." It is also interesting to read the "project business case and benefits"[10] which have a strong reputation for management focus. The first benefit for the research is "increase the visibility of your research findings, your work is easier to disseminate, easier to find and easier to read." The second emphasizes convenience: "Make it easier to manage your list of publications on your personal website and your organisation's website." For institutions, the first-listed benefit is "demonstrate to its employees, in particular the academic community, that individuals and their work are valued, by supporting mechanisms that reduce workload and maximise the benefits to them of their efforts"; and the third is to "increase the visibility, reputation and prestige of the institution."

Ranking economists and RePEc.[11] Greg Mankiw is a Harvard economist, textbook writer, high-profile blogger, and sometime chair of former president George W. Bush's Council of Economic Advisors. He refers from time to time to a ranking of economists generated by RePEc[12]. He wrote a *note*[13] about this year's Nobel Prize last week, and pointed to the RePEc ranking, noting that six out of the top ten on the list had already won. The rankings are based on data about authors who have registered with the RePEc Author Service,[14] which aims "to link economists with their research output in the RePEc bibliographic database." Authors get a profile page and also receive statistics about downloads of their papers and citations to them. Many rankings[15] are generated from the system.

Finally, I noticed the following tweet[16] from danah boyd[17]: "It pains me when academics don't take care of their search engine presence. RateMy-Teacher should never be an academic's top result."

Search engine presence is increasingly important to people and to institutions. . . . Reputation management is emerging as a new service category which should be of interest to libraries.

NOTES

1. www.oclc.org/programs/ourwork/researchinfo/default.htm
2. http://vivo.cornell.edu
3. www.oclc.org/research/announcements/2009-09-30.htm
4. http://vivo.cornell.edu/about
5. http://vitro.mannlib.cornell.edu
6. www.jobs.ac.uk/jobs/YD567/Bibliometrician
7. www.mendeley.com
8. http://hangingtogether.org/?p=740
9. https://www.escholar.manchester.ac.uk/jrul
10. www.irproject.manchester.ac.uk/about/businesscase/index.html
11. http://ideas.repec.org/top/top.person.anbcites.html
12. http://ideas.repec.org/top/top.person.anbcites.html
13. http://gregmankiw.blogspot.com/2009/09/nobel-prize-pool.html
14. http://authors.repec.org
15. http://ideas.repec.org/top
16. http://twitter.com/zephoria/status/4298093062
17. www.danah.org

NOVEMBER 2, 2009

On the discriminations of availability . . .

http://orweblog.oclc.org/archives/002019.html

Seamus Heaney[1] famously—and in poetry—complained about being included in an anthology of "British" poetry. In the course of his poem,[2] he invokes Miroslav Holub's[3] "On the necessity of truth," where a man creates a disturbance in a cinema when he sees a beaver mistakenly called a musk-rat on the screen. The man wants to set the record straight.

I don't have a copy of Heaney's work as I write this, but I can point to a <u>discussion of the passage</u>[4] in *Acting Between the Lines: The Field Day Theatre Company and Irish Cultural Politics, 1980–1984,*[5] courtesy of Google Books.

(And it would be nice to be able to easily reference the appropriate parts of both Heaney's and Holub's works on the web. I find that I am increasingly expecting to be able to find book text online—when looking for a quote, when helping with homework, etc.)

Now, a few weeks ago, Sergey Brin wrote an op-ed piece about Google Books in the *New York Times*.

He discusses the fate of books still potentially in copyright:

> But the vast majority of books ever written are not accessible to anyone except the most tenacious researchers at premier academic libraries. Books written after 1923 quickly disappear into a literary black hole. With rare exceptions, one can buy them only for the small number of years they are in print. After that, they are found only in a vanishing number of libraries and used book stores. As the years pass, contracts get lost and forgotten, authors and publishers disappear, the rights holders become impossible to track down.
>
> Inevitably, the few remaining copies of the books are left to deteriorate slowly or are lost to fires, floods and other disasters. While I was at Stanford in 1998, floods damaged or destroyed tens of thousands of books. Unfortunately, such events are not uncommon—a similar flood happened at Stanford just 20 years prior. You could read about it in *The Stanford-Lockheed Meyer Library Flood Report,* published in 1980, but this book itself is no longer available. ("A library to last forever"[6])

It was soon pointed out in the library community that *The Stanford-Lockheed Meyer Library Flood Report* was still "available" inasmuch as it was held by several libraries. WorldCat.org showed <u>four libraries</u>[7] holding it, and there are probably more. There was some discussion on the Web4lib mailing list along these lines, for example.

At the same time, on a closed mailing list in which I participate, one commenter argued that this level of availability meant that the volume was actually not available in any "practical sense."

As it is available in the "library system," the report is available to library users across the country. However, they have to be affiliated with a library which offers an interlibrary lending service, they have to know about it, they have to submit a request, and they have to wait for it to arrive.

Certainly, if the report were available through Google Books (or some other network-level repository of digital books), its availability would be greatly amplified.

It is clear that there are grades of availability. As some level, the transaction costs—or, as important, the price—of acquiring something may be considered too high for it to be considered available in a "practical sense." But your mileage may vary.

In this case, the fact that it is in the "library system" means that it is potentially "available" to library users anywhere through the interlibrary lending arrangements in which most North American libraries participate. The book is available in a very real way for somebody who wants to see it with a little persistence. And through the public availability of WorldCat and other resources, and the greater prominence and ease of use of end-user requesting, the transaction costs have gone down. And there is a link to WorldCat from the <u>Google Books record</u>[8] for the report.

However, it would seem that the transaction costs are still too high for many. Libraries do not yet appear as a "system" on the web, in the sense of being able to support well-seamed, easy-to-use discovery, request, and delivery across the system. And, of course, instant digital availability sets a different expectation than such a system currently provides.

That said, it seemed to me (as it did to the librarians on the web4lib discussion list) that saying that this volume was no longer available was a stronger statement than the situation warranted. I could go with "not easily available," but "no longer available" was too much . . .

And as I sat there looking at something being called a muskrat, I wanted to say, no, it is a beaver. . . ;-)

NOTES

1. www.worldcat.org/wcidentities/lccn-n79-99140
2. www.worldcat.org/oclc/10359386
3. www.worldcat.org/wcidentities/lccn-n50-28157

4. http://books.google.com/books?id=b_ed7AUp-hUC&lpg=PA148&dq=beaver
   %20heaney%20holub&lr=&pg=PA148#v=onepage&q=beaver%20heaney%20
   holub&f=false
5. www.worldcat.org/oclc/30508889
6. www.nytimes.com/2009/10/09/opinion/09brin.html
7. www.worldcat.org/oclc/18540285
8. http://books.google.com/books?id=D_v-HAAACAAJ&dq=The+Stanford
   -Lockheed+Meyer+Library+flood+report&ei=73_uSpaiMoWIygTww6m9Aw

MAY 2, 2010

People are entry points too . . . redux

http://orweblog.oclc.org/archives/002086.html

I have been reading *The Power of Pull*,[1] by John Hagel III, John Seely Brown, and Lang Davison. They provide a broad framework for thinking about current changes and how people and firms should position themselves to operate effectively. A major part of this is a shift from managing "knowledge stocks" to being able to participate in "knowledge flows."

John Hagel III writes[2]: "This pull approach seeks to develop scalable pull platforms that amplify our ability to draw out the people and resources when we need them and where we need them."

I was struck by this passage . . .

> We all talk loosely about information overload and assume that this is the real problem. In fact, we live in a world of increasing knowledge scarcity. The most valuable knowledge is in very short supply and is extremely hard to access. Information overload is a distraction. As we discussed in earlier chapters, in a world of accelerating change, the most valuable knowledge is highly distributed and may be embedded in the heads of people who are not well known and who are difficult to identify. . . .
>
> It's not so much about finding which information is most valuable, as many of those who fret about information overload would have it. Improving return on attention is more about finding and connecting with people who have the knowledge you need, particularly the tacit knowledge about how to do new things. The danger is that we all get so

busy assimilating explicit knowledge that we have no time to connect with people and build the relationships through which tacit knowledge flows. We get so busy reading about steampunk, or brewing, or building networks, that we don't actually find and connect with and learn from the people who are doing it. It's not so much information that we need as knowledge. And knowledge means people.

These people and the knowledge flows they generate can then become effective filters for information more broadly. By harnessing social media such as blogs, social-network platforms, and wikis, we can begin to rely on these mechanisms to expose ourselves to information that has been curated and passed on by these people. Since we deeply understand their contexts and passions, we can begin to determine when their recommendations are most reliable and increase our return on attention for both the tacit knowledge they offer and the information they recommend to us. Our personal social and professional networks will be far more effective in filtering relevant knowledge and information than any broader social-technology tools we might access.[3]

The authors talk of three "primary levels" of pull. First there is *access*, the ability to find people and resources when they are needed. The second is the ability to *attract* valuable and relevant people and resources to you. Social networking, conferences, location in relevant geographic spikes (Nashville for country music) are important here, as is the ability to be open to and develop relationships through serendipitous encounter. The third is the ability to *achieve* more by learning more effectively and translating that learning into improved performance. Interestingly, the authors discuss "creation spaces" which support this third level. Examples include the social interaction on World of Warcraft and the SAP Developer Network, which provide support for shared attention to problems.

The above passage, and the book itself, are suggestive in several ways. I thought I would mention a couple of things here.

The first is that I was interested in thinking about the three levels in relation to library expertise (if libraries want to be seen as experts, then their expertise must be seen).

1. Access: is library expertise visible when people are searching for things? I have written before—here[4] for example—about such expertise being visible on websites, and also, for example, of the nice feature on the University of Michigan website which returns appropriate library contacts[5] in searches for resources.

2. Attract: how should librarians position themselves so as to seem natural partners or collaborators?

3. Achieve: as "creation spaces" emerge, how should librarians interact with them? One thing that comes to mind here is the role of emerging social networks for researchers, and library interaction and support. Guus van den Brekel spoke about this at the recent EMTACL10 conference [Slideshare[6]].

The second is that I was struck by the extent to which success is seen by the authors to be bound up with network participation—networks of people and resources facilitated by digital networks. The future, they seem to suggest, favors—in Dave White's phrase[7]—the network residents.

NOTES

1. www.edgeperspectives.com/pop.html
2. www.edgeperspectives.typepad.com
3. John Hagel III, John Seely Brown, and Lang Davison, *The Power of Pull: How Small Moves, Smartly Made, Can Set Big Things in Motion* (New York: Basic Books, 2010).
4. http://orweblog.oclc.org/archives/001873.html
5. www.lib.umich.edu/mlibrary/search/mirlyn;website;ejournals;searchtools ;deepblue/demographics
6. www.slideshare.net/digicmb/virtual-research-networks-towards-research-20
7. http://orweblog.oclc.org/archives/001773.html

JUNE 20, 2010

Music: Marcus, Morrison, Mumford, and Carr

http://orweblog.oclc.org/archives/002107.html

I recently read Greil Marcus's book[1] on Van Morrison. While I have most of the Morrison oeuvre on some form of physical medium, it was useful to be able to refer to my aggregate digital collection, and to the Zune market-place and iTunes Store as backup.

I could quickly look up songs I couldn't remember or place, and I could confirm my memory of songs Marcus did not mention (he has a particular view of where Morrison's strengths are, and dismisses large stretches of his work).

A couple of things about this. First, I expect to be able to find—and be able to listen to—much of the stuff I look for, even though, in this case, Morrison is on record as saying that he is not a "download artist" (see this interview[2] with *Time*, for example). As I have discussed elsewhere,[3] he has also resisted the YouTubification of his work. The second is that this certainly leads to a "flattening" of one type of experience—the work involved in finding and playing music. Search and you will find, skimming over many years' work and many artists.

We went to hear Mumford & Sons in OSU a few weeks ago. I had been interested to see them compared to Crosby, Stills & Nash in an NPR story[4] before going. They responded that they had a variety of folkish influences, UK as well as US. And indeed, we thought we heard something of someone like June Tabor and a more robust version of the Waterboys in what they did. A caustic *Independent* review[5] heard the Fleet Foxes.

Again, one could trace relationships online. Here is what the Zune marketplace has to report (see figure 9.6).

Again, in one view, this represents a flattening of experience as one can quickly develop a sense of relationships or influences. This type of experience is now routine, of course. We are used to being provided with hooks and hints. Artists and artists are ranked, related, and recommended in the environments in which we discover, manage, and share music. We can let Pandora do our listening for us.

In each of these cases I was reminded of Nicholas Carr's discussion of music, from where the phrase "flattening of experience" comes, and my remarks . . .

> A while ago, Nick Carr wrote about[6] this change in our experience of music. He quoted from two BBC reports. One proclaimed "a new golden age of infinite music" in which "there's no longer any past—

mumford & sons

influenced by	related artists	related genres
The Byrds	Calexico	Blues / Folk
The Waterboys	Fleet Foxes	
Leonard Cohen	A.A. Bondy	
Fairport Convention	Johnny Flynn	
Spirit of the West	Laura Marling	
Billy Bragg	Houndmouth	
Red House Painters	Jessica Lea Mayfield	
Grant Lee Buffalo	Deer Tick	
Bert Jansch	The Unthanks	
	Sean O'Connell	
	Sam Lee	
	Lissie	
	Levek	
	Sarah Harmer	
	The Decemberists	
	Dry The River	
	Here We Go Magic	
	Ben Howard	
	Jake Bugg	
	Smoke Fairies	
	Twin Forks	
	Stornoway	

FIGURE 9.6 Mumford & Sons's page on Zune

just an endless present." By contrast, he notes, John Taylor, of Duran Duran, takes a more "nuanced view" which he describes as follows: "He wonders whether such easy abundance doesn't lead to a flattening of experience: When everything's present, nothing's new." He provides a quote from Taylor, who on the basis of the "power" of a TV experience, went on a ten-mile cycle looking for a record, and then listened to it again and again.

Taylor argues that, when it comes to music or any other form of art, the price of our "endless present" is the loss of a certain "magical power" that the artist was once able to wield over the audience. I suspect he's right. (*Be everywhere now*[7])

So, as a full range of music, movies, and maybe books becomes available to us, so too does our engagement with it change. Our sense of ownership changes, as media are delivered as a service. The work involved in assembling a personal collection diminishes. Our sense of historical perspective may change. But, I am not so sure about the loss of a certain "magical power" or the flattening of experience. Sure experiences are different. But think of an earlier transition. This magical power may also have been felt to be lost when "mechanical reproduction" allowed live performances to be shared in the first place: A recording could never take the place of a performance, could it? (*Stuff as a service*[8])

Carr is always suggestive. However, there is also a *Kulturkritik* gloominess about some of his writing. In talking about change, he quite often focuses on what we have lost, not on what we have gained.

Now, my musical experiences are limited: my knowledge and collections have been shallow. It is true that this new convenience has flattened my experience in one dimension (and I think also of Adorno's "withering of experience"). However, the online world has also enriched my sense of relationships and history and extended my experiences in important ways. I think I have gained more than I have lost. My musical appreciation is, in fact, deeper, because of the opportunities I now have. Both the volume and the variety of what I listen to, and what I buy, are greater than they used to be.

P.S. I would be interested to see a future study of how this broad availability affects the composition of music itself.

P.P.S. I am reading Nicholas Carr's *The Shallows* at the moment and was interested to see Steven Johnson's critique[9] of it in the *NYT* earlier today.

NOTES

1. www.worldcat.org/title/when-that-rough-god-goes-riding-listening-to-van
   -morrison/oclc/435418486
2. www.youtube.com/watch?v=QVHbUPNcTiU
3. http://orweblog.oclc.org/archives/001730.html
4. www.npr.org/templates/story/story.php?storyId=123891913
5. www.independent.co.uk/arts-entertainment/music/reviews/album
   -mumford—-sons-sigh-no-more-universalisland-1797620.html
6. www.roughtype.com/archives/2009/11/be_everywhere_n_1.php
7. www.roughtype.com/archives/2009/11/be_everywhere_n_1.php

8. http://orweblog.oclc.org/archives/002033.html
9. www.nytimes.com/2010/06/20/business/20unbox.html?ref=business

On the discrimination of curators and curations . . .

http://orweblog.oclc.org/archives/002119.html

As existing practices evolve and new ones emerge, it often takes time for the way in which we talk about them to settle down. There may be some interim terminological confusion. This has happened in our world with *archive* for example.

We can also see this happen with *curation/curatorial/curator*. In recent conversations, it seems to me that I hear overlapping senses radiating from three centers.

The first is a traditional one to do with the creation of collections of cultural objects and the selection, management, and care throughout their life cycle. Think of museum curators in this context, for example, or the curatorial staff at the British Library. We often hear this sense extended to the creation and care of an exhibition. I and others have used the phrase <u>curatorial traditions</u>[1] to refer to the different but related bodies of professional practice deployed in the museum, library, archive, and related domains.

The other two are newer and selectively emphasize core functions of the curatorial role suggested above.

The second emphasizes a preservation and stewardship role, acknowledging this as part of an overall management life cycle. One sometimes hears this in a restricted version of "data curation." And preservation is a central aspect, for example, of the work of the <u>Digital Curation Centre</u>[2] at Edinburgh University.

The third emphasizes the selection, organization, and presentation function, and may be coming to be the most widely used sense in which *curation* is used. Here is a recent comment of Michael Cairns, for example:

> In recent years content curation has emerged out of the wild, wild, west of "mere" content. Sites such as the Huffington Post, Red State

and Politico all represent new attempts to build audiences around curated content. While they appear to be successful, at the same time there are other sites (such as Associated Content and Demand Media) contributing to the morass of filler content that can plague the web users' experience. The buzz word "curation" does carry with it some logic: As the sheer amount of information and content grows, consumers seek help parsing the good from the bad. And that's where curation comes in.[3]

Interestingly, curation, in this sense, has been central to the value of bookstores, newspapers, and libraries, and is coming to be emphasized more. In each case, the management of supply may be moving elsewhere (to Amazon in the case of books, for example) or becoming simpler (as data is aggregated in discovery layer products for libraries, for example), leaving it important to think harder about the management of demand or consumption (providing greater support for selection, saving time, and so on . . .) of which curation, as used in this third sense, is a central part.

NOTES

1. www.google.com/search?hl=en&q=%22curatorial+traditions%22+OR+%22 curatorial+tradition%22+&btnG=Search&aq=f&aqi=&aql=&oq=&gs_rfai=
2. www.dcc.ac.uk/digital-curation/what-digital-curation
3. http://personanondata.blogspot.com/2010/06/curator-and-docent.html

FEBRUARY 18, 2011

The university's curatorial role

http://orweblog.oclc.org/archives/002156.html

I made a note in these pages[1] a couple of years ago about the University of Edinburgh's mission statement.

> The University's mission is the creation, dissemination, and curation of knowledge.

The occasion was Chris Rusbridge's justified pleasure[2] at seeing the mission changed to include "curation." At the time, Chris was the director of the Digital Curation Centre, based at the University.

At CNI, recently, I was very interested to hear Maria Bonn talk about[3] scholarly publishing strategy and infrastructure at the University of Michigan. She discussed how several areas of scholarly publishing had been consolidated into MPublishing, a division of the University Library. I thought the combination of services was fascinating. I also thought that it exemplified what Scott Walter[4] has called the service turn[5] in libraries, and, more particularly, that it was an example of leveraging several services to create a truly distinctive offering in the way he suggests will become more common for libraries.

> MPublishing is the primary academic publishing division of the University of Michigan. It creates, promotes, distributes and preserves scholarly, educational and regional materials in digital and print formats. By bringing together the talents and resources of the University of Michigan Press, the Scholarly Publishing Office, Deep Blue (the University's institutional repository service), the Copyright Office, and the Text Creation Partnership, MPublishing builds upon the traditional publishing strengths of the University of Michigan while creating and shaping sustainable publishing models for the future.
>
> MPublishing is dedicated to the integrity, persistence, and durability of the scholarly record. It combines the values and experience of publishers, librarians and information technology specialists to publish and promote the best quality scholarship. By approaching the life cycle of information at every stage, from the initial spark of an idea to its delivery and long-term preservation, MPublishing takes a holistic approach to publishing that maximizes the impact of its publications both now and in the future. (*MPublishing | MLibrary*[6])

Several organizational things struck me. One was that this was not the organizational home of the HathiTrust, although one can understand that there might be good reasons for that. The second was the mix between activities aimed at supporting effective communication and publishing of Michigan research outputs and those which involved the university as a publisher, either through the press or its journals[7]. The third is more general. Myself and Brian Lavoie recently wrote about[8] how the network is reconfiguring the organizational boundaries of the library. There is the boundary between the library and external entities; however, there is also the boundary between entities within the university. I though that this was a very interesting example of how internal university activities are being reconfigured to align related activities in new ways.

One of the particular things I liked about the presentation was how Maria aligned university, library, and MPublishing missions. The University of Michigan mission is powerfully stated:

> The mission of the University of Michigan is to serve the people of Michigan and the world through preeminence in creating, communicating, preserving and applying knowledge, art, and academic values, and in developing leaders and citizens who will challenge the present and enrich the future. (*Mission statement[9]*)

What jumped out at me was the word *preserving*, which immediately reminded me of the Edinburgh statement.

This did cause me to wonder whether Michigan and Edinburgh had explicitly provided for preservation/curation of institutional assets, and to what extent the library was seen as the place to address this issue.

Coda: I have noted[10] how the use of the word *curation* has developed recently. I read *curation* in the University of Edinburgh's mission as being aligned with the second sense I discuss there. Preservation is certainly an important interest of the Digital Curation Centre.

NOTES

1. http://orweblog.oclc.org/archives/001766.html
2. http://digitalcuration.blogspot.com/2008/09/curation-in-university-mission.html
3. www.cni.org/tfms/2010b.fall/Abstracts/PB-university-ruddy.html
4. https://netfiles.uiuc.edu/swalter/www/
5. http://orweblog.oclc.org/archives/002152.html
6. www.lib.umich.edu/mpublishing
7. www.lib.umich.edu/spo/journals.html
8. www.oclc.org/us/en/nextspace/017/research.htm
9. www.umich.edu/pres/mission.php
10. http://orweblog.oclc.org/archives/002119.html

INDEX